# Where's Me Plaid?

## A Scottish Roots Odyssey

By Scott Crawford

Where's Me Plaid?
A Scottish Roots Odyssey
2nd Edition
Author Scott Crawford
Published August 2016

ISBN-13: 978-1537349794
ISBN-10: 1537349791

The first edition of this book was published by Clan Crawford Association in August 2013 as Volume 5 of the House of Crawford series.

The map and historical timeline contained in this book, as well as the narrative, are the original work of the author.

The cover photo, "Man on the Royal Mile" was taken by Anita Pinzi, who retains the copyright. © 2016. The photo is used with permission here.

# Acknowledgments

There are many people who deserve thanks for this book. Katrina is a rather obvious one, I suppose, so I shall start with her.

Also, I must thank my first readers—my parents and my friend Morgen who patiently read every word and whose enthusiasm spurred me on, and all my other friends and family members upon whom I forced those early drafts. They may or may not have read them, but attaching them to emails and sending them off made me feel like I had an audience.

The helpful librarians of Scotland, particularly those in Kilbirnie, West Kilbride, Kilmarnock, Lanark, and Perth also deserve special mention, as they pointed me time and again toward nuggets of information or landmarks I never would have found on my own.

I would be remiss not to thank the late Peter Houison Craufurd and his lovely wife Caroline for their hospitality, welcoming me into their home at Craufurdland for tea rather than prosecuting me for trespassing after I confessed to sneaking down their driveway. Further thanks go to their son Simon not only for remembering me more than a decade later and inviting me back to Craufurdland, but for the good work he and his wife Adity are doing to ensure the estate thrives for generations to come. It was my recent visit with them which helped to inspire this second edition of *Where's Me Plaid*, as I try to make the book worthy of its place in the Craufurdland library—though it still seems a stretch to find it in the same room as a rare volume of Shakespeare and a first printing of *Tam O'Shanter*.

I wish to thank Clan Crawford Association, especially Kevan Crawford, whose book planted the seeds of my interest in Crawford history and upon which I drew heavily for my own writings, and Joanne Crawford, whose persistence and encouragement led to the publication of the first edition of *Where's Me Plaid*.

Finally, I wish to thank Anita Pinzi, who encouraged and assisted me in the publication of this second edition – the book you now hold.

# Disclaimer

This book describes the author's experiences on separate trips taken to Scotland in 2004 and 2006. Everything in it is true to the best of his memory, which is imperfect, so let's say it is more or less true. The impressions and opinions expressed about those experiences are entirely his own. Some names and identifying details of individuals have been changed to protect their privacy, giving them latitude to distance themselves from the author and his imperfect memory.

# Scotland

## Crawford Country

- Loch Katrine
- Callander
- Stirling
- Firth of Forth
- Dumbarton
- Glasgow
- Edinburgh
- Roslin
- Largs
- Kilbirnie
- Croshie
- Loudoun
- Lanark
- Crawfordjohn
- Kilmarnock
- Crawford
- Firth of Clyde
- Ayr

N
W · E
S

- Cawdor
- Culloden
- Inverness
- Loch Ness
- Balmoral
- Braemar
- Stonehaven
- Fort William
- Glencoe
- Glamis
- Dunkeld
- Perth
- Callander
- Stirling
- Firth of Forth
- Helensburgh
- Glasgow
- Edinburgh
- Largs
- Lanark
- Ayr
- *See inset map above*

## United Kingdom

- Scotland
- Northern Ireland
- Wales
- England

## The Crawford Crest

TUTUM · TE · ROBORE · REDDAM

"Tutum te robore reddam"
"I will render you safe with my strength"

5

# Where's Me Plaid?

## (A Scottish Roots Odyssey)

# Part One

## On the Crawford Trail

# Chapter 1: An Accidental Discovery

April 6 is National Tartan Day. Did you know that? If you qualify as one of the 27 million Americans who still claim some degree of Scottish ancestry, you can use this day to dress up in a plaid skirt and throw insults at the English. If you don't, perhaps you can laugh at those that do.

But maybe I've jumped ahead of myself. Do you know what tartan is? Don't feel bad if you don't. Most people don't. This is particularly true in the United States, where Americans seem to know startlingly little about all things Scottish—which is a shame, because U.S. history and culture owe much to Scotland.

For a start, take a small thing like the American economic system. The basic principles of free-enterprise society, still taught in every economic class across America, were first spelled out by a Scotsman named Adam Smith in his book *The Wealth of Nations*, published in 1776, just in time to shape the course of a new nation.

Scottish immigrants and their descendants have played similarly important roles at each stage of America's history. Jesse Chisholm, the amiable Scotch-Cherokee cowboy, pioneered the first cattle drive trail in 1867, ushering in one of the most romanticized eras of American history. Scottish immigrant turned steel tycoon Andrew Carnegie, a name practically synonymous with big business in the 19th century, developed at least three time-honored American traditions: 1) living the rags to riches dream; 2) treating his factory workers like sub-human dirt particles; and 3) making up for such behavior by donating a huge percentage of his fortune to charity, so long as his name appeared on everything built as a result. Thus Carnegie Hall, Carnegie-Mellon University, and a string of Carnegie Libraries in cities across America. And where would communications systems be today had it not been for Scottish immigrant and inventor Alexander Graham Bell, whose famous though oddly seductive words, "Watson, come here; I want you," brought the world the telephone and helped solidify America as the leading nation of invention?

This is just the briefest sampling of Scottish personalities who have left their mark on American society. Between 1715 and 1776, over a quarter of a million Scotsmen and women made their way across the Atlantic to settle in the American colonies. By 1790, over half a million people living in the United States came from Scottish or Scotch-Irish ancestry, making them the third largest ethnic group in the new nation behind English and Africans. In the late 1800s, another wave of immigration further added to the country's Scottish stock.* These new arrivals became the laborers, tradesmen, businessmen, farmers, soldiers and artists, who along with immigrants from other countries would build the United States to its present-day state.

With so much debt owed to Scotland, the average American knows little about this rugged land north of England. It seems that, once settled in America, Scottish immigrants and their descendants too quickly forgot about the country they left behind, which again I say is a shame, as the country they left behind happens to be thriving. In 1999, after nearly 300 years of union with England, Scotland regained an independent parliament to legislate on internal affairs. Edinburgh, the capital, now hosts the world's largest annual arts festival, and, in 1990, Glasgow was crowned the European City of Culture, edging out cities like Paris and Rome for the honor. All of this has led to a fifty percent rise in tourism since the start of the 21st century, with nearly twenty million people now visiting the country annually. And as these visitors inevitably discover, Scotland retains what can never be taken away: the most beautiful and haunting scenery imaginable, a romantic history full of blood, intrigue and heroism, and some of the friendliest and most fiercely loyal people in the world.

Yet, mention Scotland to almost anyone in the United States and they will likely picture one of the following: golf, whisky, a small yappy dog, bagpipes, men in skirts, a guy from Star Trek. Or perhaps they'll picture combinations thereof; there are some interesting possibilities. What they almost certainly will not be able to tell you is why any of these things are associated with Scotland. Nor will they be able to find Scotland on a map.

---

* Even more Scots emigrated to Canada, though, as a rule, people in the United States are not expected to know anything about Canada.

The level of ignorance is appalling.

I know. I've been part of the problem, though I managed to take ignorance to the next level: I didn't even know I was Scottish.

．　．　．　．　．

School teachers on a small island in the Caribbean, my wife and I had planned to travel each summer. A change of scenery is always necessary after a long year in a small place, no matter how beautiful that place may be. But as tends to happen, our lives had become busier than expected and, by the summer of 2004, several years had gone by without any major excursion from the island. Our only trips had consisted of family visits to Ohio and Florida, and no offense to Mom and Dad, but such trips cannot be spoken of in the same breath with words like "relaxing" or "rejuvenating" and, at any rate, come up a bit short in the "exotic locale" category. As a result, we were going stir crazy and becoming exceedingly cranky. We hadn't threatened to harm each other yet, but island fever had set in, adding to the tension of our daily lives. When our students began recommending we take a trip, the message hit home: we desperately needed to get off the rock.

Given where we lived, a vacation didn't require palm trees and sandy beaches. Instead, alluring destinations tended to dwell in colder climes: the mountains or deserts of the American West, or cosmopolitan cities for a dose of much-needed culture.

For reasons I no longer recall, that summer Scotland came into the discussion and quickly became an idealized destination for the perfect holiday. Images of picturesque castles to explore and dramatic highland scenery for hiking appealed to us both. And of course, there would be a convivial pub at the end of each day: someplace where we'd walk in and friendly, burly men smelling strongly of sheep would regale us with tales of highland heroism while a sassy barmaid served up pints of creamy ale around a roaring fireplace. Never mind that we'd be there in July; in my Scottish fantasy, there was always a roaring fireplace.

We both had our own private reasons as well for traveling to Scotland.

For me, a social studies teacher, it appealed to my fascination with medieval history. For my wife, Katrina, an avid and indiscriminate reader who never considered talent a prerequisite for writing (she particularly enjoys books about talking cats), it had something to do with the disproportionate number of romance novels set in Scotland. In her version of the Scottish fantasy, the burly men in the convivial pub are replaced with the brooding, Fabio-like characters that inevitably adorn the covers of these literary masterpieces.

Soon we were online booking airline tickets, an exercise followed by the next logical step in the process: learning something, anything, about the country we were about to visit. Our accumulated knowledge of Scotland consisted of a hodgepodge of generic information obtained through pop culture in our thirty-plus years of life. This amounted to remarkably little, but did include a warm appreciation for the Saturday Night Live skit, *If It's Not Scottish It's Crap*, featuring Mike Myers. To expand on this, we ordered a slew of books on Scottish history, culture and travel to begin planning our trip.

While waiting for these to arrive, I undertook some preliminary research online. I'm not sure how this developed—perhaps on a tip from an acquaintance, perhaps by sheer dumb luck—but at some point while I was supposed to be looking for places to see and stay in Scotland, I discovered that my last name, Crawford, is a Scottish name. This may seem obvious to some, but to a guy from Ohio, whose parents, grandparents and great-grandparents were all also from Ohio, the question of family roots just hadn't progressed beyond: "What part of Ohio are we from?" With this newfound information, our upcoming Scottish excursion took on an interesting twist. It got even more interesting when I happened across a photograph of what was supposedly a Crawford castle. Apparently, we Crawfords were not just lowly peasants over there in Scotland. I immediately pictured myself knocking on the door, announcing my Crawfordness, and being ushered to a chair of honor beside the roaring fireplace while a sassy maid served me creamy ale.

Such visions set off a frenzy of research with each fact painting a nobler and more colorful picture of family history. Tales surfaced of Crawfords hunting with kings, battling Vikings, storming castles, and then…holy bagpipes! …William Wallace was a Crawford! That's right. William Wallace, the 13th century Guardian of Scotland who battled against English tyranny, was immortalized by Hollywood in the movie *Braveheart*, and is revered above all other Scottish heroes by men and women to this day…*he* was a Crawford. At least his mother, Margaret Crawford, was, which makes Wallace a half-Crawford, and that ain't bad. I remained naturally dubious at first; anyone can put anything on the internet and I didn't want to get too excited only to find that my family roots had been manufactured by a 13-year old *Braveheart* fanatic for a school project. Thus, I cautiously dug deeper on various websites, but in each case the story held up. William Wallace, it seemed, was indeed a Crawford.

I'm sure the reader, being a member of the human race, understands the magnitude of such a discovery. We humans have an inherent need for a sense of identity, a feeling of importance in this world. Every kid who fantasizes hitting the winning homerun in the World Series or draining the last second shot in the NCAA tournament knows this instinctively.

Of course, the next best thing to actually being a hero is being related to a hero. Come to think of it, being related to a hero may be even better. It somehow identifies you as somebody important without going to the trouble of earning such distinction yourself. Sort of riding your ancestor's coattails, if you will. I now stood in a position to do just that. No more did I have to shrink beside the guy whose ancestors came over on the Mayflower, or whose grandfather stormed the beaches at Normandy, or whose second cousin invented the Styrofoam cup. I was a relative, however distant, of William Wallace, the great Scottish warrior and patriot portrayed by Mel Gibson in *Braveheart*. When Mel Gibson is playing your ancestor, you know you're from a line of badasses. I started to walk with a swagger.[*]

By the time the travel books arrived in the mail, our coming trip had

---

[*] I beg the reader to keep in mind that this and all other references to Mel Gibson were written before his career took a slight downturn, by which I mean nosedive. So please think Lethal Weapon/Braveheart Mel Gibson, and not drunk, bigotry-spewing, mugshot Mel Gibson.

acquired a fresh purpose: I was going to discover my Scottish roots. Katrina, who was watching her much-anticipated, romantic holiday morph into a decidedly unromantic, though highly romanticized whirlwind of genealogical research, remained remarkably tolerant of my fanaticism, which is the only way my behavior prior to the trip can be described. She didn't even protest when I started planning an itinerary around Crawford sites of interest, though she did raise an eyebrow at my terribly affected Scottish accent and flat-out refused to address me as Sir Scott.

Somewhere in the next two weeks, sense did return, and in the end I checked my enthusiasm enough to reduce the "roots" portion of our trip down to three days. The remaining week and a half would be spent as originally planned, exploring the streets of Edinburgh, marveling over castles and cathedrals, hiking in the highlands, and—a "must do" on our list—attending a highland games festival. The opportunity of seeing large men in plaid skirts heaving unbelievably heavy objects unbelievably far distances was simply too tempting to miss. Fortunately, highland games are a rather ubiquitous part of Scottish summers: there is always a festival going on somewhere, and not just in the highlands, we discovered. Katrina zeroed in on one in the Trossachs where we planned to end our trip. The festival was scheduled for our last weekend in Scotland, so we booked a reservation at a nearby Bed & Breakfast and called the trip planned. It was the only reservation we had.

Having struck this fine balance of research and adventure, we anxiously awaited our departure date. What I didn't know at the time, but would discover in the course of the trip, is something that everyone who has dabbled in genealogy probably knows already: that a family's roots are inevitably intertwined with its country's history and culture, so that the research of one automatically leads to the discovery and appreciation of the other. I was about to learn a lot about Crawfords and even more about Scotland. It was fascinating, as it turns out, and I think even non-Crawfords will enjoy hearing about it, though they might not swagger as much the next day.

And at the very least, they'll learn once and for all what tartan is.

# Chapter 2: Necessary Adjustments

(Arrival in Scotland)

One inescapable truth about travel is that between the excitement of leaving on a trip and the excitement of arriving at one's destination lurks the seemingly interminable process of getting there. This is a dilemma made more severe when one starts from a small island in the Caribbean. Any trip beginning from such an island means travelers can pretty much write-off a day of their lives. It doesn't matter where one's final destination may be or how long it should take to get there; once connecting flights, ferry trips, goat-inspired traffic jams, sleeping attendants, and any number of other possible diversions are factored in, the trip will always qualify as an all-day event. It once took me twelve hours to get to Puerto Rico, and I can see Puerto Rico from my island on a clear day. I could have backstroked faster. Now, with an entire ocean between Scotland and me, I knew I'd have some time to kill.

Fortunately, I had the perfect book to occupy my time: a history of the Crawfords of Scotland, joyously discovered during my flurry of internet research prior to the trip. Hours passed virtually unnoticed as I read the book cover to cover on the long flights from San Juan to New York and New York to London. By the time we boarded our last plane for the short hop to Glasgow, day had passed to night and night showed signs of giving way to yet another day. Flying north, I watched out the window with fascination as a paling sky revealed rolling hills below, gray at first, but slowly taking on the greens and golds of pastures and fields.

We touched down in Glasgow under a beautiful sunrise promising a clear, full day ahead. I had only slept a few restless hours on the plane, but, remarkably, I didn't feel tired. Outside waited the land of my ancestors. I prepared to be welcomed with open arms.

The customs official had other ideas.

"What is the purpose of your stay in Scotland?" a uniformed man, whom I shall refer to as Officer MacDung, asked upon arrival. MacDung's ruddy face was all business beneath a set of bushy eyebrows, made all the bushier by their contrast with the thin wisps of gray hair combed optimistically across the bald-patch crowning his head. His tone held more than a hint of boredom, as might be expected from someone who spends his entire day asking the same questions.

"Holiday," I replied, trying out the British term for vacation. Katrina, standing next to me at the counter, rolled her eyes.

"An' where will ye be staying?" MacDung continued flatly.

Hmmm. I hadn't expected that. I glanced at Katrina to see what assistance she might offer, but found her enjoying this interrogation much more than me. She met my gaze with arched eyebrows and an amused smirk, indicating that she too was rather curious about the details of our accommodation. I was apparently on my own here.

"Uh, we don't have any reservations until the second week," I volunteered helpfully. "We plan on just playing it by ear until then." I said this last with as much upbeat optimism as I could muster, hoping MacDung had a little spirit of adventure tucked away beneath that stiff collar and balding pate. Such spontaneity had after all been my idea, not Katrina's, to accommodate the fact that I had no certainty of where my "roots journey" might take us.

MacDung raised a bushy eyebrow. "Tha' willna dae" he informed me. "Withoot an address, I canna allow ye t' enter the United Kingdom. Ye will hae t' be taken ootside and shot." That last part may not be an exact quote. To be honest, I was having trouble making out the accent.

I swallowed hard. This was not going well. Didn't he see my last name on my passport? It's Crawford, dammit! We've got castles all over this place! Somehow, this didn't strike me as the right approach, but it did give me an idea. The book I'd read on the plane contained a picture of a tavern in the town of Crawford. I didn't know if the place even rented rooms, but it was a legitimate location we would visit in the next few days—a fact which managed to erase any guilt for what came out of my mouth next.

"The Crawford Arms Hotel," I stammered, "in the town of Crawford. That's where we're going." I hoped my voice sounded more confident than

I felt. I could sense MacDung's ruddy stare and the impatient shuffle of feet behind me. "Shoot 'im, already," the feet seemed to say. I looked meekly at Katrina to see how she was taking the news that her long-awaited Scottish holiday may be over before it began. Her expression was not hard to read: "Shoot 'im, already."

After an infinite pause during which I breathed not at all, MacDung looked back at my passport before penciling the name "Crawford Arms" on a form. "Plan tae see a bit o' your ancestry, d' ye?" he said and smiled. He wasn't so bad after all.

"That's right," I murmured, emitting a long overdue breath and trying not to vomit on the counter.

"Guid luck t' ye then," he said, handing back our passports. And with a wave we entered Scotland.

•   •   •   •   •

Cars in Europe are not like cars in the United States. Despite rising fuel costs, global warming, and any number of other reasons why oversized cars don't make sense, Americans still love big cars. The bigger the better, in fact. My favorite ad for an American car promoted the Chevrolet Avalanche, a vehicle so big its advertisement read: "All the utility of a yak train, without the yak train smell." I got a kick out of that ad every time I saw it, but it never inspired visions of a fuel-efficient car. Nor was it meant to. That's the whole point. Americans adore big, fat cars.

Europeans take the exact opposite approach to vehicles. "The smaller the better" seems to be the motto east of the Atlantic, a land of very tiny, very puntable cars. I've seen skateboards in the U.S. bigger than some European cars. Even the model names reflect this trend: whereas American cars are named after mountain ranges and natural disasters, European cars sport cute names, like "Mini" or "Punto". These sound like cars you can put in your pocket. And, in fact, you nearly can.

I bring this up because our first stop upon leaving the airport was the rental car agency, a short shuttle bus ride away. The prospect of driving a car that barely fit around my body fascinated me, and I waited with giddy anticipation as the agent finished the paperwork and then pointed outside at what was to be our means of transportation for the next two weeks. Perfect. A tiny red car—a Fiat Crumb or some such model—bigger than a breadbox, but not much. Fortunately, we packed light.

Katrina and I squeezed our bags into the trunk and contorted our bodies until we found ourselves upright in the front seat. Once we had giggled and commented over "just how darn cute" the car was, we sobered up and tried to prepare ourselves for the experience of driving in a foreign country.

For driving, like so many other tasks, is a habitual process. At home, most of us drive so often we don't really have to think about it. We know where we're going, where all the controls are, exactly how much pressure to apply to the pedals, and who has the right-of-way at an intersection, so we can pretty much spend all our time in the car doing other important tasks, such as talking, singing off key with the radio, or moving an arm up and down on the air flow outside the window. But throw us into a different car in a different country with different rules of the road, and suddenly driving requires total concentration. I was tense.

One piece of good news was that I didn't have to get used to driving on the opposite side of the road. We drive on the left in the Caribbean, so I could set that aside as a factor of worry. Other considerations would require adjustment, however. First of all, the steering wheel was on the opposite side of the car. This *was* different from the islands, and gave rise to a further complication: I now had to shift gears with my left hand. Being a decidedly right-handed person, this gave me great worry. I can go months at a time without using my left hand. How could I rely on it to distinguish between first and third gear on the fly when I was in unfamiliar country and trying to figure out where the heck I was going?

For a few humbling minutes, I circled, or rather hopped, around the parking lot, entertaining the attendants with a chorus of grinding gears. I had hoped to stay in the lot until I felt comfortable, but the pained look on the agent's face staring aghast from the office window caused me to change strategy mid-grind and hop prematurely toward the lot's exit—a rash action that only served to hasten my encounter with the next demon of driving in Scotland: round-a-bouts.

Round-a-bouts, or traffic circles, exist in the United States, but prove far less common than standard intersections with stop signs or traffic signals. In Scotland, round-a-bouts reign supreme. This we discovered quite unexpectedly within a few hundred yards of leaving the rental agency. We felt smug in our Fiat Crumb as we took to the Scottish highway—me adjusting the mirrors while Katrina looked over the map—when seemingly out of nowhere the first round-a-bout appeared. It loomed up ahead like a mirage in a desert, an indistinct smudge smacking of danger on the horizon. I slowed down as we approached and asked pertinent questions in my head. "Let's see, I merge left, but if I'm going straight through, do I stay left the whole way around? Or do I have to get on to the left, merge right as I make my way around, and then merge back left before I turn? And what about other cars getting on as I go around?" In a panic, scenes from *National Lampoon's European Vacation* flashed before my eyes. I saw myself as Chevy Chase, trapped in an endless London round-a-bout, pointing out Big Ben and Parliament again and again to his family while trying futilely to merge left.

Fortunately for me, this was not a London round-a-bout; this was a round-a-bout on the outskirts of Glasgow in the wee hours of the morning, and there wasn't another car in sight. My panic proved a bit misplaced as we hopped safely through, gears grinding, and a hint of smugness began to return.

Shortly after this, Katrina announced we were driving in the wrong direction.

The rental agent had given us directions to the town of Kilbirnie, which was to be the first stop on our Crawford tour. Unfortunately, I didn't make out everything he said and was too proud to ask him to repeat himself. He probably said something to the effect of, "Take a left at the first round-a-bout; it'll take you to Kilbirnie." What I heard sounded more like, "You look like a duck and smell funny." Sighing, we pulled over to the side of the road and consulted the map.

"You're doing great, honey," Katrina mused, ruffling the map in her lap. "You seem to have a real kinship with this place."

"C'mon," I pleaded. "New places always require adjustments." This was true for me even when visiting the next town over. Considering we had crossed an ocean to a foreign land, I felt I was doing quite well.

"Yep," she went on, as if I hadn't spoken, "a real homing pigeon…"

"At least we're finally in Scotland."

"…heeding the call of your ancestral roots." Her voice was full of feigned awe, but I noticed she was smiling. With thirty minutes of stress and confusion coming on the heels of twenty hours of tedious travel, she remained in good enough spirits to mock me. I took this as a good sign, as I hopped the car back onto the road.

Safely en route to Kilbirnie, it seemed our Scottish holiday had finally begun. The stress of driving faded with each passing mile, and we settled back to take in the scenery. A crumbling stone wall followed the roadside, separating the highway from the low hills beyond. Small houses dotted the countryside, which lay neatly divided into green and brown fields. I was thinking it looked a lot like Ohio when, with a suddenness which left us scratching our heads and consulting the map, a road sign announced we had arrived at our destination.

We hadn't been driving more than twenty minutes.

This would happen again and again during our trip. We would chart a route for the day, setting aside hours for the drive, and then, twenty minutes later, arrive unexpectedly and seemingly prematurely at our destination. This shouldn't have surprised me. I am, after all, a social studies teacher and am supposed to understand basic geographic conventions such as scales on maps. But somehow, I just couldn't get my head around the fact that Scotland is not a big country. It didn't fit any of the templates I had in my head. Katrina and I live on an island where we can be anywhere in forty minutes or less, but it *looks* like a place where we can be anywhere in forty minutes or less. With only twenty-one square miles in area, one side looks very like the next. But we had also lived in the American West, where just driving to the grocery can be an all day affair requiring provisions and an extra tank of gas. But again, the West *looks* like a place where it should take all day to drive somewhere. There are mountains and deserts and canyons and plains; a region encompassing such variety has to be huge.

Scotland, given its diverse landscape, gives off the impression that it is a much bigger place than it is. Within its borders, one finds rugged mountains, rolling hills, treeless moors, thick forests, meandering rivers, rich farmland, two major cities, a plethora of towns and hamlets, and hundreds of lochs, at least two of which have surface areas of over twenty square miles each. These are not the features of a small country. Yet Scotland is a small country. In area, it contains just over 30,000 square miles. That's considerably smaller than Ohio, which boasts an area of nearly 45,000 square miles, yet was still small enough for me to jump into a car on a whim and drive halfway across the state with friends to catch a baseball game or eat a chilidog at a favorite spot, only to return later in the day in time to tell our mothers what a lovely time we'd had at the local mall, where we had supposedly been for the afternoon. Scottish teenagers must be doing this kind of thing all the time, except substitute soccer and whisky for baseball and chilidogs and remember they can only fit one other person in the car.

Think of it this way: if Scotland were a U.S. state, it would rank 41st in size, being a little bigger than West Virginia, but a little smaller than South Carolina. Scotland is, in fact, a country one can drive across in a day—a fact which, once embraced, has tremendous advantages for two people in a Fiat Crumb trying to explore as much of the country as possible on a two week holiday.

# Chapter 3: Gauntlets the Castle Stormer

## (A morning in Kilbirnie)

In the early morning hours of April 1, 1571, the lone guard patrolling the north ramparts of Dumbarton Castle, fourteen miles northwest of Glasgow on the River Clyde, was startled to see an armed man leap over the top of the castle wall. He was somewhat more startled when forty-nine others followed. Considering the other side of this particular wall formed the top edge of a sheer cliff over two hundred feet high, I think it's safe to say he was not expecting company.

Much to the guard's disappointment, the intruders did not shout "April Fools!" and then have a good laugh at his expense, slapping his back and checking his underpants. Rather, they shouted "A Darnley! A Darnley!"—the name of the former king, murdered four years earlier—and proceeded to capture the castle. The surprise was so total, the victory so complete, the invading party did not lose a man.

The person responsible for this rout was a military captain by the name of Sir Thomas Crawford, a swashbuckling character who had, at some point in his career, earned the endearing nickname of "Gauntlets." His story has all the makings of a Hollywood screenplay.

As the sixth son of Lawrence Crawford of Kilbirnie, Sir Thomas did not have a lot of prospects before him. Scottish law and tradition gave the eldest son the right to inheritance of land and titles, while younger sons were left to make their own way. Many went into the clergy; others hung around the manor and mooched off their elder brother; the rest went looking for adventure. Sir Thomas was of the latter ilk.

Fortunately for him, adventure was not hard to find in 16th century Scotland. This was the time of the "Rough Wooing", a wonderfully descriptive name given by Sir Walter Scott, the 19th century Scottish writer, to describe attempts by England's King Henry VIII to steal away Scotland's child queen to marry his own young son and heir. Little Mary had been crowned Queen of Scots upon the death of her father when she was only six days old, and almost immediately became a subject of intrigue and power struggle for foreign powers and the Scottish nobility, a state of affairs that would last her entire tragic life. Henry VIII's violent campaign—a campaign continued by his successors after his death—ultimately failed to bring young Mary to England, but did succeed in bringing death and destruction to many Scots and their towns during a series of raids between 1544 and 1548.

One of the most devastating of these raids was the Battle of Pinkie Cleugh, an English rout of the Scottish that gives us our first historical glimpse of Sir Thomas Crawford. In this battle, Sir Thomas was taken captive, which proved about as good as one could hope for in a battle leaving 15,000 less fortunate Scots dead. Crawford was ransomed and then spent the next eleven years honing his military skills in France as a member of the Scottish Archers, an elite fighting unit responsible for guarding the French royal family, Scotland's closest ally.

Crawford returned to Scotland just in time to get caught up in the Protestant Reformation, where Catholics were having great fun accusing Protestants of being heretics and Protestants were returning the favor by calling Catholics whoremongers and idolators. In this tense environment, Sir Thomas rubbed shoulders with friends in high places, becoming a close confidante of Henry Stuart, better known as Lord Darnley, the good looking, arrogant young man who married a finally grown up Mary, Queen of Scots, and became a very meddlesome king.

Crawford's friendship with Darnley ended abruptly when the latter was murdered at Kirk o' Field in 1567. Actually, Darnley wasn't just murdered. He was strangled in bed and then extravagantly blown up in an explosion that rocked all of nearby Edinburgh. His body landed in an orchard across the street from the house he had been sleeping in, which of course was now just a pile of rubble. At any rate, the young king was quite dead.

The mystery of Darnley's murder has never been definitively solved, though history points to a conspiracy involving a number of Protestant nobles led by the Lord Bothwell, all of whom wanted the young Catholic king out of the way. Mary herself was suspected of complicity in the plot, though actual evidence for her involvement remains scant and unreliable. The most damning evidence against Mary proved circumstantial. She had had a rocky marriage to Darnley, which included periods of estrangement and, incredibly, the murder of her secretary by Darnley and some fellow nobles (more on this later). Given this, many believed she wouldn't mind being rid of her husband. But even more damning in the eyes of the Scottish people was her subsequent marriage, within a few short months of Darnley's death, to Lord Bothwell, the leading suspect in the king's murder! What inspired such an incredibly foolhardy and shortsighted move on Mary's part remains unclear, but to many the marriage served as proof that the Queen had taken part in the plot.

This left an opening for her enemies, of which she had many, to exploit, and they took to arms against her. Mary was forced to abdicate, leaving her toddler son, James VI, on the throne. In reality, however, Protestant nobles now ruled the country and set about chipping away at Mary's remaining supporters who had holed up in various castles and strongholds across Scotland.

Re-enter Sir Thomas Crawford. Disgusted by Mary's behavior, or maybe just wanting to be on the winning side, Crawford allied himself with the Protestant nobles. By 1571, only a couple of strongholds remained in the hands of Mary's supporters, one of which was the supposedly impregnable Dumbarton Castle. Sir Thomas would change that. Having received inside information from a soldier formerly stationed at Dumbarton concerning the layout of the castle fortifications and the positioning of guards, Crawford developed a plan that was so preposterous, so outlandish, it actually worked.

Approaching under cover of darkness, Crawford and his band of fifty men huddled at the base of the cliff beneath the northeast side of Dumbarton Castle, the side deemed so inaccessible it was manned by only one guard. Without the aid of even moonlight, Crawford and his men set up a specially constructed ladder that reached to a high ledge on the cliff face. At least it was supposed to reach to the high ledge. When Crawford arrived at the top of the ladder, he was actually short of the ledge and so, with his sword and firearm strapped to his back, had to free climb the rest of the way up the rocks, throw down a length of rope, and help secure the ladder a little higher so the rest of the men could ascend.

Once the party had assembled on the ledge, they hoisted the ladder up, leaned it against the rock face, and began the exercise all over again to get to the next level. Unfortunately, Crawford had not screened the men of his merry band for phobias, and therefore missed the somewhat important fact that one of them suffered from an acute fear of heights. Somewhere along the way, this man panicked and froze on the ladder, unable to move forward and unable to climb back down. As he was now directly in the way of the rest of the men, Crawford had to do something or else be caught trapped on the face of the cliff when the sun rose, which of course would be rather difficult to explain. The easiest thing, one could be forgiven for thinking, would have been to duct tape the man's mouth shut and knock him off the ladder to the rocks below. Given the absence of duct tape, Crawford chose a more humane solution and had the man lashed to the ladder where he had frozen in a panic. The ladder was then turned over so the man was on the backside, enabling the remaining members of the party to scramble up, undoubtedly stomping on the poor man's fingers every chance they got.

The party reached the top of the cliff and the castle wall without further incident, and, well, you know how it turned out from there. Crawford succeeded in capturing the castle for the Protestant nobles, and for his efforts, was awarded the lands of Jordanhill near Glasgow, making him Sir Thomas Crawford of Jordanhill, though I'd like to believe his friends still called him Gauntlets. And Crawford didn't stop there. Two years after his capture of Dumbarton, he would lead a force to capture Edinburgh Castle, the last stronghold of Mary's supporters. This attack would prove likewise successful, albeit in a much bloodier fashion.

This sixth son now had a title and land of his own, and the respect of the most powerful men in the country. Much of his exploits regarding the capture of the castle are known through his correspondence with none other than John Knox, the famous fire and brimstone preacher who led the

Protestant Reformation in Scotland and loved the word whoremonger above all others. Crawford also received a letter from King James VI, the monarch who would successfully unite Scotland and England under a common crown, thanking him for his service to the kingdom.

At the end of his long and distinguished career, Sir Thomas returned to Kilbirnie, land of his childhood, and had a mausoleum built for him and his wife where they remain in silent repose today in a quiet churchyard not far from the stately Crawford manor home of Kilbirnie Castle. It was therefore in Kilbirnie that Katrina and I would start our tour of Scotland, paying our respects at this hero's grave and exploring the halls of an old family estate.

But first we had to find them.

.    .    .    .    .

Driving into Kilbirnie, Katrina and I were treated to our first view of a Scottish town. It did not disappoint. Stone buildings, quaint and cozy looking, lined the streets, built directly adjacent to one another like a row of townhouses. We followed the road toward the center of town, me trying not to run onto the sidewalk as I craned my neck to glimpse down the side streets.

We didn't really know what we were looking for. We had a guidebook with us, but Kilbirnie, which apparently isn't a major tourist destination for anyone but Crawfords, wasn't listed in the index. Thanks to my prior research, I knew that the church where Sir Thomas was buried was called the Auld Kirk,* but I had no idea where it was located or where the castle would be in relation to it. Given our driving experiences thus far, an aimless navigation of Kilbirnie's streets and round-a-bouts seemed a poor way to spend a morning.

"Why don't we park the car and walk a bit?" Katrina suggested.

I didn't need convincing. Downshifting with an extravagant raking of gears, I steered the car into the first available spot.

---

* "Auld Kirk" is Scottish for "old church".

This proved to be a great decision. The sky was clear and the air pleasant and cool, despite being July.* We pulled on sweaters and began ambling up and down the streets, past the stone facades of the buildings, which I imagined all had neat little gardens in the back. After exploring the better part of downtown without any sign of the Auld Kirk, we picked a main looking road and began walking away from the town center.

The road led up a gentle hill, and, after a quarter of a mile or so, the buildings started to change. Smaller, disconnected structures with yards replaced the connected stone houses. We were clearly nearing the edge of town and were about to turn around when we spied, not the kirk, but a building offering a ray of hope: a public library.

Upon closer inspection, the library was closed, but we noticed an elderly gentleman in the parking lot unpacking books from his car (a Peugeot Halfpint, I believe). Thinking the man might be the librarian, I approached him and asked if the library were about to open. Smiling, he turned around and responded, and I got my first taste of a full-blown, down home Scottish accent.

Fortunately, Katrina was there. She has a much better grasp of languages and dialects than I do, probably because she grew up in a military family and spent significant time in Turkey, Germany, Italy and Croatia all before she was six, whereas I grew up in Ohio and spoke nothing but Ohioan to Ohioans until I was twenty. While I stared at the man as if he were speaking Swahili, she determined that he did not work at the library, but was simply returning books through the drop slot. The library didn't open for another hour.

While I was fascinated, if a bit stymied, by his accent, he was likewise intrigued by ours, which clearly gave us away as Americans.

"Whit're ye dae'n in Kilbirnie?" he asked, squinting at us and pulling off his well-worn cap. His face was kindly enough, its wrinkles and complexion suggesting a life spent largely outdoors.

Katrina gave him the short story: first trip to Scotland, family roots,

---

* The average summer temperature in central Scotland is 65° F, a cool summer by almost any measure. Still, the perception of just how cool is a very relative notion. Most locals we met wore short sleeves.

old church nearby with some dead Crawfords in it, and so on.

He looked interested, in an amused sort of way. "Did ye see the kirk yet?" he asked.

"Actually, we were having trouble finding it," Katrina replied. "Can you tell us where it is?"

"I could dae tha'," he said, tapping his cap against his leg, "but I may as well take ye there. Come on." And he motioned toward his Peugeot Halfpint.

I looked at him stupidly, not sure I had understood correctly. He repeated the words "Come on" and added some hand gestures for my benefit, and I realized that, yes indeed, this man was inviting two strangers into his car. I would soon learn that this was not unusual in Scotland. Katrina and I, who spent a good deal of time being lost over the next two weeks, would occasionally stop to ask a passerby for directions—almost always an elderly gentleman—only to find him bending over backwards to set us on the right path, as if he had no matter more pressing than making sure we two travelers found our way to our next destination. In the town of Kilmarnock, one man even got into our car, rode with us a few blocks to make sure we knew where we were going, and then popped out at a traffic light saying he'd make his own way back home. I don't know if this is universal across the country or not, but it certainly left us with the impression that Scots are some of the friendliest, most helpful people on Earth.

Not knowing this yet, Katrina and I looked at each other apprehensively, both shrugged with a "what the hell, you only get a chance to be axe-murdered in Scotland once" sort of expression, and got in the car. Within minutes, we were at the Auld Kirk.

Records show that a church has stood on the site of the Auld Kirk since at least 1127, though the oldest part of the current structure was the nave, constructed of beautiful, sturdy looking stonework in 1470—still pretty old by any standard. Over the years, additions were made, all in the same stonework style: a bell tower in 1490, a wing in 1597, and so on. Most recently, an organ chamber was added in 1910. But the most famous addition of all was built in 1642 by the Crawfords of Kilbirnie. Lords of the surrounding region—a sizable tract of meadows, woodland and arable land—the Crawfords financed an elaborate wing containing an ornately carved balcony, crafted of oak, with the family's armorial crest affixed to the front. The book I'd read on the plane featured a photo of this balcony, now known as the Crawford Gallery. It was beautiful and I longed to see it.

Unfortunately, the kirk was not open. An iron fence enclosed the building and the surrounding grounds, and the gate was locked. Crestfallen, we followed the sidewalk around back to at least get a glimpse of the graveyard. There we found a gap in the fence and, not knowing how Scots felt about foreigners trespassing on sacred ground, cautiously slipped through. No alarms sounded; no dogs attacked; no surly undertaker chased us off with his shovel. Instead, a man on a riding mower gave us a kindly wave and kept on going, leaving a path of freshly cut grass behind as he headed off to a far section of the graveyard. It looked like our visit wouldn't be all for naught, after all.

We walked toward the church, and immediately saw what we were looking for: Thomas Crawford's mausoleum. A large rectangular tomb built of moss-covered stone blocks, the structure stood close to the Auld Kirk. Openings in the sides allowed curious visitors to look inside the tomb where stone effigies of Sir Thomas and his wife lay above whatever was left of their four hundred year old remains. The whole thing was very cool in a creepy sort of way. On the outside, a stone plaque read as follows:

*God schaw ye richt.*
*Heir lyis Thomas Cravfvrd of Iordanhil,*
*sext son to Lavrence Cravfvrd of Kilbirny,*
*and Ionet Ker his spovs, eldest dochter to*
*Robert Ker of Kerrisland, 1594.*

I thought about the man and his adventures: friend of kings, prisoner of war, stormer of castles. How proud he must have been of his accomplishments to have come home and have this mausoleum built for his posterity. I wondered what his eldest brother who had inherited the Kilbirnie lands thought of his younger sibling's exploits. Was he buried here as well? We saw other tombstones with Crawford inscriptions, but most were hard to read. Half a millennium had taken its toll.

These were old graves. Much older than anything we are accustomed to in America. 15th century, 14th century. I even saw one with a crude sword carved into it that I later learned may have dated from the Crusades. I could have lingered all day.

Rejuvenated, we walked back to the now open library, which turned out to be just down the street. There we got our first glimpse of another wonderful quirk of Scottish culture: fantastic public libraries staffed, of course, with friendly Scottish people. The librarians at Kilbirnie, two kindly, bespectacled ladies, welcomed us in with a smile. They listened attentively as I told them of my quest for family history, before ushering us into the local history room with some encouraging chatter and advice. There they turned us loose.

The room was spectacular, a veritable treasure trove of information. Volumes of old documents, photographs, drawings, genealogies, legal papers and more lined the bookcases and spilled out of boxes onto the floor. There seemed to be no end to the information contained in this room, where the curious visitor could obtain quaint tidbits of local history ("In the matter of Lord Badluck's stolen goat, M. MacFraud was convicted of producing forged papers, for which he was drawn and quartered, with his body parts being subsequently banished from the realm for a period of fourteen years." And so on.). We would soon find that, like friendly people bending over backwards to give us directions, local history sections in libraries were not unusual in Scotland. We visited libraries in towns throughout our trip—little towns, big towns, it didn't matter—they all had local history rooms full of wonderful information about the surrounding area.

I am useless in such rooms. I get overwhelmed by the prospect of all that information and start looking for the nearest picture book. Katrina, on the other hand, has a knack for research and can skim through paper after paper, somehow gleaning important facts from each. She was soon turning up fascinating information about the history of the Kilbirnie Crawfords: legal documents detailing a feud over ownership of a nearby loch; a genealogy highlighting men such as John Crawford, chosen for Parliament in 1693 and later elevated to the title of Viscount; and a lithograph of the remains of Kilbirnie Castle, the family's manor home, along with an account of its burning in 1757. As Katrina uncovered story after story, I finally accepted my role as note taker, and was writing furiously when the door opened and one of the librarians entered the room.

"I tho' ye might wan tae ken," she said, "I rang the Auld Kirk and they're open, if ye still wan tae see it."

Katrina translated for me and we thanked the thoughtful librarian profusely. I mean it. Some of the nicest people in the world.

Minutes later we were back at the Auld Kirk. Passing through the now open gate, we wandered inside only to find—can you guess?—more friendly people. Two church ladies, which should be adequate description, welcomed us in and beckoned us over to sign the guestbook. Their names were Edith and Ardith or something similarly appropriate, and they were both well over 200 years old. Frail enough to have been sent airborne by the lightest of breezes, they nonetheless met our arrival with a twittering display of energy and animation. It had been days since anyone had signed in.

"How lovely to see you," announced Edith, the wispier of the two, clutching my arm with a bony hand. The strength of her grip suggested its purpose was less to stabilize her own stance and more to keep me from slipping away.

"Lovely indeed," Ardith echoed, latching onto Katrina in similar fashion. We had found our guides.

I briefly introduced the subject of family history and the Church Ladies nearly fell over themselves to instill me with Crawford-related trivia facts about the kirk.

Pointing at the Crawford Gallery above—the highlight I'd come to see—Edith asked: "Did ye ken it was built higher than the pulpit tae remind the preacher tha' he was subordinate tae the Crawford laird?" This was voiced in a hushed tone accompanied by a knowing look so that the scandalous nature of the information could sink in.

"No, I didn't know that," I replied, "but I like the thought very much."

This sent Edith and Ardith twittering, as they led us to the Gallery stairs, encouraging us to go up for a closer look. Temporarily releasing us from their grasp, they stayed below, calling up information in loud whispered voices.

"The wood was carved by hired Italian craftsmen," Ardith remarked. "Be sure tae look a' the detail."

It was hard not to. The entire balcony was intricately carved with biblical inscriptions, family mottoes, coats of arms, and decorative flourishes.

"The family vault is beneath your feet," Edith added, causing Katrina to recoil slightly.

"Don't even think about going down there," Katrina whispered to me, though she needn't have bothered. According to Edith, the vault had been sealed years ago, once it had grown too full and, presumably, aromatic.

"The plain bench in the back was for the servants," Ardith continued from below, "an' the kitchen is behind the gallery."

"I'm sorry, did you say kitchen?" I asked, feeling I must have misheard.

"Oh aye," she said, "Sunday mass was an all-day event. The servants would have had t' prepare a meal mid-way through."

As I digested this last bit of information, I studied the detailed carvings with a whole new sense of appreciation. Knowing how long even an hour at church could seem when I was young, I suspected the diversion such carvings provided was about the only thing keeping children sane in 1642. I tried to imagine myself sitting for hours on a wooden bench above a pile of dead relatives, listening to a preacher drone on and on about whoremongers and hellfire while the smell of food wafted out of the kitchen. I'm not sure I would have had much of an appetite.

Edith and Ardith twittered away when I expressed as much.

We had left our camera in the firm grip of Edith, and before we left the Gallery she offered to take our picture from below.

"Don't forget to pose as though you were lording over the pulpit," Ardith recommended encouragingly.

I put on my best lordly face, but only succeeded—as Katrina was quick to point out—in looking like I had to take a royal dump. Edith and Ardith were still twittering about it as we left the Auld Kirk, tremendously pleased with our visit.

Back in the car, we began driving out of Kilbirnie, though we hoped to catch a glimpse of the castle before leaving the area. Edith had given us directions, which we tried our best to follow. It seemed the ruins stood just out of town, conveniently located along the road to our next destination. With Kilbirnie disappearing behind us, we were beginning to fear we'd missed the castle when Katrina glimpsed some crumbled stone walls beneath a growth of twisting vines and small trees.

Edith hadn't mentioned the golf course separating the ruins from the road.

As we sat in the car lamenting the fact that the castle appeared off limits, we noticed two men walking along the road ahead abruptly turn and disappear into the roadside hedge. A moment later they emerged on the other side and started walking across the golf course. They carried guns. We watched their progress as they cut across a fairway, idly shouldering their rifles, and, upon reaching a gate on the far side, slipped through and entered the property of the castle ruins.

Now, I think the reader would agree that a rational person would not get out of the car, trespass across a golf course, and purposefully hail the attention of two scruffy looking strangers with guns. A rational person would step on the gas and send his Fiat Crumb screeching back onto the highway, leaving the librarians and church ladies of Kilbirnie to deal with such ruffians. I don't know if it was the luck we'd had with friendly people all morning that clouded our judgment or the fact that we'd spent the last twenty-four hours traveling across an ocean to get our first glimpse of a Crawford castle, but we were suddenly seized with the same delirious irrationality that must have led Sir Thomas to scale a cliff toward a heavily fortified castle in the dark. We found ourselves out of the car, across the golf course, and calling to the armed men before we realized just how stupid this probably was.

Fortunately for us, the ranks of friendly Scots included scruffy looking characters with guns. At least, I think they were friendly. Predictably, I couldn't understand a word they said, and remarkably this time neither could Katrina. Their accents were far thicker than anything we'd heard thus far. We carried on a brief dialogue, though this is a generous usage of the word. Katrina's and my role in the conversation consisted mostly of vague head nods, bewildered looks, and the mantra: "I'm sorry, could you repeat that?"

Eventually, we determined that the thinner and scruffier of the two men now owned the land housing the castle ruins and that he and his friend were presently hunting rabbits—the latter made clear when one of them abruptly broke off speech, pointed at a copse of bushes and raised his rifle, only to mutter under his breath as a rabbit hopped smartly into the safety of cover. Thinking I may have stumbled across a distant relative, I told the landowner that I was a Crawford and asked if he was, too. Regrettably, the response was never a simple "aye" or "nae", but always a rambling, unintelligible exposition much longer than would have seemed necessary. In this case, I assumed we were not kin as his response didn't include embracing me in a bear hug and pulling out a flask of whisky to share. We likewise didn't understand his response to our request to explore the ruins, but as we wandered off toward the crumbling walls neither man took a shot at us. Under the circumstances, this qualified them as friendly people.

The castle itself was in pretty bad shape, as far as castles go. Once the great manor home of the Crawfords of Kilbirnie, that powerful clan that stormed castles in the night and made preacher's sweat in their pulpits, Kilbirnie Castle was now a pile of rubble in a field. In 1757, when the castle was already over four hundred years old, a fire had rendered the structure uninhabitable, ironically just as it was undergoing restoration. No one is certain how the fire started. One story claims a spark from a chimney wafted through an opening in the partially reconstructed roof, igniting the rooms below. Another blames the incident on a maid carelessly disposing of melted candle grease. However it started, the fire took hold in a big way, consuming the roof structure, the towers, and the great hall and giving George, the 19th Earl, barely enough time to save his infant daughter and get out.

Having read at the library about the fire, I hadn't expected a complete castle. Still, I had expected to be able to wander through a series of rooms and, with a little imagination, picture what the structure may have looked like when it served as the home of barons and viscounts. Instead, Katrina and I picked over the crumbling walls, making brilliantly insightful comments like, "This circular group of stones may have been the base of a round tower," or "This rectangular gap in the wall may have been a doorway," though we were never really certain.

In the end, crumbling ruins on a golf course were not the mental image I wanted to preserve of the family castle, and we didn't linger too long. Still, I had found tangible evidence of former grandeur, and the Auld Kirk had been resplendent with Crawford history. We drove away from Kilbirnie feeling pretty smug. It had been a good first stop.

# Chapter 4: Vikings on an Angry Sea

## (An afternoon in Largs)

On October 2, 1263, King Haakon of Norway must have looked to the heavens with growing concern. With the wind picking up and the sky growing ominously darker, his armada of Viking longships standing off the western coast of Scotland rocked furiously on the suddenly choppy sea. As the gale intensified, the king struggled to keep order as one after another the anchors gave way and carried the dozens of longships towards the coast of Largs where a Scottish army waited on shore. The Viking warriors who manned these ships were ready for battle; that was after all why they had come.

But not on these terms.

With their boats washed aground, the Vikings had no choice but to jump out and begin the struggle toward shore through the pounding surf, only to be met by the shouts and blades of fresh and heavily armed Scots. The slaughter was awful, with heavy losses on both sides. The churning sea turned red with blood as it washed ashore on the rocks. Both sides fought well, but in the end, the Vikings were forced into a confused and dangerous retreat to their boats, in which they rowed away as the storm abated.

King Haakon would never make it back to Norway. He died on the return journey, and his son, succeeding to the throne, quickly signed a peace treaty relinquishing Norwegian claims to the western isles of Scotland, ending once and for all the Norse occupation of Scottish territory.* Still, it had been a good ride. Prior to the Battle of Largs, Vikings had occupied Scotland for nearly 500 years, long enough to have a significant and lasting cultural influence that continues to this day—not the least of which is evident in a town name like Largs, a name that can't help but conjure up images of fierce dragon-headed ships, helmeted men swinging double-bladed axes and braided women sporting metallic bras.

---

* It should be noted that Norwegians continued to occupy the Shetland and Orkney islands in the north for another two hundred years, but these were not considered part of Scotland at the time.

When Katrina and I planned our Scottish holiday, Largs had landed on our list of destinations not because of any particular Viking fetish we shared, but because of an obscure fact found on the internet regarding the battle. According to a website I had stumbled upon, there was a reason the Scots were so prepared for the Vikings that day in 1263: it seems a Crawford had predicted the storm.

For some reason, this story intrigued me as much as any I had uncovered in my brief foray into Crawford history. I had read of heroic deeds and feats of arms, but this, this was something altogether different: a Crawford employing an aptitude for natural science with a bit of trickery and strategy to outwit the enemy. It was like an episode of *The A-Team*. I intended to find out more about this meteorologically inclined ancestor of mine. Did he have an old knee injury that acted up when the weather was about to change? Had he consulted with druids at a nearby henge? Or was he just one of those dreamy types that spent his days watching the sky?

We were on our way to Largs to find out.

• • • • •

The road from Kilbirnie to Largs was a quiet, pleasant highway following a low stone wall through hilly country. Within twenty minutes we caught our first glimpse of the sea and were soon winding our way down to the coast. The sun danced on the water below.

Largs is a coastal village, nestled on the shore of the Firth of Clyde* in western Scotland. A picturesque, prosperous little town, it capitalizes on its seaside location and Viking history, the latter captured in a Disney-esque, multimedia exposition center called Vikingar!. That exclamation point is not my emphasis by the way. It's actually part of the name of the exposition center. That's how excited Largs is about its Viking roots.

Katrina and I planned to spend the night in Largs, so we set about the

---

* A firth (which is really just fun to say, especially when coupled with similarly fun words, such as in the Firth of Forth), is a long, wide mouth of a river that opens up to the sea at one end, much like a bay, and narrows at the other end, where it meets the river emerging from the mainland. In this case, the Firth of Clyde is the great big mouth of the River Clyde, which flows through Glasgow amongst other places.

business of finding lodging. The main road through town runs parallel to the coast, and we drove the length of it and back to get a sense of the area. A historic district comprised the town center, nestled against the shore with shops, restaurants and all the other amenities one would expect in a place making its living off tourists. Neat houses dotted the surrounding hillsides. We settled on a small bed and breakfast just south of the town center and checked in. The room, like most in Europe, was roughly the size of our Fiat Crumb. We put our bags down and then scrambled over them to get back out the door. It was only mid-afternoon so we still had plenty of time to explore.

Our first stop, as it had to be, was Vikingar!, located just to the north of town along the water. A replica Viking longship anchored out front of a large modern building suggested we had arrived at our destination, but we still had no idea what wonders awaited. I expected a small museum focused mainly on the Battle of Largs, preferably with an entire room dedicated to Crawford contributions to the victory. Instead, we found ourselves in a modern multimedia complex, complete with a main exhibition tour, cinema, gift shop and cafeteria all dedicated to the celebration of Vikinghood. It was marvelous. Sort of a Colonial Williamsburg meets IMAX concept with all the cheesiness and kitsch one would expect of such a place.

We purchased tickets for the next tour, which didn't begin for half an hour. This time was easily passed in the gift shop, which offered for sale everything a tourist who knew nothing about Vikings could possibly want: plastic swords and battle axes, horned helmets, books on how to write your name with runes, and so on. I browsed through a shelf of books on Viking life and Norse mythology, and found a few that discussed the Battle of Largs. None mentioned anything about Crawford weathermen, however. I pointed out this bit of disturbing news to Katrina.

"They're just keeping you in suspense," she surmised, trying on a horned helmet and poking me with a plastic sword. "If they gave away all the brilliant plot twists in the gift shop, no one would buy a ticket for the exhibition."

I waited until she turned around and clubbed her on the helmet with a plastic battle axe. Such action did little to convince Katrina of Crawford heroics, but did elicit a polite cough from the store's cashier, causing us to sheepishly return our weapons to the bin and hasten over to the tour waiting area where a small group had assembled.

When the appointed time arrived, a door swung open and out shuffled a droopy young man dressed like Hagar the Horrible: furry tunic, furry boots, helmet, shield…you know the look. Hagar greeted us with a resigned expression that said, "I know I look stupid, but its part of the job, so shut up already," before introducing himself as our guide and ushering us through the door. Crossing the threshold, we traveled back in time and found ourselves in a small rustic room simulating a Viking farmhouse. The room was littered with cooking implements, crude benches, weapons and bits of dried food. As we took in the surroundings, Hagar began speaking about daily life as a Viking.

Judging by the reactions of the other tourists in our group, his oral tale proved fascinating. I assume he revealed that Vikings, despite being forever depicted as marauding sea warriors, spent the majority of their days as peaceful farmers, providing for their families through the tedious cultivation of crops—an activity which seldom required the donning of horned helmets or metallic bras. I can't say with more certainty because Hagar, despite the Viking get up, was every bit Scottish when it came to his speech patterns. Catching only one out of every five words he uttered, I had to piece together the narrative with a combination of hand gestures and my own patchy understanding of Norse history. Mostly, I contented myself with looking around at the contrived scenery, which was diverting enough all by itself.

After the farmhouse, the tour continued through a succession of rooms, all with a different Viking theme: the Hall of Gods, a longship, the shores of Largs. Special effects incorporated along the way enhanced the experience. These consisted of light projections, video screens, dramatic theme music, and, on the simulated shores of Largs, life-sized warriors with creepy projected faces that spoke—sort of like mannequins with ghostly, animated expressions. Our tour group shuffled through in awe.

The exhibition's only disappointment was the lack of any mention of a Crawford with an uncanny knack for weather patterns. The omission proved a bit disconcerting and made me wonder if I had indeed been duped by an overzealous Crawford posting phony websites. I considered asking Hagar about the matter at the end of the tour, but was pretty sure I wouldn't have understood his answer.

· · · · ·

Back outside the sky was still gloriously blue. Having done enough research for the day, Katrina and I wandered over to the waterfront for a leisurely stroll. We didn't make it far. An opportunistic ice cream vendor had set up shop directly across from Vikingar!, and we felt the need to sample a dish.

Sitting on the waterfront at Largs with a bowl of ice cream will long be a favorite memory of mine. A paved path stretched down the waterfront to the town center where the church spires and gabled roofs presented a view that was both quaint and magnificent at the same time. To the west, the isle of Great Cumbrae, just a couple miles off the coast, shone in the sun. Everywhere there were people: strolling, biking, waiting for the ferry, or just sitting and eating ice cream like us. It was the first time we had stopped moving all day.

"Now *this* feels like vacation," Katrina mused, finishing her bowl and leaning over to sample a spoonful from mine.

The ice cream having just whet our appetites, we meandered back to town in search of dinner, settling on an unremarkable restaurant chosen mostly for its offering of fish and chips and availability of malt vinegar, for which I had a hankering. When Katrina proved less decisive about her order, the waiter, a chatty young man who could obviously sense new blood in his country, attempted to steer her toward some more traditional Scottish fare.

"Perhaps ye'd like to try a haggis?" he offered smiling. Something about his expression spoke of foreboding.

"And what exactly is haggis?" Katrina asked warily.

"It's a type of sausage, really," he replied brightly, "mixed in with tasty things like onion, oatmeal and liver bits."

"Liver *bits*?" Katrina repeated.

"Tha's right," he continued, clearly enjoying the opportunity to educate. "An' in keeping wi' tradition, we prepare it in a sheep's stomach for added flavor." Here he held out his hands as if he were holding a basketball, apparently to help us envision the dimensions of an inflated sheep's stomach.

A brief pause followed, allowing the appropriate mental image to form.

"Is tha' right," Katrina finally responded with mock interest barely concealing disgust. "In that case, the salmon sounds great."

The waiter shrugged his shoulders and headed off to the kitchen. One sensed this was part of a nightly routine performed for tourists.

"Haggis really is the quintessential Scottish dish," I observed to Katrina, "I'm surprised you didn't go for it." Of the two of us, she was the much more adventurous eater.

"Let's just say that anything prepared in the innards of a sheep ranks low on my 'things to try in Scotland' list," she replied.

"Well, it's supposed to be quite tasty," I pressed.

"Tasty?"

"Yes."

"Really?"

"That's what the guidebook says."

"Then I wonder," Katrina said in the tone of a lawyer about to deliver a coup de grace, "with all those Scottish immigrants flooding into the United States, why haggis didn't catch on over there?"

I had to admit, it was a good point.

After dinner, we headed back outside for a stroll: the first of what would become a sacred nightly ritual for us, enjoying the last hours of daylight each evening. Scotland is a country that seems to encourage walking, and everywhere we found paths inviting us to do so. On this night we walked along the shore where the battle had taken place. Shallow water lapped against a tumbled field of rocks, tiny pools providing a haven for waving seaweed and crustaceans. The sun low over the water turned the water blood red, but other than this detail, it was difficult to imagine a battle taking place here. Everything felt so peaceful.

As if sensing my doubt, the path ended at a monument built to commemorate the defeat of the Vikings. The tall, round tower of stone had been dubbed the Pencil Monument, and it contained plaques at its base describing the events which took place on the surrounding shore. There was no mention of Crawford, but by this point, I wasn't really expecting any.

"Do you realize how long we've been up?" Katrina asked with a yawn, as we turned to follow the path back to town. "Don't take this the wrong way, but I think this officially ranks as the longest day of my life."

I knew what she meant. After traveling through the previous day and night, we had been on the go since sunrise that morning. It was now after 9:00pm, and the sun was still up.

"Back home, the sun would have set two hours ago," Katrina observed sleepily, leaning into me as she walked.

She was right. In the tropics, the days show little change in length throughout the year—just a couple of hours from the height of winter to the height of summer—so we had forgotten the pleasures of long, sunlit summer evenings.

Scotland is about as far away as one can get from the tropics. Walking on the shore at Largs we stood at 55° north latitude. If we had kept walking west, circling the globe at that latitude, we would have passed two degrees north of Edmonton, Canada and just one degree below Sitka, Alaska. Continuing on, we would have been well in the north of Siberia, passing two degrees above Moscow and directly through Copenhagen before returning to Largs, probably in time for a spectacular sunset. Scotland is way up there.

The upshot of this northern latitude is a huge shift in the amount of daylight the country gets between summer and winter: about ten hours in fact. In the dead of winter, the sun rises as late as 9:00am and sets by 4:00pm, which undoubtedly helps explain the popularity of pubs. Throughout our trip, however, the sun was up by 5:00am and didn't set until nearly 10:00pm, with twilight lingering until nearly midnight.

These long days, combined with the short distances between destinations, meant that two travelers like us could get a lot out of our time in Scotland. But after a full day of travel followed by a full day of exploration, we were ready for our first day in Scotland to end. We wandered back to our hotel and went to bed about as content as we could be, and didn't even notice that our toes touched the opposite wall of the room.

# Chapter 5: Lord of the Trailer Park

## (From Crosbie to Craufurdland)

I have specific expectations when it comes to lodging in various regions of the world. Such expectations were not consciously formed, yet somewhere along the way became cemented in my head and now help to reinforce the stereotypes I associate with each region.

For me, Western America will always mean camping. If I find myself somewhere between the Rocky Mountains and the Sierra Nevadas, I expect to hike with a fifty pound pack on my back to my place of lodging, which will likely be a clearing in the woods miles from anywhere, set up my own tent, chop my own firewood, cook my own meal, and at some point, leave my mark in nature while trying to avoid getting eaten by Bigfoot.

This contrasts sharply in my mind with everything east of the Rockies, which is defined by roadside chain hotels with names like "Comfort Inn", "EconoLodge" or "Generic Hotel By Highway". These hotels are all the same. They have the same beds, the same non-descript decorations, the same invisible maids, the same sad-looking swimming pools that nobody uses. At these hotels, I expect to drive up in my car, carry my suitcase to a featureless room, eat dinner at a fast food restaurant located within fifty yards of the entrance, and then return to my featureless room where the remote control will adhere to my hand for the rest of the night as I search for a decent movie on HBO but instead get a bad Chuck Norris film, and thus resign myself to watching reruns of sitcoms I never liked in the first place on Nickelodeon.

Europe presents a different scenario altogether in my mind, though this scenario has varied with age. My last trip to Europe took place in my early twenties, and Europe meant youth hostels. On that trip, I wandered with a rucksack on my back, bouncing from one seedy hostel to another, meeting other seedy characters like myself with whom I could explore. The idea was always to meet an exotic beauty from some far-flung region of the world (who was just dying to meet a guy from Ohio) with whom I could philosophize over wine at a sidewalk café before strolling hand in hand among street musicians and artists. In reality, I'd end up hanging out with a pack of Canadians, wishing I could afford cheese to go with my dry bread for lunch. Thus I learned that American ignorance of Canada is reciprocated by a Canadian disdain for the United States. Canadians I met throughout the trip invariably had a maple leaf flag sewn prominently onto their backpacks, not out of some inflamed Canadian pride—which would be difficult to come by in a country that still has the British monarch on its money—but for the sole purpose of distinguishing them from Americans like myself. So there you go.

Ten years later, I felt ready to step up my European experience a notch or two above hostels. With just enough income to not have to sleep with a pack of Canadians who openly loathe me, the natural choice for lodging became the bed and breakfast. Bed and breakfasts, or B&B's, have a culture about them all their own. The very term bed and breakfast has a romantic quality to it and conjures up a picture of an old stately home, large without being intimidating, full of cozy rooms, friendly, doting proprietors, and a handful of other guests who are always charming without being overbearing and certainly don't have flags sewn on their luggage to distinguish them from myself.

Katrina and I had looked forward to the B&B experience on our trip, though I should note my one trepidation: I'm not much for small talk. I get this honestly. My father, who loathes small talk so much that he can't even remember the correct term for it (he calls it "short talk"), goes to great lengths to avoid such pointless interaction. This is perhaps best demonstrated by his annual outing taken shortly before Christmas to the much dreaded shopping mall in our hometown. Each year, he parks near the anchor store at one end, briefly shops at just that store, and then returns to his car and drives two hundred yards to the anchor store at the other end of the mall to continue shopping, thus avoiding any chance encounter with an acquaintance during the two-minute walk through the interior of the mall. I am much of the same mould.

So it was with eagerness tinged by just a shade of anxiety that, upon waking up in the morning at the B&B in Largs, we stepped out of our room and wandered to the communal dining room.

I am pleased to say that, in this particular case, the romantic image held up. We entered a welcoming, wood paneled room filled with cloth-covered tables of varying size. Out the window the Firth of Clyde sparkled in the morning sunlight. The handful of guests occupying the room looked up, mumbled good morning in a kindly but non-engaging way, and turned their attention back to the food on their plates. Everyone seemed quite content to go about his or her own business, and the little bit of small talk—or short talk, if you prefer—that occurred was brief and pleasant. ("So, you're from America, are you?... Oh, the Caribbean. Goodness, you're quite far from home. Well then, have a pleasant holiday in Scotland. You have a rare day of sun, you know.") Then it was back to their plates in a very unhurried fashion.

And the food, I should note, was delicious. A wonderful assortment of cold food was already laid out on a common table: fruit, wedges of cheese, pitchers of juice, some sort of cereal grain. After we helped ourselves to a plate, a server brought out a hot meal of eggs, sausage and mushrooms—all very tasty. On this occasion and several others throughout the trip, Katrina and I ate so much at breakfast that we skipped lunch and didn't eat again until the evening, which enabled us to pack even more into the day.

The only drawback to the morning was trying to shower in a stall smaller than a phone booth, a standard feature of every B&B in Scotland so far as I can tell. This was a very funny and somewhat bruising experience, involving my knocking helplessly into the shower walls as I tried to maneuver my arms, irretrievably bent at the elbow and thus reduced to T-Rex-like stubs, into various scrubbing positions. After great commotion, I pronounced myself wet enough to be most likely clean, and stepped out of the shower to begin the equally difficult task of drying off with a towel the size of a postage stamp.

Full, well rested and eighty-five percent clean, we were ready to start our second day in Scotland.

· · · · ·

My mission for the day was to restore some family honor by solving the mystery of the victory at Largs. The lack of any mention the previous day of a Crawford at the Viking battle had made me dubious of any family role, but I was not ready to give up on my storm-predicting ancestor. I still had one avenue to explore.

The website where I had found the only mention of a Crawford at Largs had also mentioned that, as a reward for his services, this particular Crawford had received the lands of Crosbie, upon which he had built a castle called Crosbie Tower. Crosbie, according to the website, was located just outside the village of West Kilbride, which itself was less than ten miles south of Largs. I confirmed the location on our map before squeezing into our Fiat Crumb in the highest of spirits. We were in Scotland; the sun was shining; we had a castle to find and a mystery to solve. This promised to be a great day.

The road followed the coast south from Largs. We meandered along enjoying beautiful views of the Firth of Clyde as we headed toward West Kilbride. Our plan was simple: we would drive into the town and seek out the public library, hoping to find information on a Crawford connection to Crosbie and directions to Crosbie Tower, if indeed it still existed. The latter question was resolved unexpectedly as we came to a fork in the road on the approach to West Kilbride. A sign post told us that one direction would take us to the town, while the other would take us to—can you believe it?— Crosbie Tower.

We marveled at our luck as we took the road to the castle. A very narrow back road little more than one lane wide, it twisted through the countryside into a wooded glen. After a few minutes, a driveway turned off and another signpost announced our arrival at something called "Crosbie Tower Caravan Park." Hmmm. I hadn't expected the Caravan Park part. Nor did I really know what it meant. Perhaps a band of gypsies had taken up residence in the castle? The question was soon answered.

The driveway wound its way up a gentle hill, and on either side of the road we began to pass a series of trailer homes tucked into the woods. That's right, trailer homes. Mobile homes, homes on wheels, tornado bait— call them what you will, but at the end of the day, a caravan park turns out to be just a fancy Scottish euphemism for a trailer park. Well, I'd seen these before. I'm from Ohio after all. I had relatives that lived in trailer parks. They all lived next to some guy named Eddie who, besides owning a trailer, also possessed a beer gut, a car on cinder blocks, and a third wife who screamed a lot: "Eddie, get your damn feet off the sofa! Eddie, where were you last night?! Eddie, put that crowbar down!" Eddie would spend his time getting exercise at the bowling alley or in bar fights until finally a tornado blew away his trailer or he ended up in prison. Then a new guy named Eddie would move next door and begin the cycle all over again.

Driving by the rows of trailers at Crosbie, I noted that both the yards and homes—and, I assume, the inhabitants—looked neater and tidier than their counterparts in America. Yet still, it would take a very generous definition of castle to think I was on the right track in my search.

But then Katrina, a little too smugly, called my attention to a detail I'd overlooked. A side street broke off from the main road to create a little trailer neighborhood within the caravan park. A sign, upon closer study, indicated the name of the street as—and this is rich—Crauford Court. A variant on the spelling perhaps, but unmistakably a tip of the hat to the family name. It may not have been what I expected to find, but it did serve as a pretty strong indication that the Crawford family had done something important here, or at least important enough to justify commemoration by a trailer park. Our curiosity piqued, we drove forward hoping to find either a castle or a bowling alley, whichever came first.

When the road dead-ended at the top of the hill, we found what we had come for. Crosbie Tower, or what we presumed was Crosbie Tower, stood on a crest of land lording over the trailer park. A stately three-storey manor home that had obviously been added to over time, the castle stood in pretty good repair considering its counterpart in Kilbirnie. A relatively new looking wing of reddish brick and bay windows protruded from an older looking structure of grayish stone and tiny windows. The reddish brick part, despite being newer, had obviously suffered a fire some time ago, and was now roofless and somewhat dilapidated. The original gray structure, however, looked remarkably intact.

We parked the car and wandered around the ruins, looking up at the windows. A mound of gravel had been dumped in the front yard as if work was being done and the doors to the castle had been sealed off. No signs offered any information about the structure, but this had to be it.

A somewhat humbler though decidedly more modern building across the street appeared to be the headquarters of the caravan park, so we walked over to see if anyone was around. Knocking persistently on a door marked "Office", we eventually heard signs of life, and moments later a tired looking middle-aged man came to the door. He looked surprised to see a young couple at his door, and for a moment—I swear I saw his eyes light up—he probably thought he was about to make a sale.

If he was disappointed when I instead asked about the history of the castle, he hid it well. Rather, he launched into a succinct explanation of the castle's history as if his job as manager of the caravan park also included guided history tours, which it may well have. We listened intently as he related a fascinating—and to me, very satisfying—tale.

According to the caravan park manager, a castle had been on this site since the late 13th century, built by Sir Reginald Crawford, who held the title of Sheriff of Ayr. This particular Reginald Crawford was the brother of Margaret Crawford, mother of that greatest Scottish hero William Wallace. Legends abound about Wallace's connection to the castle. One claims he was actually born in the castle. Another says he jumped out of a third storey window to escape the English during a surprise raid. The manager proudly pointed out this window to us, despite the fact that the current castle almost certainly dated later than the 13th century. At any rate, Wallace appears to have been a regular at Crosbie, visiting his ol' Uncle Reggie. A rather famous incident regarding the Barns of Ayr, of which more will be told shortly, seemed to confirm this.

In the meantime, the reader can imagine my elation upon learning this news. The manager didn't know of any connection to the Battle of Largs, but surely this couldn't be a coincidence. Historians place Wallace's birth somewhere between 1270 and 1276, within a decade or so of the Battle of Largs. The timing would have been perfect for Reginald Crawford or possibly his father Hugh, one of whom appeared to be the lost weatherman I was looking for, to have acquired the lands of Crosbie after the battle in 1263 and to have built a brand new castle just in time to house the daredevil antics of a young William Wallace. I was beginning to feel vindicated, but wanted to find out more to be certain.

We left the caravan park, and found our way to West Kilbride, a quaint hilltop village replete with gray stonework and winding streets. The public library stood just off the main street, and we were soon inside talking to the librarian, who proved to be every bit as friendly and helpful as those in Kilbirnie. She eagerly directed us to the local history section of the West Kilbride library, and even suggested some of her favorite sources for local history, one of which, titled *Our Village: The Story of West Kilbride*, proved particularly helpful.

Flipping through its pages, I learned many nuggets of useful information regarding Crosbie Tower, including the fact that it had remained in the Crawford family for 600 years before being sold in the 19th century. Reading on, I learned that, for an 18-year period in the 1940s and 50s, the castle operated as a youth hostel. I pictured packs of seedy, young Canadians lodging at the ol' family estate, throwing their maple leaf bags onto the floor of the Great Hall, and came to the conclusion that the castle's ultimate fate as the centerpiece of a caravan park constituted a definite improvement over its operation as a hostel.

Slipped in amongst these facts, I finally found confirmation of my meteorologically-inclined ancestor. At least I found near confirmation. What the book actually said was that the lands of Crosbie had been given to the Crawford family "for good service at the Battle of Largs in 1263." Now, I know this doesn't actually say that Uncle Reggie or Grandpa Hugh predicted the storm, but what else could "good service" mean given the website I had seen? Certainly, no one would have read "good service" and then made up some far-fetched scenario about predicting a storm. Someone wanting to bend the truth to glorify an ancestor would have created a tale about swimming out to drill holes in the Viking longships, or losing his weapon on the beach but continuing to fight off Vikings with nothing but a chunk of driftwood and the carcass of a dead fish, but surely not predicting a storm. For me, "good service" confirmed the website's reliability.

I walked out of the library satisfied, my swagger back and slightly amplified. I even considered returning to Crosbie Tower to claim the castle and take up life ruling over the serfs in my feudal trailer park. All the cars on blocks and cheap grills and tin homes would be mine, and their occupants would form my peasant army that I would raise to hold off encroaching nobles in some ongoing neighborly feud over sheep or boundaries. After a day of good fighting, I'd invite my people back to the castle for a day of revelry, but not too much, lest they become spoiled and dissatisfied with their own menial lives. To keep them satisfied, I would build them a bowling alley.

Such were my thoughts as I drove away from West Kilbride. I tried to share them with Katrina, who, ever a good sport, nonetheless stared at me with a pitying glance and moved as far away as one can get in a Fiat Crumb.

·   ·   ·   ·   ·

We were making our way to Ayr, another twenty miles down the coast from West Kilbride, which in Scotland qualifies as quite a distance indeed. Rather than be daring and try to make the entire thirty-minute journey in one stretch, we decided to detour slightly inland to the town of Kilmarnock, breaking the long drive into more manageable fifteen or twenty minute chunks. Kilmarnock ranked as the largest town we had visited yet, described by our guidebook as "by and large, a shabby and depressed manufacturing town," so I'm sure the reader understands our desire to visit.

Needless to say, Kilmarnock's manufacturing highlights were not what drew us to the city. Rather we hoped to gain directions to a nearby site of interest called—and I'm not making this up—Craufurdland Castle. I had learned about this particular castle in the book I'd read on the plane. It proved noteworthy not just because it was a beautiful old castle, but because, of all the castles we could see in Scotland, it stood as the only one still in Crawford hands. In fact, Crawfords still inhabited it. There were probably Crawfords home right now. This was the one castle where I could conceivably knock on the door, announce my Crawfordness and, like in my Scottish fantasy, be ushered into the room by grateful kin and given a seat of honor beside the roaring fireplace while their sassy maid served me creamy ale.

Of course, we first had to find the castle, which as a still-inhabited residence was not marked as a tourist attraction on our map. Given our successes of the last two days, the library of Kilmarnock struck us as a good place to look for guidance—which meant we first had to find the library.

Kilmarnock is a tourist's nightmare. The entire downtown district consists of a mess of one way streets that suck in passing cars, spin them in a pre-determined pattern through a cycle of chaotic traffic, and then shoot them back out again roughly where they started. If a tourist proves unlucky, as we did several times, the car will then be sucked back into the course to repeat the cycle.

When we finally extricated ourselves from the vicious loop, we pulled over near a convenience store to ask directions to the library. As the reader may recognize, this is the part of the story when Katrina returned to the car, not with directions, but with a sympathetic elderly gentleman who had literally put his groceries down on the floor in the middle of his shopping and left the convenience store to help us find our way. He nimbly climbed into the car with us, directed me into the one-way chute of death, and helped me successfully navigate until he was able to point out the way to the library along with a recommendation of where to park. As I thanked him profusely, he opened the door, stepped out with a wave, and began making his way back to the convenience store to continue his shopping.

This turned out to be premature, as I then missed the entrance to the parking lot and was forced to bob along in the traffic back to our original starting point near the convenience store. Fortunately, I was getting to know the route fairly well at this point, and steered back into the loop, sheepishly waving to the surprised gentleman as we passed him on the sidewalk, and this time successfully entered the lot and walked to the library.

The library was of course fantastic and worth all the trouble. The librarian could not direct us to Craufurdland Castle, but did direct us to a magnificent local map section which broke the surrounding areas down by district with the most minute details. While Katrina combed through the various maps to pinpoint our destination, I browsed through the stacks, finding tidbits of information, fascinating to no one but a Crawford, from which I will spare the reader. I have no idea how much time passed, but I was happily engaged in a genealogy of the Crawfords of Loudoun when Katrina came to find me, triumphantly clutching a copy of a map in her hand.

Back in the car, we set off in search of the castle, which even with the map proved difficult to find. We were well into the countryside surrounding Kilmarnock when we finally spotted a sign for Craufurdland and turned down the road. Like the approach to Crosbie Tower, the road to Craufurdland proved long and narrow. It took us through what appeared to be a private nature preserve surrounding the castle. A tiny river—a creek, really—called Craufurdland Water ran through the preserve, and we passed several cars loaded with fishing gear parked along the roadside. We continued a long way and hadn't seen any signs of life in some time when the road suddenly narrowed further and large "No Trespassing" signs were posted at the edges. It was pretty clear that we were close to the castle, and also pretty clear that these Crawfords valued their privacy. Sensitive people that we were, Katrina and I got out of the car and continued on foot.

I want to make it clear from the start that I felt very guilty about this. Still, I had come pretty far to take a little peek, and maybe stay for just one pint. We tiptoed down the hedge-trimmed driveway, apprehensive of every noise. After a hundred yards or so, the hedge on the left stopped and we poked our heads around. There, startlingly close, stood a stately, intact, fully inhabited Crawford castle. It was beautiful. Built of light brown stones, the castle sported a turreted façade with small paned windows and a large arched entryway. It looked like a castle out of a fairy tale, only this one had cars parked out front.

People were home. It was just as I had hoped—better, really—but suddenly I felt stupid and small. Katrina urged me to knock on the door and introduce myself.

"I can't do it," I muttered.

Katrina stared at me as if I had just kicked a puppy.

"I can't do it," I repeated. And I couldn't.

For some reason, seeing those cars in the driveway brought it home to me that these were real people living their lives, albeit in grander fashion than most. I pictured myself at home in the islands enjoying our waterfront cottage only to have some tourist from Nebraska show up and say, "Hey there, I thought I'd come butt in on your day, hang out on your beach and otherwise disrupt your privacy, because after all I'm a Crawford like you. Say, do you have any creamy ale?" I didn't want to be that guy, regardless of how much I wanted to be inside that castle. So, contenting myself with a surreptitious photo taken from behind the hedge, I turned and walked away—though as I did I could have sworn I saw a shadow of a maid pass the window carrying a tray of pints.

Still, it was hard to be disappointed. After seeing dilapidated family estates littered across golf courses and trailer parks, we had found one that remained just as a castle should be: well-maintained, surrounded by beautiful grounds, and occupied by Crawfords. It was only early afternoon and we had already resolved the mystery of Largs and found proof that, at least in one corner of Scotland, the family name continued to thrive. I vowed to call ahead to Craufurdland next time.

Returning to the car, we began the short journey to Ayr. All those thoughts of creamy ale had put me in the mood for a pub, and with evening coming on we were determined to find one.

# Chapter 6: Swinging Uncles and Bonnie Lasses
## (An evening in Ayr)

On the morning of June 18, 1297, Sir Reginald Crawford and his nephew, William Wallace, set out from Crosbie Tower on the road to Ayr. As Sheriff of Ayr and a leading noble in Scotland, Crawford had been summoned to a meeting between Scottish and English lords to discuss peace between the two lands. This was welcome news after years of turmoil during which England, led by the ruthless Edward I, or Longshanks, as he was known, had reached north and tried to bring Scotland under its control.

What caused this turmoil makes for a fascinating story in itself. Eleven years earlier, the reign of the successful and very popular Scottish king, Alexander III, had come to a rather unexpected end when he rode his horse over a coastal cliff on his way home from a meeting and ignominiously plummeted to his death. Apparently such bad luck ran in the family because all of his children had preceded him to the grave, leaving only a three-year old granddaughter living in Norway to succeed him to the throne. This "Maid of Norway," as she was known, had a short and ineffective reign herself, dying at the age of seven without ever stepping foot on Scottish soil. Thus, in 1290, Scotland found itself fresh out of royals, with a handful of squabbling nobles claiming the right to the vacant throne.

For two years, Edward of England feigned concern for his northerly neighbor, offering to act as arbitrator between the nobles to help restore order and just rule to Scotland. It soon became clear, however, that Longshanks was far more intent on establishing a puppet king in Scotland that would pay homage to England and ultimately render Scotland a vassal state of its southern neighbor. Needless to say, many Scots were not pleased with this arrangement. Resistance had mounted, with skirmishes between Scots and English soldiers becoming more and more frequent.

It was under these conditions that Longshanks invited leading members of the Scottish nobility to a council at Ayr to discuss peace. To ensure their safety, the English king had issued a charter of peace some months prior, signed by many of the Scottish nobility.

Thus, we find Sir Reginald and his nephew riding toward Ayr on the appointed day. At some point during the journey it occurred to Reginald, who possessed a copy of the peace charter, that perhaps the document would be a good thing to have with him as he rode toward a city occupied by English soldiers. Thus, he sent his nephew, William Wallace, back to Crosbie Tower to retrieve the document while he himself continued on to the meeting. It was the last time Wallace would see his uncle alive.

Arriving on schedule to a meeting called under the guise of peace, Sir Reginald found himself seized by English soldiers, who promptly slipped a noose around his neck and hung him from the rafters of the meeting room. The council had served as a ruse to gather the leading nobles of Ayr in one place where they could be treacherously murdered one by one upon their arrival. Sir Reginald proved to be the first of many nobles who would die that day.

When Wallace finally approached with the useless charter, he was intercepted on the outskirts of the city by friends who warned him of what had occurred. Wallace, who had already lost his father to skirmishes with the English, did not take the news of Uncle Reggie's death well. Waiting until nightfall, he and a band of followers approached the Barns of Ayr, where the meeting was to have taken place and where the English soldiers now drunkenly celebrated the deaths of the Scottish nobles. A man of efficiency, Wallace barricaded the doors, trapping the English inside, and set fire to the buildings, which soon blazed furiously out of control. As the soldiers perished in the flames, Wallace's fate was sealed.

Prior to the incident, he was little more than an upstart rebel, more of a nuisance, really, than a serious threat to English rule in Scotland. Afterwards, however, Wallace was a full-blown revolutionary who three months later would lead a ragtag army at Stirling Bridge to one of Scotland's greatest victories. It would seem Longshanks had tangled with the wrong family.

• • • • •

Today, Ayr, the county town of Ayrshire, is a city of consequence. With 50,000 residents, it ranks as the largest city on the Firth of Clyde coast, and has the rich and turbulent history one would expect of a major seaport. I was obviously keen to visit the site of the burning of the Barns of Ayr, the brutal and bloody event just described in which my ancestors had served as both victim and avenger. Consulting my guidebook, however, I found that Ayr had more to offer than just the memory of hanging Crawfords and frying English soldiers.

The city had been the stomping grounds of Robert Burns, Scotland's poet laureate, who rattled the ears of the 18th century aristocracy with romantic poetry written in raw Scottish dialect rather than the polished King's English. As a consequence, the city provided the setting of some of Burns's greatest works and now serves as an essential stop on the Robbie Burns trail, a path followed by Burns fanatics who wish to visit sites of interest associated with the poet.

I knew very little of the poet at the time other than what the guidebook told me, but have learned more since. Burns, who was born in the town of Alloway just to the south in 1759, clearly revered the city, musing:

*Auld Ayr, wham ne'er a town surpasses*
*For honest men and bonnie lasses.*

We can take Burns at his word when it comes to bonnie lasses, for by all accounts, he was an expert on the subject, fathering illegitimate children throughout the area.

The eldest son of a bankrupt farmer, Burns became a ploughman himself, supporting his family after his father's death in 1784. This earthy existence kept him close to the common man and shaped his poetry, which he had already begun to write before his father's death. Just two years later, he published his first work, titled *Poems, Chiefly in the Scottish Dialect*, featuring poems such as "To a Mouse, on Turning her up in her Nest with the

Plough, November, 1785" and making him a sensation amongst common and educated Scots alike.

As his stature increased, Burns traveled throughout the country collecting traditional songs and lyrics, which eventually led to the composition of his own songs. Some of these became quite famous throughout Scotland and beyond and even endure today. In fact, most of us, whether we have ever heard of Robert Burns or not, are familiar with at least one of his works: "Auld Lang Syne", a song sung around the English-speaking world every New Year's Eve. Everybody knows the tune, though nobody quite knows the words. It seems that every December 31, I join a pack of drunken celebrants mumbling something along the lines of: "Should auld acquaintance be forgot, blah blah flub blub bub bah! Should auld acquaintance be forgot blah blah for Auld Lang Syne." Sound familiar? I thought so.*

At any rate, upon checking into a B&B near Ayr's central district, Katrina and I decided to take in a bit of the Robbie Burns trail while strolling through the streets and finding our bearings. We walked north along the main road, stopping to dally in Wellington Square, a flowery plaza full of war memorials and statues and lined with attractive old buildings. We continued on past St. John's Tower, a gated ruin of a church old enough to have provided a meeting place for the Scottish parliament in 1315, following Robert the Bruce's victory at Bannockburn, of which more later.

A few blocks further, we arrived at the banks of the River Ayr and one of the major stops on the Robbie Burns trail: the Brigs of Ayr. Two bridges (brigs in the Scottish dialect) spanned the river just a block apart, connecting the downtown district with the northern bank. The bridge nearest us was known as New Brig, while the one a block further on was known as Auld Brig. Of course, new and old here take on relative measures. Both qualified as quite old by American standards, where we consider old anything built before our own births. (Anything built before our parents'

---

* So that you can impress your friends this New Year's Eve, I've included the complete lyrics for *Auld Lang Syne* at the back of this book. I don't advise learning more than the first couple of verses for two reasons: 1) your friends will likely be too drunk to remember your feat anyway, and 2) unless you speak native Scots you won't understand the words even after reading them.

births is ancient. Anything from our grandparents' time will likely contain dinosaur fossils.)

Burns immortalized these two particular bridges in his poem, "The Brigs of Ayr", in which Auld Brig and New Brig debate a number of issues, including which is the more bridge-worthy. I was intrigued by the following excerpt, contained in our guidebook:

New Brig:   *Will your poor narrow foot-path of a street,*
      *Where twa wheel-barrows tremble when they meet,*
      *Your ruin'd formless bulk o' stane and lime,*
      *Compare wi' bonnie brigs o' modern time?...*

Auld Brig:   *Conceited gowk! puff'd up wi' windy pride!*
      *This mony a year I've stood the flood an' tide;*
      *And tho' wi' crazy eild I'm sair forfairn,*
      *I'll be brig, when ye're a shapeless cairn!*

Burns, who died in 1796, didn't live long enough to find out just how prophetic his poem would be. The New Brig, built in 1787, lasted less than a century before being replaced with an even newer bridge (the new New Brig?) in 1877, which is the New Brig seen today. The Auld Brig, an arched stone structure built in the late 15th or early 16th century, continues to stand half a millennium later. Katrina and I took a stroll across the Auld Brig just for kicks. It held.

By this point, we'd worked up a fairly good appetite, so we set off to find some fare. In keeping with the Burns theme, we selected a pub on the High Street called the Tam O'Shanter. Tam O'Shanter was the title of one of Burns's most famous poems, and the pub served as a sort of shrine to the poet, with verses from his poetry covering the rafters. The menu offered traditional Scottish fare, which is to be expected of a pub honoring a poet whose works include "Ode to a Haggis". I settled on a shepherd's pie, made with local Scottish lamb, and Katrina ordered salmon. More importantly, I ordered up a pint of creamy ale.

With full bellies we wandered back out to the High Street to continue our stroll. After just a few blocks, we came upon the Wallace Tower, the monument built to commemorate the Barns of Ayr incident. The monument, which consists of a large, grey stone tower sporting a statue of Wallace on the façade, was built in 1828 on what is believed to be the site of the incident. Remarkably, no one is quite sure it's in the right spot, which I suppose is forgivable given that Wallace burned the Barns to oblivion more than 500 years before the monument's construction.

Katrina and I walked around the base of the tower, which boasted plaques relating the brutal tale of the events of 1297. I read them all. Then I read them again... Something was missing, something of the utmost importance: my family name. Somehow the city fathers who erected this monument had managed to tell the story of Wallace's burning of the Barns of Ayr without mentioning the name Crawford once. Instead, they merely make mention of an "uncle" who had been hung, precipitating Wallace's rage.

Now, I realize I'm not the most unbiased person to be critiquing this subject, but this oversight seemed a trifle unfair to me. The fact that Sir Reginald Crawford was the Sheriff of Ayr and the first noble to be killed on that fateful day seems like it should have been enough to garner a mention. But when you add to this the fact that Reginald was Wallace's uncle, and that it was his death that affected Wallace so deeply that he went on to burn scores of English soldiers alive, it seems almost impossible to not mention him. Yet, the monument did not.

Still, at least it contained a vague reference to my ancestor hidden behind the term "uncle". That was better than Vikingar! and the Pencil Monument in Largs which offered absolutely no clue that a Crawford had played a key role in the events transpiring there. As we walked away from the Wallace Tower, I felt the need to consider this disturbing trend over another pint.

Fortunately, pubs proved rather easy to find in the town center of Ayr. We picked one that looked inviting, but whose name I can't recall. (It was one of those typically clever names for which British pubs are famous, such as *The Impaled Knight* or *The Crippled Nun*.) Like most pubs we would enter throughout the trip, this one contained a long wooden bar with an array of taps offering beers I had never heard of. I loved this about Scotland. The only problem, I would discover as time went on, was that each pub seemed to offer a different selection from the last, as if every town had its own breweries that stocked the local pubs but weren't shipped anywhere else. For example, I would spend all night drinking Greenmantle Ale at a pub and decide it was the best beer I had ever tasted. Then the next night, I would enter a pub in a different town that didn't have Greenmantle Ale. So I'd try their selections until I settled on another pleasing choice, say Skye Cuillin or Red MacGregor, only to discover in the next town that I had to start all over again because they had all new beers. Come to think of it, this really is quite a nice problem to have to work through.

It was not so nice for Katrina, who isn't fond of dark or flavorful beers. Her beer of choice is Coors Light, which tastes like tap water that someone accidentally spilled a couple of drops of stale beer into while cleaning up the day after a party. So Scotland's selections of rich ales that actually measure the "heaviness" of the beer by a number, such as 70 or 80 (the higher the number, the heavier the beer), offered no special treat for her. She watched with an expression bordering on horror as the bartender poured me a Caledonian 80, pausing halfway to let the dark ale settle.

"And what'll ye have, luv?" he asked.

"How about a Caledonian -10?" Katrina ventured.

"Canna help ye there," he replied, topping off my pint and sliding it toward me. The deep amber color ale was crowned with a good half inch of creamy head.

I gratefully took my first sip while Katrina puzzled over the choices. Something in her face told me that I should savor this pint, for my much-anticipated pub time might be limited by this unforeseen crisis. I took another tentative sip. But then the bartender, who obviously had been faced with such a dilemma before, came to the rescue.

"Have ye tried hard cider, then?" he asked, gesturing toward a tap labeled "Strongbow".

Katrina had not tried hard cider, but when the bartender poured the light, clean beverage into a glass and pushed it across the bar, it was an instant hit. I took a big gulp of ale.

Hard cider is perhaps best described as apple juice with a kick. It tastes so sweet one can almost forget it's alcoholic, which would be a mistake because it contains every bit as much alcohol as the strongest beer. By the end of the pint, Katrina had pronounced it "even better than Coors Light." Perhaps not a phrase Strongbow will use in their next advertising campaign, but a ringing endorsement nonetheless. Ordering another round, we settled in and passed a pleasant evening in the pub with the handful of local patrons present.

I can't overstate the importance of Katrina's cider discovery. Finding a beverage that came out of a tap that she enjoyed meant I could look forward to guiltless pub experiences throughout the trip. I was ecstatic, and by the time we stumbled back to our room a couple of hours later, I had nearly forgotten all about the evening's slight at the Wallace Tower. In fact, far from feeling wounded, I now celebrated a personal triumph. Amidst conversation at the pub, it had occurred to me that I was actually starting to understand people when they spoke. Of course, three pints of Caledonian 80 probably helped.

# Chapter 7: The Common Root

## (Adventures in Loudoun, Crawford and Crawfordjohn)

If I wished to honor my family ancestry through the names of my children, I could do no better than to christen my sons Reginald, Hugh or Galfridus, though this may not do them any favors on the school playground. All daughters, incidentally, would be named Margaret.

If the Crawfords of Scotland provide any indication, families in the Middle Ages were not particularly creative when it came to naming children. I make this claim after reviewing a genealogy covering nine generations—and several branches—of Crawford lineage. Of the thirty-six male Crawfords featured on the page, twenty-five share just four names: Reginald, Hugh, John and Galfridus. Of course, this is refreshingly diverse compared to the names of the women on the page, fully half of which are—can you guess?—that's right, Margaret.

This contrasts sharply with the baby naming process of today in which parents-to-be, in an effort to be unique and hip, thumb furiously through baby naming books searching for that perfect name, obscure but acceptable, with which to christen their new progeny. This is a process involving fierce debate between couples, and inevitably results in adorable children named Chandler or Britney who grow into resentful teens that hate their parents and dress like Marilyn Manson.

Considering this, I enjoy the simplicity of the older tradition, naming children to remember honored ancestors, though it should be noted that such patterns bring just a touch of confusion to genealogical research. In my time spent in the libraries of Scotland, I was forever coming across paragraphs like the following: "Hugh Crawford had two sons, Hugh and Reginald, and it was Hugh, grandson of Reginald and Margaret, who succeeded to the Estates of Loudoun. This Sir Hugh Crawford had two children, Reginald and Margaret...it was Reginald who was next in line and by 1283 he was Sir Reginald Crawford of Loudoun, Sheriff of Ayr...His son was another Sir Reginald Crawford of Loudoun." And I'd bet my house young Reggie either married or fathered a Margaret.

All of this is a long way of introducing our adventures for the day. We were on our way to the town of Crawford, the heart of the barony where the family name originated many moons ago and began the spawning of all these Reggies, Hughs and Margarets. On our way there, however, I noticed that, with a slight detour, we could pass through the very Loudoun mentioned in the confusing paragraph referenced above. This seemed worth doing as it meant taking in another family castle.

The time and manner that Loudoun came into Crawford hands proved a bit confusing at first, given the plethora of Reggies and Hughs involved, but once I got it sorted out, it shed some interesting light on an aspect of Scottish society that is often overlooked: the crucial role women played in the passing of lands and power from one family to another. In a nutshell the story goes as follows:

Sometime prior to 1189, a Norman named James de Lambinus, who had won the favor of the Scottish king for one reason or another, received a grant for extensive lands in Ayrshire. This James de Lambinus did two things of note: 1) change his name to de Loudoun to reflect the name of his new barony, and 2) manage to die leaving no male issue to inherit the Loudoun lands. Fortunately, James had a daughter, Margaret (of course), who was still very much alive and who happened to fancy a Sir Reginald Crawford, then Sheriff of Ayr. With their marriage, the Loudoun lands passed into the hands of the Crawford family—or more accurately, a succession of two Hughs and three Reginalds—who would control the barony throughout the 13th century.

Crawford control ended in the early 14th century, when the last Reginald was executed by the English for his support of his cousin, William Wallace. This Reginald, incidentally, was the son of the Reginald who had been hung at the Barns of Ayr. Confused yet? At any rate, this last Reggie had no surviving sons. Thus, the Loudoun lands passed into the hands of Susanna, most likely Reggie's niece, who married a Campbell and subsequently ushered in an era of Campbell control over the estate.

Thus, we have a barony passing into and out of family hands through women of the line. Apparently this happened frequently throughout Scotland, creating blood ties and alliances between families and realigning power bases from time to time. If a daughter of a powerful family married a husband of a less powerful family, it was not unheard of for her husband to even adopt her family name, as happened at least once with the Crawfords of Kilbirnie over the years. I found this rather progressive for a time in which people were still executed by having their bodies torn apart with horses.

As Katrina and I drove toward Loudoun, the barony had been out of Crawford hands for nearly seven hundred years, so I had low expectations for what we'd find. More rubble perhaps? Such doubts disintegrated into piqued curiosity when Katrina noted a strange symbol—different than the symbol used for other castles—marking Loudoun on the map.

"It lists the castle as an 'other attraction'," she muttered, checking the map key.

We speculated optimistically as to what this might mean.

"Perhaps a museum?" I ventured.

Katrina hoped for a preserved medieval village inhabited by people in full costume. No amount of speculation, however, could have prepared us for the cheerful glow of a brightly painted sign announcing the entrance to—God help us—Loudoun Castle Family Theme Park.

This was too much. Driving on the highway, I had mentally prepared myself for a humbling experience. In a corner of my mind, I had pictured another family castle in the middle of a trailer park or flanking the fairway of a golf course. What I had not pictured was a castle surrounded by roller coasters, carnival games and candy-popping children.

We parked in the enormous parking lot and walked toward the park's entrance, not knowing what to expect. Actually, we should have known exactly what to expect, because, as it turns out, amusement parks in Scotland are not so different from their counterparts in America. They feature all the same elements: huge crowds at the entry gate, exorbitant admission fees, the aroma of tasty food that will clog your arteries like a cork, and a few shameless adults running around in animal suits terrorizing young children. In this case, the animal suit was cutely named "Rory the Lion" and was worn by an adult clearly high on cocaine. As we approached the gate, Rory was jumping up and down waving at a group of children who spontaneously burst into tears and ran crying to their parents.

A map of the park posted outside the entrance showed that inside waited magnificent rides, each of which would inevitably offer visitors the opportunity to wait in a thirty-minute line for forty seconds of thrilling excitement. Of course, to get to these rides, visitors must make their way through a series of food stands and carnival games, the latter offering the chance to part with large sums of money while trying to defy the odds of a rigged game to win a cheap stuffed dog or cheetah. This prize, when won, would be presented by the lucky winner to a child or girlfriend who would have approximately five minutes to enjoy it before its head fell off.

Without going in, I knew this was all true. I am, after all, from Ohio where people buy season passes to amusement parks and get out of school for the county fair. In fact, the more family castles we saw, the more I was beginning to understand why Crawfords felt so at home in Ohio. How comforting the state's trailer parks, golf courses and county fairs must have appeared to my migrating ancestors. I could just hear the conversation.

"Well I'll be, Margaret. Is that the smell of cotton candy and waffle fries wafting over yonder hill?"

"By gum, Reggie, I believe it is. Park the trailer next to those other ones, and go win me a stuffed cheetah at the ring toss. I think we've found our new home."

Given the above description, the reader may come to the conclusion that I am a bit scornful of amusement parks. That would be a grave error, for I am actually a huge fan of amusement parks and all they contain. The long lines for short rides, the rigged games and worthless prizes, the junk food are all part of the romantic carnival culture that make the parks so endearing. As I stared at the Loudoun park entrance, I felt a tinge of nostalgia that nearly made me reach into my wallet and purchase a ticket.

This foolhardy move was forestalled by Katrina, who was not raised in Ohio and didn't share my fondness for fried cheese on a stick and other such foods. When I tentatively suggested we enter, she looked at me with a "you've got to be kidding me" glance and assured me that she didn't desire a headless cheetah as a souvenir from Scotland.

Fortunately, entry proved unnecessary as we could actually see Loudoun Castle from the gate: a turreted façade of brown stone blocks peeking out from behind trees and carnival games. I snapped a quick photo and walked dejectedly back to the car, which was just as well as I later discovered that the only part of the castle dating back to Crawford times lay buried beneath the current structure and wouldn't have been visible anyway. Remarkably, I learned this from the park's website, which actually contained a history section, showing that there is at least one difference between Scottish amusement parks and their American counterparts and raising my respect for the former considerably.

• • • • •

In order to pass a standardized history test in the United States, only the most superficial understanding of events is required. To illustrate this, every year I would introduce the landmark Supreme Court case *Marbury v. Madison* to my U.S. History students in the following manner:

"Today, we will discuss the ins and outs of the case and its subsequent effect on U.S. history, which is a useful thing to know and will make you impressive at parties; however, for the purposes of national standardized tests, including the AP test which will actually earn you college credit, you will only be required to know one thing: *Marbury v. Madison* established the policy of judicial review. Period. You will not be required to define judicial review or to give examples of judicial review in action, and you will certainly not need to know who either Madison or Marbury was. The question will usually be phrased in the following manner:

*Which Supreme Court case established the policy of judicial review?*

a. *Plessy v. Ferguson*

b. *Brown v. Board of Education*

c. *Marbury v. Madison*

d. *Frazier v. Ali*

When you see that question (and you will), you'd better get it right and come thank me." (And they do.)

I bring this up not because I wish to trash the testing authorities of America, though they could use a good drubbing, nor because I expect the reader to be taking an AP History test soon, though if you do, you'll be ready. Rather, the anecdote provides a pleasant little segue into another commonly known but poorly understood trivia fact that actually bears some relevance to our current story: that is, the Battle of Hastings.

Despite the fact that the Battle of Hastings ranks as one of the single most important events in the history of Europe, for American standardized tests one need know only that the battle occurred in the year 1066. In extreme cases where the test is asking for very advanced knowledge, students should know that it was William, Duke of Normandy (subsequently called William the Conqueror), who invaded from France, crossing the English Channel and subjecting England to Norman control. Students will probably not need to know that the monarch he defeated was the Anglo-Saxon King Harold of England, and will certainly not need to know the tale I am about to tell, though it has significant relevance to thousands of families, including the Crawfords of Scotland.

After William's defeat of King Harold, the Normans didn't just congratulate themselves and go home. They had come to stay. In order to quell resistance to Norman rule, William began the systematic purging of English landholders who remained loyal to the former Anglo-Saxon monarchy. With their lands and power lost, many of these nobles, largely Saxons and Danes, fled north to friendlier pastures.

The Scottish king, Malcolm Canmore, had married the sister of King Harold (another Margaret, of course) when she had fled north to escape the wrath of William in 1068. To please his new wife and, more importantly, to beef up his defenses against the new Norman threat with as many powerful figures as possible, Malcolm welcomed many other refugee nobles into Scotland, adding slews of Saxons, Angles and Danes to the already resident Picts and Scots.

Many of these newcomers settled into Scottish life quite comfortably, intermarrying with locals, having families, and eventually receiving grants of lands and titles as years went by. One such newcomer, a Dane by the name of Thorlongus (Thor the Tall), received a grant for land near the English border from the new Scottish King Edgar, who reigned in the waning years of the 11<sup>th</sup> century, although Thor appears to have donated much of this land to the church. What *is* certain, however, is that Thor's son, Swane, was also granted land by Edgar and became known as the Overlord of Crawford in Lanarkshire.

The origins of the name Crawford are disputed, but the most popular and plausible claim notes that the name stems from two terms, *cru* and *ford* meaning "bloody crossing". Adding strength to this claim is the fact that a Roman fort, built on the banks of the River Clyde and likely a scene of armed conflict in years long past, stood in the region that came to be called Crawford. Whatever its origin, the name appears to have already been in place and must have been adopted by the family when Swane gained control of the land. Swane's son, Galfridus, comes down to us in history as Galfridus de Crawford and is generally considered to be the progenitor of the House of Crawford.*

Over the last nine centuries the family tree has branched significantly until, today, Crawfords span the globe. Supposedly, however, Crawfords throughout time and space, from William Wallace to Joan Crawford to my cousin Danny can all trace our family trees back to this one common root. I think that's pretty darn cool.

I was now on my way to see where this common root hung his hat.

---

* There are conflicting accounts of the origins of both the Crawford name and family. I have chosen to stick to the most widely accepted versions. Anyone having hard, fast evidence proving these versions incorrect and another version correct should contact me and Crawfords around the world immediately.

Somewhere on the road after Loudoun, we left the hills of Ayrshire behind and crossed into Lanarkshire. Lanarkshire is a large county, just east of Ayrshire, roughly encompassing the watershed of the River Clyde. It is the most populous county in Scotland, thanks to the city of Glasgow, which lies in northwestern Lanarkshire where the river widens before emptying into the Firth of Clyde. Glasgow is not the county town, however. That honor falls, rather obviously I suppose, to the town of Lanark, situated further upriver and not far from the town of Crawford.

We stopped in Lanark to grab a quick lunch and do some preliminary research at the library. The town was of decent size with an old, attractive town center situated on a hilltop. Katrina and I walked around briefly, particularly enjoying the narrow, medieval side streets, until we found the library, just down the hill from the town center.

Considering Lanarkshire contains Scotland's biggest city, the Lanark library was substantial, and this proved particularly true of its local history section. It contained way too much information to comb through, but the librarian, a kind, middle-aged gentleman who clearly had his own fascination with genealogical research, put me on the track of some useful sources. These not only confirmed much of what I had already read regarding Crawford origins but also broadened my knowledge of this hill country, highlighting its rich mining history. It seemed my ancestral lands had sat atop some of the largest gold and silver deposits in all of Britain, though the mines had long since depleted the land of its wealth.

Armed with such information, we left Lanark and drove south toward Crawford. With each mile the countryside grew more and more charming. The road wound its way through rolling hills, larger than those of Ayrshire, with grazing sheep strewn out amongst the shades of green and gold. Streams flowed through the valleys. Every now and again, a wooded glen would appear. Houses were scarce.

Crawford proved to be a small town tucked neatly into the hills near the River Clyde. We drove down the main street taking in the surroundings of this place that gave rise to my family name. I particularly enjoyed the ego-boosting thrill of having my name plastered on building after building: the Crawford Kirk, the Crawford Post Office, and, finally, at the other end of town, the Crawford Arms Hotel, the place where customs officials currently had us residing. From the look of the building, it was more of a tavern than a hotel, which suited me just fine. I longed to go in, order up a pint, and trade stories with the proprietor, putting aside my usual disdain of short talk. There were lights on inside, but the door was locked. A handwritten sign said "back shortly". We waited ten minutes, but no one returned.

Feeling a bit conspicuous lurking outside a tavern door in a small town, we reluctantly climbed back into the car to go in search of the barony's original castle. If I couldn't lift a glass in a pub of my namesake, at least I could poke around the halls of a Crawford castle that was actually called, well, Crawford Castle.

A sign pointed us onto a side road, taking us out of town and closer to the banks of the Clyde. The road, keeping with the pattern of those leading to family castles, was long and narrow, just wide enough for one car, and that being a Fiat Crumb or Peugeot Halfpint, not a GMC Earthquake. The road crossed through open fields and then entered a small, wooded grove. Just inside the copse of trees, a driveway turned off to the left serving a two-storey stone farmhouse, surrounded by a series of barns and other outlying farm-like buildings. A sign at the driveway announced this as Crawford Castle.

Hmmm.

I looked again at the farmhouse. It was on the large side for a regular house, was made out of stone, and could have been quite old, but that was where any similarity to a castle stopped. There were no turrets, no defensive walls, no indications of a ditch or moat to slow the approach of an attacking force. Instead, it looked every bit as welcoming and approachable as farmhouses should. It most certainly was not an 11th or 12th century keep, built to protect the progenitors of the Crawford name. It was a farmhouse, pure and simple.

Confused, we parked the car and got out. In the process my gaze crossed to the other side of the road, and there I finally saw what I had been missing. The castle perched on the crest of a hill across the road, camouflaged by the overgrown trees and the fact that there was almost nothing left of it. A dilapidated keep known as Tower Lindsay, according to a posted sign, was all that remained.

This proved more along the lines of what I expected. The castle, after all, was over eight hundred years old and had been through some rough times, including being burned by William Wallace in the late 13th century, a fact I found just a bit ironic given Wallace's own Crawford roots.

This story, which I had come across in Lanark, was told by Blind Harry, the wandering poet who chronicled Wallace's adventures in his epic poem, appropriately titled *Wallace*. Blind Harry lived in the 15th century and comes down to us in history as a sort of Scottish Homer—a rather apt comparison given his lack of sight and tremendous penchant for hyperbole. He claims to have based his poem, written more than 150 years after Wallace's death, on the Latin text of the warrior's chaplain, a man named Blair. Blair's work has subsequently been lost to history, leaving Blind Harry's poem as the leading authority on Scotland's greatest hero. His work is undoubtedly exaggerated, but considered accurate enough in its relaying of the sequence of events that made up Wallace's adventures.

For centuries, the epic poem was recited around the firesides of Scotland. In the romantic days before television and video games, its daring verse describing sword play and castle sieges would have provided unparalleled entertainment to peasant and noble alike. It also bred a patriotic spirit and an inherent disdain for all things English in the children of Scotland.

I would love nothing more than to relate the tale of Wallace's burning of Crawford Castle here in Blind Harry's original verse. Unfortunately, its usage of medieval, native Scots makes the poem all but incomprehensible. Thus, I have paraphrased the story as follows:*

---

* The tale in Wallace's original verse is included in Appendix C of this book. If one can learn to pronounce everything correctly in a rich Scottish brogue—a feat I have yet to achieve—it would remain excellent fireside entertainment today, whether or not anyone understands a word.

Towards the end of the 13$^{th}$ century, as Wallace was gaining notoriety for his exploits against the English, his travels took him near the town of Crawford, land of his maternal ancestors. Both the castle and the town had fallen into the hands of English soldiers, which must have annoyed Wallace tremendously, and he vowed to clear his ancestral land of such rabble. Entering the town disguised as a blind beggar, he learned from a woman he met along the road that the English captain, a man named Martindale, was carousing with English soldiers in a nearby townhouse and had recently been bragging about how he would teach Wallace a lesson if he dared show his face.

Wallace approached the house with just one other man, Edward Little, whereupon he entered the room, announced his greeting, and proceeded to slaughter the twenty men single-handedly with his sword. Actually, in an effort to keep the story in the realm of realism, Blind Harry claims that Wallace killed only fifteen of the men himself, while Edward Little polished off the other five. Meanwhile, Wallace's second in command, a man named Sir John Graham, took the rest of Wallace's men to the castle, which they proceeded to set alight. As it burned, Wallace rejoined his band, presumably with a very bloody sword, and helped himself to the spoils of his ancestral castle before retiring to the countryside of Lanarkshire for a little respite.

At the time of this incident, the Crawford barony was only about two hundred years old, yet it had already undergone significant change. For starters, it was no longer one barony. Galfridus, the original Crawford, had split the barony into two parishes, giving the larger parish containing the town of Crawford to his first son, Hugh. The other, he gave to his second son, Reginald. This smaller parish would become known as Crawfordjohn, named for Reginald's eldest son, John, who inherited the land upon his father's death. The descendants of the Crawfordjohn parish would go on to form the most famous branches of the Crawford family. In fact, all the family lands we'd visited thus far on our trip—Kilbirnie, Crosbie, Loudoun, Craufurdland—were acquired by the offspring of this Crawfordjohn line.

The larger parish of the original barony kept the name of Crawford, but would pass out of Crawford hands within a few generations when the great-grandson of the original Hugh, another John, died without any male heirs. John's daughter married Sir David Lindsay, transferring control of the barony to the Lindsay family. Thus, Lindsays for centuries thereafter held the title of Earl of Crawford, even after the barony was transferred to the region of Angus, well to the northeast of the original lands. I mention this now for two reasons: 1) it allows all Crawfords to claim kinship with the famous poet, Davie Lindsay, born centuries later and whose works were so well loved by the Scottish people that the expression, "It's neither in the Bible nor in Davie Lindsay," was enough to condemn a new idea or prove a notion false, and 2) it is a long way of explaining why the crumbled pile of rubble Katrina and I now viewed was known as Tower Lindsay.

We poked around the ruins a bit, but there was not much to see. Time had launched the ultimate assault on the castle, and its remains served as another reminder that the heyday of the Crawfords of Scotland had long since passed. I snapped a picture of the ruins and, for good measure, the sign in front of the farmhouse before climbing back into the car.

What happened next, I cannot explain and will not try. Suffice it to say that, in my attempts to maneuver back onto the road, our car became irretrievably lodged in a ditch. Thanks to the fact that a Fiat Crumb has just enough clearance to slide a penny between the road and the undercarriage, our front end had lodged on a seemingly unthreatening protrusion of rock, causing the wheels to spin uselessly in the air as I tried to back us out of the predicament.

Seeing no solution at hand, we did what most people would do in the situation. That is, we got out of the car and stared at the front end with a dumbfounded expression, scratching our heads and hoping the car would magically extricate itself from the ditch. It did not. We did, however, receive a miracle of another sort.

Having not seen another car or even another human being since turning off the main road in Crawford, imagine our pleasant surprise when, within minutes of putting the car into the ditch, an old, battered pick-up truck came sputtering down the road toward us. Imagine our further good fortune as the driver of the pick-up truck ascertained that our car, despite being lodged in a ditch, stuck out into the road just enough to prevent his truck from passing. Certainly our eyes were deceiving us when the doors of the truck opened and three strong-looking adult men climbed out to survey the situation. Perhaps not a miracle, but by any standard a very fortunate turn of events.

Having tried all conventional methods of removing the car from the ditch, our newly assembled group hatched a desperate plan: the four men would lift the front end of the Fiat Crumb while Katrina, sitting in the driver's seat gunned the car in reverse, being careful to give it enough power to get back on the road, but not so much power that she careened into the ditch on the other side, less than half a car-length away. This plan was not warmly embraced by Katrina, who had yet to drive in Scotland and did not fancy her first experience shifting with her left hand to be quite as harrowing as this promised to be. Reluctantly, she climbed into the driver's seat.

I'm happy to report that all went well. The Fiat Crumb weighed approximately twelve pounds and was lifted easily by four grown men. Katrina drove like a pro, stopping the car on a dime in the middle of the road much to the admiration of her Scottish rescuers. I offered to buy everyone a pint at the Crawford Arms Hotel, but they declined, saying they had to move on and anyway the Crawford Arms was still closed. They had just driven by a moment before.

I took this as a sign it was time to move on to Crawfordjohn.

•   •   •   •   •

If Crawford seemed like a remote town, the village of Crawfordjohn, just two miles to the northwest, was infinitely more so. A book I had come across in the Lanark library told of an old expression inspired by this isolation: "Out of the world and into Crawfordjohn." I liked this very much. The same book, written in 1928, contained this description of the area: "Its hills re-echo with the bleating of sheep and lowing of kine, and are vocal with the song of birds or the pleasant ripple of its numerous rills.

The piercing warning whistle of the locomotive engine and discordant rush of railway traffic do not disturb the tranquility of its glades and glens; even the toot of the ubiquitous motor-car only subserves to emphasise the pleasurable and restful calm of its haughs and hills." Happily, things appeared not to have changed much in the seventy-six years since.

The town itself was just a cluster of buildings tucked into a hillside lining the road. It was exactly what I have always pictured when somebody says the word hamlet. This particular hamlet contained a tavern, a church, a graveyard and enough homes to hold its forty-six residents—a number so startlingly low, the entire town could fit on a single motorbus, should they fancy an outing.

We parked the car near the tavern and got out to walk. A woman, about our age, was gardening in front of her house and spoke to us as we passed.

"Lost, are ye?" she asked.

"No, not lost," I replied. "We just wanted to see the town."

The woman eyed me suspiciously, so I went on to explain my situation, concluding by asking her if she knew anything about the town's history.

"Ye've managed to find the yin person who doesnae," she replied. "My husband and I just moved here fi Glasgow. Matthew should ken a bit. He grew up near enough." With that, she brushed off her hands and went to find her husband, indicating us to follow.

We had stumbled across the newest residents of Crawfordjohn. Two people moving in must have caused quite a sensation in this town. I imagined it as the kind of place which twenty years later would still refer to Matthew and his wife as the "new folks". As we walked, I asked the woman, Becky, what had induced them to leave the city and come to such a small, isolated town.

"We both come fi country towns," she explained, "but met in Glasgow where we'd moved for a wee bit ae craic. It didnae take long tae get our fill ae that."

Now it was my turn to eye Becky suspiciously. She looked young, fit and healthy rather than emaciated and strung out. Not exactly the crackhead type. She must have noted my confusion.

"Craic is an expression we Scots use for excitement," she explained, reassuring me that she had not spent her time in Glasgow getting acquainted with the gutters. "But Matthew and I like the quiet ae the countryside. And excitement isnae far if we fancy it."

I reflected on this. As isolated as Crawfordjohn seemed, it lay less than thirty miles from Glasgow and only slightly further from Edinburgh. I tried to imagine a town within thirty miles of Manhattan feeling so isolated.

The back of the house bordered the churchyard, and there we found Matthew cleaning up sticks. He didn't look too excited about dropping the armful he'd gathered back to the ground and coming over to speak with us, but he humored us nonetheless.

"Crawford," he said, after he heard the tale. "That's a riever name."

"A river name?" I asked, a bit confused.

"No, a riever name," he repeated. "Cattle thieves."

I was getting quite a vocabulary lesson here. Still, a riever name didn't make any more sense to me than a river name, but Matthew mistook my confusion for disappointment.

"Don't worry," he said, clapping me on the shoulder, "we were all cattle thieves."

Rieving, Matthew explained, referred to the practice of stealing cattle and was practically a national pastime in Scotland in centuries gone by. I would find out more about this practice toward the end of our trip when we visited the Rob Roy Visitor Center and heard the story of Rob Roy MacGregor, the most famous cattle riever of them all. Rob Roy was a national hero, so it seemed that rieving was nothing a family had to hide. I hadn't read of any connection between Crawfords and rieving, but for now, I decided to take Matthew's word on the matter.

We chatted for a while longer, and Matthew showed me some graves in the cemetery with Crawford names on them. There were plenty of them, though Matthew didn't think any Crawfords still lived in the town.

"Ye'd git more information if the museum were open," Becky piped in at one point.

I looked at her dubiously. "The museum?"

She pointed to a building just behind the church. A sign in the window advertised a local history exhibit. It was only open on certain days, and unfortunately today wasn't one of them. Still, it spoke volumes that a museum existed in this town of forty-six people. Who visited it? If every resident in town spent a week in the museum separately each year, there would still be six weeks with no one to visit. Yet, Scotland seems to be exactly the kind of place where such a museum could exist. Time and again on our trip, we would find evidence that local history is treasured throughout the country.

On our way back to the car, we detoured onto a hillside beside the town where Matthew had indicated the castle once stood. No evidence of the structure remained, though Katrina and I took great pleasure in standing on the hilltop overlooking the surrounding countryside and musing at what a great spot for a castle it must have been. We'd had terrific luck with weather so far, and the blue sky allowed for a wonderful clear view. No attacking forces would approach unnoticed today.

It was now mid-afternoon. We thought about sitting for a pint at the local tavern, but like the Crawford Arms Hotel earlier and the church museum just now, the tavern was closed. Unseen forces seemed to be telling us to move on. We had spent the better part of three days in small, obscure towns researching family history, and had uncovered much more than I ever would have expected in such a short time. Katrina had remained remarkably patient throughout, and, to be honest, had seemed to enjoy the experience as much as I had. But there was no need to push my luck.

As we got back in the car and drove away from Crawfordjohn, I felt like we were starting a new phase of the trip. It was time to leave behind the libraries and graveyards of family history and embrace the raw excitement Scotland had to offer. Tonight, we would sleep in a city 10,000 times bigger than the hamlet we'd just left.

We were headed to Edinburgh.

# Part Two

## Edinburgh to Fairyland

# Chapter 8: Volcanoes and M.C. Escher

## (Arrival in Old Town Edinburgh)

This I understand: towns change.

I have a vivid memory from my childhood of riding in a car on Route 33, the federal highway that passes through my hometown of Lancaster, Ohio. My father, who was driving, points at the Plaza shopping center as we drive by and says, "I remember when that whole thing was a cornfield and all of this was country. It was nothing but fields." By "all of this" he meant not only the Plaza, but the other shopping center and plethora of gas stations and fast food restaurants that had sprung up around it. This building boom had pushed the frontier of town a half mile further out on the highway, all the way to the intersection with Pierce Road. Pierce Road was where the cornfields started when I was a kid.

I remember trying to imagine what the town and countryside must have looked like during my father's childhood, but it was hard to picture with all the pavement and signs in the way. The image became a little less abstract a few years later when the farm bordering Pierce Road was sold to a developer who promptly paved over the cornfields to support a new indoor shopping mall. Suddenly, the line separating town and country had moved again. I can see myself in a few years driving by with my kid in the car, pointing at the mall and saying, "I remember when that whole thing was a cornfield and all of this was country." By "all of this", I would mean the host of superstores, Olive Gardens, Red Lobsters, and cheap housing developments that, fungus like, have grown up around the mall.

By the time my kid drives on Route 33 with his kid, I expect it will just be one constant stream of chain stores all the way to Columbus twenty-five miles up the road. It is all quite depressing.

Still, I like to revisit the original town center and imagine what it was like when this was all there was. Lancaster has a classic Midwestern downtown that has retained enough of its original architecture and buildings that even today, if a 19th century Lancastrian was dropped off at the corner of Main and Broad, he'd know where he was—though he might wonder why all the windows were boarded up and where all the people had gone.

Edinburgh*, the capital of Scotland, has a similar story, though on a much larger scale and having had nearly two thousand years to evolve instead of a mere two hundred. Starting as a crude Celtic fort atop a volcanic outcropping in the early Dark Ages, the city now boasts a population of 450,000 spread over a hundred square miles. As it has grown, Edinburgh has swallowed up outlying communities, such as the port of Leith which used to be a separate town altogether. The community of Kirk o' Field, where you'll recall Lord Darnley met his end in 1567, is not only in Edinburgh today, it is closer to the town center than the city's outskirts. I can just hear Ol' Darnley telling his kids now, "When I was strangled and then blasted from an exploding house over four hundred years ago, this was nothing but fields." And the kids would try to envision it (the fields, not their father blowing up), but would be unable to, of course, because Scotland's capital now has all the trappings of a modern city, along with the convenience and ugliness this implies.

Yet, amongst the sprawl, it is still possible to see Edinburgh as it once was. Drop a 16th century resident back in Old Town, and he'd feel right at home amongst the gothic architecture and narrow streets. He could reminisce as he explored the same closes and wynds** where he used to engage in swordplay, hail friends in the warmth of a tavern, or slip discreetly to the doorstep of a waiting lassie. Sure, he'd notice a few things amiss. He may be puzzled to find that, in lieu of horseshoes or poultry, all stores now sell family crest refrigerator magnets. He would likely smile to discover that the stench of human feces, horse urine and chimney smoke that once earned the city the nickname "Auld Reekie" seemed to be missing. Yet, all

---

* The pronunciation of Edinburgh is a bit tricky. No matter how much it looks like it should be pronounced "Edin-berg", it is not. The official pronunciation, so far as I can tell, is "Edinburra" or "Edinboro" or Edinbra" or "Edinbro" or something like that. In a pinch, mumbling and hurrying on to the next word also seems to work.

** A close is a medieval alleyway often opening up into a slightly wider courtyard behind the buildings of the main street. A wynd is a narrow lane.

in all, he would be on very familiar ground.

Driving into Edinburgh, it didn't take me long to determine that Old Town was where I wanted to be.

. . . . .

The approach to Edinburgh provided our most harrowing experience yet on the roads of Scotland. In order to navigate, Katrina juggled three maps: a large fold-up map of Scotland, a map of Edinburgh printed on the back of that map, and an even more detailed street map found in our guidebook. Each new intersection or road sign we approached triggered a flailing of arms and a rustle of paper, followed by a suggested course of action, usually phrased more like a question ("Go straight?") than a definitive conclusion. Adding to the stress, the route took us through a series of enormous and heavily trafficked round-a-bouts, which I passed through with my hands clenched tightly on the wheel, swiveling my head like one of those toy dogs on a dashboard as I merged in and out of traffic. Thus, it was with some relief that we finally arrived in Old Town and were able to park the car to get our bearings—though the feeling quickly changed to one of wonder.

We had stopped in an area called the Grassmarket, a long, narrow plaza where city dwellers of old could buy a pig and watch a good public execution all in one trip. Immediately to the north, Edinburgh Castle perched on a high outcropping of rock, its cliffs and medieval walls looming over the plaza. Surveying the scene, I felt it was about as dramatic an entry point as we could have hoped for in the Scottish capital.

Our guidebook had noted the Grassmarket as a good place to find hotels, pubs and restaurants. Glancing around at the old buildings lining the street, I fixed on one called the White Hart Inn and crossed over to inquire about a room for the evening. Entering, I found myself in a dimly lit, crowded pub, with a wooden bar lining one wall. Ignoring the obvious, I walked over and inquired of the bartender if I could get a room for the night.

"'Fraid ye're a wee late," he replied, pouring a drink. "We rented our last room a few decades back." He passed the pint to a patron down the bar and turned to me with an amused expression. "We're just a pub now, mate, an' a crackin' guid ane a' that." Helpfully, he pointed out the window to the tallest and newest building in the plaza. "Tha's a hotel."

Thanking him sheepishly, I walked back outside and crossed the plaza. The hotel, sporting a modern façade decked with chrome and plate glass, was a bit swanky for my taste, but it was late afternoon and I was anxious to get situated so we could enjoy the evening.

We walked into the lobby which, with its chrome trim and cold tile, looked about as unwelcoming as possible after two nights in bed and breakfasts. Fashionable, young couples looking like they'd just returned from a magazine shoot adorned a trendy bar adjoining the lobby. We felt tremendously out of place. Standing at the registration desk, our old backpacks leaning against the counter, I kept waiting for the clerk to call security, having deemed us too un-hip to patronize the establishment. Thus, it was with genuine surprise that we instead received a working key to what would be our room for the next two nights. Throwing down our bags on furniture fashioned more for style than comfort, we felt no need to linger and headed back out to the Grassmarket, hurrying through the lobby so as not to subject the atmosphere to our contaminating presence longer than necessary.

It was now dinnertime, and we were ready for a good old-fashioned pub. Luckily, I knew of "a crackin' guid ane" across the street.

Written records show that the White Hart Inn has been in existence since the year 1516, though the pub may be quite older still. Think about that. Scotsmen were drinking at the White Hart Inn while Leonardo da Vinci was painting in Italy. The pub had been in business at least a year when Martin Luther nailed his "Ninety-five Theses" to the church door in Wittenberg, Germany, sending the pope into a tizzy and launching the Protestant Reformation throughout Europe. When Sir Thomas Crawford captured Edinburgh Castle in 1573, he could have celebrated with a pint at the White Hart Inn, which had already been in business for over a half-century just down the hill. It is an old tavern.

The only thing remaining of the original structure is the cellar (the current building dates to 1740), but that doesn't stop the proprietors from claiming to be "Edinburgh's oldest surviving public house." At least two other establishments debate this claim, but no one denies the White Hart is a historic place. It serves as a stop on the city's Literary Pub Tour, a fantastic concept pulling together literary types who want the experience of hoisting a pint in the very pubs where famous poets and authors once did the same. The White Hart earned its spot on the tour thanks to visits from both Robbie Burns in 1791 and William Wordsworth in 1803. Burns stayed for a full week, during which time he wrote a love song, "Ae Fond Kiss", and presumably received that and more from the lover he was visiting. Like those of the Tam O' Shanter in Ayr, the rafters of the White Hart Inn are adorned with lines from his poetry.

On a slightly less romantic note, the pub claims to have been frequented by the famous 19th century bodysnatchers of Edinburgh, William Burke and William Hare. The Irish duo spent much of 1828 befriending strangers in pubs for the sole purpose of luring them back to a Grassmarket flat, murdering them in cold blood, and then selling their corpses to a prominent doctor at Edinburgh Medical School for experimentation. Apparently this kept them flush with pub money for most of the year until Hare finally betrayed his own partner to the authorities. Burke was executed for the crimes, but Hare, amazingly, was allowed to flee the city. Today, White Hart patrons can enjoy caricatures of both Burke and Hare carved into the wall near the door, which I suppose serves as a good reminder to watch who you leave the pub with.

I learned all of this, or most of it, from the back of a menu while enjoying a pint in front of the Inn. It was a beautiful day, and all up and down the Grassmarket the pubs had put out tables so patrons could sit and enjoy their food and drink in the sunshine. Sitting in the warmth of the sun with a pint of creamy ale and a diverting, history-filled menu, I was content. As I read, most of the stories were of course new to me. One, however, sounded strangely familiar. It explained that the White Hart Inn was called the White Hart Inn to commemorate the following event:

In 1127, King David I was hunting in the woods outside Edinburgh when he gave chase to a white stag. In the course of the chase, David was thrown from his horse, at which point the stag turned and began charging the king. Helpless on the ground, David, who comes down to us in history as a particularly pious king, frantically prayed to God for salvation. As a result of the strength of his prayers, claims the menu, a crucifix appeared briefly between the stag's antlers and then the charging animal vanished from sight. To show his gratitude for this miracle, which occurred upon the Feast Day of the Holy Rood,* King David founded Holyrood Abbey, the ruins of which can still be seen today.

Hmmm.

Yes, I had heard this story before. Except, in the version I had read, the part of God was played by—can you see it coming?—a bloody Crawford! What was this? Here I sat trying to enjoy a good pint in Edinburgh, the family roots portion of my trip now behind me, only to find further evidence of my ancestry being written out of Scottish history in the first pub I visited.

Incredulously, I showed the menu to Katrina.

"In the real story," I told her, "King David takes a hunting party with him, which includes Sir Gregan Crawford, the younger son of the original Reginald Crawford, who received the Crawfordjohn property when Galfridus divided up his barony."

Blank look.

"Okay, the important part is this: It was Sir Gregan who saved the king! Sir Gregan turned the charging stag and kept the king from being trampled!"

"Yes, of course, dear," said Katrina, sipping her cider. "Go get the manager. I'm sure they'll reprint the menus. It's a much better story anyway with Sir Grego."

"Gregan," I said, but I got her point. Every country needs its legends.

---

* Rood means cross. Thus, the Feast Day of the Holy Rood is the Feast Day of the Holy Cross.

The disappearing stag story is one of Scotland's. Still, they didn't have to write the Crawfords completely out of it. They could have footnoted it or something—a little explanation saying: "Obviously, the above story is complete rubbish. What really happened was King David sat down and wet his pants while Sir Gregan rode his horse between him and the charging stag, keeping Scotland from losing its beloved and soggy monarch." Or something to that effect.

Sir Gregan's heroics were at least preserved in other ways. Most visibly, the Crawford family crest features a stag with a cross between the antlers along with the motto, *Tuttum Te Robore Reddam*, which roughly translates to: "I will render you safe with my strength." Both crest and motto stem from the Holyrood incident. More tangibly still, Sir Gregan received lands in Ayrshire for his service to the king, starting the Dalmagregan branch of the Crawfords. It was all there in the libraries and public records, but like the Crawfords at Largs and Ayr, Sir Gregan had somehow disappeared from popular history.

I put down the menu and finished my drink, sensing a conspiracy.

• • • • •

Over 350 million years ago, before the age of dinosaurs or the White Hart Inn, Edinburgh would have been a pretty hot place to be. This is partly because Edinburgh, or at least the land that would become Edinburgh, was located near the equator on the enormous supercontinent of Pangaea. It is also because, at that time, volcanoes were turning the area into a boiling cauldron of lava. Fortunately, for the Edinburgh Tourist Board, this condition did not last.

In the millennia since, the continents have gone about their busy lives—drifting, colliding, breaking apart, drifting some more—until we find the world as it is today, with the land surrounding Edinburgh comfortably located in the northern climes and its volcanoes long since extinct. Yet, evidence of the fiery past remains.

The city today is built on and around the remnants of these extinct volcanoes, which now take the form of massive crags of rock jutting up from the ground. The Castle Rock provides one dramatic example of these, but more striking still is an 823 ft. behemoth called Arthur's Seat. This prominent crag juts up just to the east of Old Town, and forms the centerpiece of Holyrood Park, a nearly four square mile wilderness within the city. Thanks to Arthur's Seat and Holyrood Park, city dwellers can enjoy hiking, rock climbing and magnificent views of the city's spires and rooftops, and even the sea beyond.

Not all the crags have been left wilderness, however. In fact, most have been incorporated into Edinburgh's structure as the city has grown outward from the Castle Rock. The result today is a city of many levels, resembling more an M.C. Escher sketch than the grid-patterns of most modern cities. This holds particularly true in Old Town where curving streets and staircases take pedestrians up and down the slopes. Attractive bridges span low areas, connecting the neighborhoods of one high ridge with another, while separate neighborhoods bustle below. These features, when combined with the spires and masonry of its medieval architecture, imbue the city with character, beauty and endless diversions.

All of this makes Edinburgh a fantastically interesting city to see on foot, as Katrina and I would soon discover, so long as one takes it slow and doesn't mind a little exertion. Taking it slow would prove to be no problem for us that first evening, thanks to a hearty meal of steak and potatoes which had buoyed my spirits considerably after the discovery of another slighted ancestor, but now sat heavily in my stomach as we set out from the White Hart Inn for a stroll through Old Town.

Reasons to tarry proved easy to come by. Strolling to the east end of the Grassmarket, we paused to read a plaque marking the site where the public gallows once stood. In centuries past, hundreds of people accused of heresy, treason and a host of other transgressions had been hung in the square. Supposedly, the surrounding pubs did brisk business on execution days, as townspeople filled the marketplace waiting for the entertainment the gallows provided. Grimly, I pictured throngs of drunken peasants—struck by the same sick impulse to bear witness to other people's tragedy that leads millions today to watch cable news—clinking ale mugs while jeering at a condemned heretic on the scaffold. Shivering with the thought, we moved on.

At the end of the plaza, we passed under the George IV Bridge and entered the Cowgate, a street currently undergoing a revival after more than a century as a seedy underworld. Once one of the city's most prestigious sectors, the Cowgate fell from grace when the bridges were built, allowing pedestrians to pass over the neighborhood on their way to or from the High Street, which runs along the elevated spine of the Castle Rock's eastern slope. Out of sight, out of mind seems to have been the city's attitude toward the Cowgate, and the low-lying street became a haven of crime and neglect. Our guidebook quoted a 19th century writer who once said of the Cowgate: "the condition of the inhabitants is as little known to respectable Edinburgh as are the habits of moles, earthworms, and the mining population"—a comment which must have thrilled the mining population as much as it did the inhabitants of the Cowgate.

Nevertheless, according to the guidebook, subterranean has become hip, and the street now blossoms with nightclubs and artsy venues. Wandering down the street, we saw a lot of handbills posted for what looked like punk or indie bands, but there weren't many inviting doorways and everything looked fairly bleak. The street still had a definite underworld feel to it—the kind of place where someone might step out of the shadows and demand the keys to our Fiat Crumb. We turned around.[*]

Back at the edge of the Grassmarket we turned this time up Victoria Street. This was a good choice. Victoria Street curves up the slope of the Castle Rock towards the High Street and contains a singular, fascinating feature: it is a two-tiered street. Sidewalks and stores line both sides at street level, but—here's the cool thing—on top of the stores on the north side of the street, one finds another sidewalk and more stores. Arched openings at intervals along the north side of the street lead to stairways between the two

---

[*] This should not be taken to imply that the guidebook was incorrect regarding the revival of the Cowgate. It is far more likely that the revival is absolutely real and that the Cowgate was at that very moment the hippest street in Edinburgh, and that I was simply too unhip to realize this fact. Given my experience at the hotel, I would say this is probable. *(See Epilogue for more on the Cowgate.)*

levels.

I had great fun walking up one side, enjoying the storefronts at street level, which featured an odd assortment of trendy tea rooms, costume shops, and a store advertising witchery tours, only to cross and climb to the upper level on the other side of the street, taking in a whole new perspective. The upper level offers the curious pedestrian an unusual vantage point from which to study the architecture of Old Town. Because we were one level up, I found myself looking not at storefronts but at the details of the upper level masonry, niches, and windows of the buildings located immediately across the narrow street. I studied various features—a stone carving here, a bay window there—remarking on how cool some of the apartments would be to live in, so long as the windows came equipped with a good set of blinds. This was brought home when a young man reading on his couch looked up and gave me an ironic wave as I pointed and admired the woodwork of his apartment. Sheepishly, we moved on.

Eventually, our meandering took us back to the White Hart Inn where live music had begun. The pub was now heaving and we squeezed into two seats at a shared table. A guitarist and a fiddler, seated on benches in a corner of the room, played traditional folk music to a lively crowd.

The other couple at our table turned out to be Americans, the first we'd met on our trip. They hailed originally from North Carolina, but now lived outside of London, having been transferred by their company two years ago. They loved living in the U.K. and had no plans to return to the States anytime soon. This was their first trip to Scotland.

We chatted for a while about things to do in Edinburgh, but the conversation inevitably drifted toward the differences between the States and the U.K. We discussed round-a-bouts, the relative meaning of old, and the merits of British healthcare.

Overhearing our conversation, a man standing behind our table kept leaning down and adding slurred comments about his experiences in the United States. Mostly these centered around the awfulness of American beer.

"Pisswater," he would say, leaning down toward the table. "I couldna drink the stuff. It was the langest I'd gan' withoot beer since I wa' a wee bairn. Bloody awful country."

He was somehow attached to the music industry—a sound guy or groupie or something—and had been part of an American tour with a mildly famous European musician. Bjork, I think it was.

"Ye've probably nae heard 'er, but she tuk me aroun' the world," he slurred. "Worst beer of all in America."

I informed him I had heard of Bjork, though I couldn't name a song she sang, and agreed that the beer in America tasted like pisswater. Katrina recommended he try Coors Light on his next visit. He turned back to the bar, but would continue to lean back from time to time to reinforce his opinion.

"See tha', mates," he would say, holding his pint glass up to the light to show how dark it was. "Light canna e'en penetrate it. Tha's a guid beer. Try tha' wi' Coors Light an' ye'll gae blind."

And so the evening continued. The music was very good, though I didn't recognize many of the songs. This would change by the time we left Scotland ten days later. It is a country that treasures its folk music, and rightly so.

Stumbling back outside, darkness had finally descended on the night. Walking across the plaza to our hotel, we turned and were struck by the beauty of the scene. All along the north edge of the Grassmarket, soft light glowed through the small paned windows of the pubs, while the hum of voices and music floated out of doorways to mingle in the night air. Behind the buildings, spotlights illuminated Edinburgh Castle, leaving the cliffs lost in the darkness below and giving the castle a haunted look, as if it floated above the city.

I took a picture that had no chance of turning out (it didn't), and we entered the hotel. The swanky bar was empty as we crossed the lobby, the clientele having presumably moved on to the nightclubs of the Cowgate. We, on the other hand, went gratefully to bed, finding it hard to believe our day had started in Ayr. Tomorrow would be our first day staying in one place, and we looked forward to it.

# Chapter 9: Hidden Treasures, Stolen Stones

## (A tour of Edinburgh Castle)

On Christmas Day, 1950, four men crept unseen into London's Westminster Abbey, approached the coronation chair, that famed seat of Britain's monarchs, and made off with a three hundred pound hunk of rock. An impressive feat, if not a legal one. This hunk of rock was no ordinary rock; it was the Stone of Destiny, the sacred stone used in the coronation ceremonies of every English monarch for the past seven centuries. The men who made off with this priceless and weighty relic were Scottish nationalists, and in their eyes they weren't stealing it. They were taking it back.

The Stone of Destiny, also known as the Stone of Scone, had arrived in London in 1296 thanks to our old friend Longshanks (Edward I), the same cranky English king who hung Uncle Reggie at Ayr and fueled the unfettered wrath of William Wallace. Edward's troops stole it from the Scottish abbey at Scone, where it had resided for nearly 500 years and had been used in the coronation of every Scottish king since Kenneth MacAlpin, the first king of a united Scotland, in the middle 9th century. The theft of the Stone did nothing to further endear Edward to his northern neighbors, and I suspect that was just fine by him. Indeed, the very clear message he hoped to send—in case people didn't get the message a few months earlier when he hung the Scottish nobles at Ayr—was that Scotland was to have no more independent kings. The reader will be happy to know that ol' Crankyshanks was wrong, and that Scotland would, in fact, enjoy independent monarchs for another three centuries. Thanks to him, however, none of these would be crowned on the Stone of Scone.

But the history of the Stone of Destiny precedes even the Scottish kings, though the facts get murkier the further we go back. Stories claim that the Stone arrived in Scotland from Ireland, where it had previously been used in the coronation of Irish kings. Others say that before arriving in Ireland, it had originated in the Middle East, and was actually the rock used as a pillow by Jacob when dreaming about a ladder to heaven in the biblical Book of Genesis. Whatever the Stone's origins, it was a rock with considerable history and its theft from Westminster Abbey in 1950 caused quite an uproar.

Learning of the crime, British authorities scoured the countryside for four months to no avail until, quite unexpectedly, the Stone turned up on the altar of an abbey in Scotland. It was quickly returned to Westminster Abbey, where it was used two years later at the coronation of Queen Elizabeth II, and all was presumed back to normal.

Finally, in 1996, exactly 700 years after Edward I had stolen the Stone from Scone, the British Parliament as a show of good faith transferred it back to Scotland in an elaborate, but short-sighted procession that would have been much better received had it actually continued on to Scone, the Stone's rightful resting place, rather than terminating in Edinburgh. Nevertheless, Edinburgh, which at least stood within Scotland's borders, was infinitely preferable to Westminster Abbey as a home for the Stone, and it was proudly placed on display in the Crown Room of the Royal Palace in Edinburgh Castle where it remains today.

But here's the thing: No one is sure it's the right stone.

When the Stone disappeared in 1950, it remained missing for four months: plenty of time to make a copy of the crude stone block, which, being sandstone, is impossible to date. Therefore, no one can be sure that the stone that was eventually found and returned to Westminster Abbey was in fact the real Stone of Scone, rather than a copy, with the real stone remaining hidden somewhere in Scotland under the watchful eye of a chosen few.

But it gets even better: Nobody is even sure that the stone stolen from Westminster Abbey by the Scottish nationalists was the true stone in the first place! In fact, the real Stone of Scone may have never been in Westminster Abbey at all. An old rumor claims that Scottish monks may have hidden the real Stone prior to the arrival of Edward's troops in 1296, and that what was carried back to London was actually an impostor rock (perhaps even a cesspit lid!) which the monks had passed off as the real

Stone to the troops, who wouldn't have known the difference—which of course would mean that every English king after Longshanks had been crowned on the cover of a medieval monk's sewer.

If either of these stories is true, the location of the real Stone remains unknown today or at least known only by a chosen few—sort of like a Scottish version of the Holy Grail. We will probably never know the truth of the Stone's authenticity, but the mere possibility that the stone currently on display in Edinburgh Castle is a fake is enough to suggest two intriguing conclusions: 1) it is only a matter of time before someone follows up the smash success of *The DaVinci Code* with a best-selling novel on the mystery of the Stone of Scone, and 2) the thousands of visitors filing through the Crown Room every year may very well be looking at an ordinary hunk of rock.

Either way, I think it's a great story. I get just as much joy thinking of the stone as a medieval cesspit lid that fooled the English king who hung a Crawford as I do from the possibility that it is a sacred stone once graced by the derrieres and feet of Scotland's most ancient kings. Perhaps even more so, come to think of it.

Of course, when I woke up on my second day in Edinburgh, I didn't know this story at all. It was just one of many I would learn on our trip to the castle that day.

• • • • •

But first things first.

Our hotel redeemed itself in the morning. Swankiness aside, it provided one of the best breakfast experiences of the trip. The food had little to do with it. Oh, it was tasty and filling like one would expect of a Scottish breakfast, but what truly set the morning apart was the view. Breakfast was served on the top floor of the hotel where a wall of windows presented a stunning prospect of the gothic spires of Old Town. We had a table next to the windows, where we could look straight down on the Grassmarket or out on the Castle, giving us a preview of what lay ahead for the day. We ate well and sipped our coffee, anticipatory but unhurried. There was no need to rush off to the Fiat Crumb today.

Later that morning, ascending the stone steps that led from the Grassmarket to the Castle Rock, I felt as excited as I'd been yet on the trip. The reader will recall that the castles in Crawford country fell into one of three categories: ruins, centerpiece of park (trailer or amusement), or private home—none very conducive to touring. Edinburgh Castle, on the other hand, was huge, very much intact, and open to the public. It was where we would start our day.

It is hard to say how old Edinburgh Castle is mainly because the castle, which actually consists of an entire complex of buildings and fortifications, is a product of many ages. A fortress has stood on the site for nearly two thousand years, yet the oldest part of the current structure, St. Margaret's Chapel, dates only to the 12th century. The main buildings of Crown Square, the heart of the complex containing the Royal Palace and Great Hall, were constructed in the 15th century. Numerous other additions were made over the years, some as recently as the early 20th century. To complicate matters, nearly every inch of the castle has at some point undergone extensive renovation, an action followed almost inevitably by an eventual restoration. Add to this the fact that in the last half millennium the castle has served as fortress, royal residence, parliament, hospital, prison, museum and any number of other functions, and one begins to sense a place with a varied and complex history. Its story simply cannot be grasped in a morning.

Fortunately, we didn't try.

After waiting for a time in one of those winding lines common at airports and amusement parks, we entered the castle and immediately had to make a choice: to explore on our own or join a tour group. Guides offered free tours which left from the gate every so often. Our guidebook described these guides as enthusiastic storytellers who told lively tales of castle sieges, describing in detail the smell of burning oil and the roar of the cannon, which had me picturing a pleasant cross between Garrison Keillor and my high school history teacher. This image was tempered by the knowledge that mixed in with these action stories would be slightly less riveting tales of the castle's time as a hospital and maybe an in-depth discussion on medals in the War Museum. I'm sure fascinating stories abound from this more recent history, but on this particular morning Katrina and I wanted to focus on the Middle Ages and the Renaissance: the time when the castle was a castle.

We thus skipped the services of the guide and set off with a map to explore, taking delight in the simple stereotypes one associates with a castle. At the entryway, we had already passed over a drawbridge, guarded on either side by carved statues of Robert the Bruce and William Wallace, Scotland's greatest heroes. A few steps beyond the drawbridge, we passed under a portcullis, the big iron grate that could be lowered to seal off a passageway and keep out intruders. I was ecstatic.

We made a beeline for the Great Hall, which topped my list of castle attractions. For some reason, I had a fascination with such rooms and the romantic images of revelry they inspired. No matter how many times I have read about the cold and draughty rooms in medieval castles, in my mind great halls were always warm, lively places. Beneath a vaulted ceiling, noblemen and women would sit at a huge oaken table, drinking wine while a wandering bard played idly on a lyre. A bloated king seated on an elevated dais at one end of the room would wave a lazy hand and bellow, "Bring out the serving wenches!" A trumpet would then announce the entrance of several haggy looking women, missing teeth and carrying platters containing whole pigs. Throughout the meal, a court jester would make fun of the guests, belittling them all with comments that would cost a normal person his head. In the corner, a dwarf would turn somersaults.

With these images in mind, we arrived in the Crown Square where the Great Hall was located. I think I half expected a feast to be in progress as we entered. Well, it wasn't, but the scene proved easy enough to picture. The Great Hall, which had undergone restoration in the 19th century, stood as one of the best preserved in all of Scotland. An enormous room, it had a vaulted ceiling, intricately supported with beautiful wooden rafters. Vertical windows lined the walls, inlaid with stained glass depicting coats of arms.

Between the windows, weapons were hung: shields, swords, lances and axes, ready to be wielded at the first sign of danger. An enormous stone fireplace, suitable for burning whole trees, dominated the far end of the room, guarded on either side by two suits of armor—the kind that would turn their heads as Scooby Doo passed by. The whole scene was fantastic, as if a bloated king or at least a somersaulting dwarf might show up at any moment.

Thus, imagine my delight when two armed men, clothed in Renaissance dress, did enter the room. Engaged in conversation, they walked briskly toward the fireplace. As they neared the center of the room, however, they abruptly stopped and turned to face one another, their voices suddenly raised as if a quarrel had ensued. In a flash, broadswords were drawn, and the two men entered into a dazzling display of swordplay that ranged through the middle of the Great Hall.

I looked around to see if I alone had carelessly slipped through a time portal and was relieved to see everyone else in the room likewise enthralled by the duel.

What we were witnessing constituted a regularly scheduled show that just happened to be timed perfectly for our visit. It was cheesy, of course, but well done and I loved it. After the swordplay ended, the two men took a bow and fielded questions from the crowd that had gathered around them—a crowd that, besides us, consisted mostly of small children and their parents. I easily qualified as the most excited of the bunch, and it was with no small effort that Katrina finally managed to extricate me from the Great Hall. Thrilled beyond measure with the experience, we continued on.

Our next stop was the Royal Palace, located adjacent to the Great Hall in the Crown Square. The Palace was the royal residence, though it hadn't been used as such in nearly 400 years. These days, it housed the Stone of Scone, previously described, among other national treasures, and as such, ranked as one of the most popular attractions in the castle, which of course meant we had to wait in another line. This was a bit of a drag, but would turn out to be well worth the wait—and besides gives me the opportunity now, while we wait, to tell the reader how the Palace ceased to be a royal residence all those years ago.

For this story we must go back to the 16th century and check in on that woman of intrigue, Mary, Queen of Scots. When we last left her, she had just lost her husband, Lord Darnley, due to the sensational and mysterious murder already described. How much Mary may have loved Darnley can be debated, but one thing seems clear: she did love his genes. Darnley was, after all, the great-grandson of Henry VII of England, and as such, had some claim to the English throne. This would have been very attractive to Mary, who herself was a great-granddaughter of Henry VII, and coveted the English throne throughout her career as Scotland's Queen. If you read those last two sentences closely, you will have realized that Mary and Darnley were in fact cousins as well as husband and wife—a situation that achieves an odd acceptance within the otherwise dissimilar social circles of British nobility and backwoods America. The marriage of these cousins produced a son, James, who was not a mutant as one might expect, but a royal heir rather well positioned to stake his claim on the thrones of both England and Scotland, given the combined lineage of his parents.

While all of this inbreeding for power took place, the throne of England was already occupied by someone who had no intention of vacating the seat anytime soon: Queen Elizabeth I, the famed first cousin once-removed to Mary and Darnley in this strange family circle of royalty. Elizabeth reigned for nearly fifty years, from 1558 to 1603, a time period that saw the flowering of Shakespeare and the destruction of the Spanish Armada. Yet, remarkably in all that time she never married nor produced an heir—a fact that earned her the endearing, and almost certainly inaccurate, moniker "the Virgin Queen".

Mary, a catholic, and Elizabeth, a protestant, had a curious relationship. They never met face to face, though they often corresponded, with their letters alternating between sisterly, heartfelt gushiness and terse, accusatory admonishment. They plotted against one another relentlessly, and it was common knowledge that Mary wanted Elizabeth's throne. So it comes as a bit of surprise that Mary fled to England after abdicating her throne in Scotland. It is less of a surprise that Elizabeth, far from offering Mary refuge and a tray of crumpets, threw her in prison, keeping her there for twenty years and refusing to give her an audience. Their relationship ended on a somewhat sour note in 1587 when Elizabeth had Mary beheaded. It seems that Mary had been plotting Elizabeth's assassination from jail, and, as I mentioned earlier, Elizabeth was not ready to give up her throne just yet.

Of course, Elizabeth eventually would die, and upon doing so named Mary's son James as her heir. James already ruled as King of Scotland, having been crowned James VI when Mary abdicated her throne following Darnley's murder. Thus, with Elizabeth's passing in 1603, James VI of Scotland also became James I of England, and Mary's desire to have her line on both thrones was realized, though she was rather too headless at the time to appreciate it.

It is ironic that, after hundreds of years of English attempts to control Scotland, a Scottish king finally united the two countries under a common throne. Still, the effect proved the same as if Scotland had been conquered by its southern neighbor. When James VI of Scotland became James I of England, he left Edinburgh to take up permanent residence in cosmopolitan London. The Scottish parliament would retain its independence for another century, but for all intents and purposes from the reign of King James VI forward Scotland would be ruled from London, more than 300 miles to the south.

In 1617, after being away for fourteen years, James returned to Scotland for a visit and slept in the Royal Palace at Edinburgh Castle. It was the last time a Scottish monarch would do so. On future visits, which were few and far between, reigning monarchs would stay in other locales, such as the pleasant palace of Holyrood and, more recently, Balmoral Castle in the highlands. But mostly, they stayed away from Scotland altogether.

Thus, it should come as no surprise that as Katrina and I entered the Palace strikingly little remained to speak of the building's history as a residence. We saw the room in which Mary gave birth to James and other sentimental reminders of Scotland's tragic monarchs, such as a stone carving set above a doorway featuring the initials of Mary and Darnley. The true highlight of the palace, however, and the point where the line slowed down to a snail's pace as visitors gawked and pointed, was the viewing of something I hadn't known existed: the Honours of Scotland.

Thankfully, the considerate curators of the palace had suspected my ignorance and created an audiovisual presentation relating the story of these most revered symbols of Scottish royalty for visitors to watch before entering the room of their keeping. Thus, I learned that the Honours of Scotland consisted of three sacred treasures—a crown, a scepter and a sword—presented to Scottish monarchs at their coronations.

Filing past, I stood in awe of the craftsmanship of these ceremonial symbols of royal power. These were the very objects that make a king look like a king. The scepter and sword were both of the finest metals, with a crystal sphere topping the scepter. They had both been created for James IV in the 15th century, presented to him by two different popes during his reign. The crown was made in the early 16th century for James V, though it incorporated the gold circlet which had adorned the heads of kings since Robert the Bruce in the 14th century.

Despite their considerable beauty and value, the most amazing thing about the Honours of Scotland was that they were still around to be viewed at all. After being presented to five successive monarchs, the Honours' existence had been put in jeopardy when they were presented to Charles II in 1651. Charles II was the son of King Charles I, who had recently been beheaded in London by Oliver Cromwell. A blazing hypocrite who proved to be as tyrannical as the man he overthrew, Cromwell had risen to power after years of civil war waged by the English Parliament to break the power of Britain's absolute monarchy. The last thing Cromwell wanted was another king after he had finally lopped off the head of the last one. Thus, he grew furious when Scotland crowned Charles II, and vowed to capture and melt down the Honours to rid Britain once and for all of such symbols of oppressive monarchy.* Fortunately, Scottish patriots narrowly saved the

---

* Cromwell had already destroyed the English crown jewels, making the Honours of Scotland the only remaining such relics in Britain.

98

Honours from such a fate by smuggling them out of Edinburgh and hiding them in the stronghold of Dunottar Castle to the northeast and later in a rural church, while Cromwell's henchmen scoured Scotland in vain.

Having thus saved the priceless articles, one would expect them to be well looked after from there on out. And for a time, they were. The Honours were displayed at the Scottish Parliament to represent the absent monarch until the Act of Union dissolved the Parliament in 1707, merging it with the English Parliament in London. Not wanting to transfer the Honours to London where they could fall into English hands, Scottish leaders instead put the crown, sword and scepter away for safekeeping. This sounds normal enough so far, but here's the amazing part: before long, no one could remember where they'd put them. The Honours of Scotland had been lost.

I find this absolutely amazing: that objects once deemed important enough to be smuggled out of a city at great risk to avoid being melted down could just a few years later be carelessly misplaced, like a set of car keys or sunglasses. I don't want to be too critical here. I'm as guilty as the next person when it comes to losing things, especially car keys and sunglasses. I'd like to think, however, that I might be a bit more mindful of where I lay my priceless crown, sword and scepter.

Fortunately, like most car keys and sunglasses, the Honours turned up in the end, though it took a bit longer than one might expect, as no one seemed to be looking very hard. In 1818, this changed as the great Scottish author Sir Walter Scott, fueled by the same romantic patriotism that inspired his writings, led a search for the famed treasures, dramatically uncovering them in an old chest in the Crown Room of the Royal Palace of Edinburgh Castle. At the time of his discovery, the Honours of Scotland had not been seen in over a century. Simply remarkable.

Today, these royal treasures sit on display in the very same room where Scott found them. Shuffling by, I noted that the old chest had been replaced by a bulletproof glass case and modern alarm system, giving hope that the Honours might now make it a few more years without being melted down or misplaced.

While in the Crown Room, our attention was called to another object on display with the Honours of Scotland. Next to these beautifully crafted treasures sat what can only be described as a hunk of very ordinary looking rock, hewn into a rough block. This rock, as the reader may have guessed, was the Stone of Scone previously described, and it demanded our attention more for its contrast to the other objects in the case than for any inherent beauty it possessed. The Stone was a simple sandstone block, 26" long, 16" across and 10½" inches deep, weighing over 300 pounds. How four men could have removed such a stone from the coronation chair of Westminster Abbey without attracting notice boggles the mind. It would be like sneaking into the Oval Office and making off with the president's desk. Of course, this was in 1950 when the world didn't have today's high tech security devices, but how high tech does one have to be to spot four guys carrying the equivalent of an NFL offensive lineman out of England's most famous church? We stood there marveling over the stone and the mysteries surrounding it until polite coughs reminded us that the long line of people behind us might fancy a look as well.

• • • • •

"Okay, my mind needs a break," Katrina announced as we emerged from the Royal Palace, bursting with newfound knowledge. "Oh look, a view."

She made a beeline for the castle walls.

"We haven't even scratched the surface of this place," I noted, joining her a moment later to follow her gaze out over the rooftops of Edinburgh.

The view from the ramparts was spectacular. The Firth of Forth sparkled in the late morning sun, and the spires of cathedrals and monuments rose here and there, casting a gothic mood over much of the city.

"Mmm," said a half-listening Katrina. "That looks like a pretty area." She pointed down at a neighborhood with broad avenues and ample gardens just to the north of the castle.

"That's New Town," I informed her, feeling very useful with my guidebook in hand.

"Doesn't look very new to me," she retorted.

In fact, New Town was well-over 200 years old, an amusing reminder of just how old Old Town was and how Americans need to continually adjust their perspective when traveling in Scotland.

"I guess we could call it Less Old Town," I suggested.

"Mmm." My wit went unnoticed as Katrina gazed trancelike from the city walls. She always reached her saturation point for history well before I reached mine. I would never notice this until way too late, of course, but disaster was usually avoided thanks to a very effective coping technique she had developed: tuning me out. We demonstrated our respective talents now.

"Three hundred years ago, we wouldn't be looking down at New Town at all," I explained, showing off my guidebook comprehension. "Instead, we'd be looking at a man-made lake called the Nor' Loch, constructed hundreds of years earlier to protect the northern approach to the castle."

"Mmm."

"When 18th century breakthroughs in weaponry made castle warfare obsolete, the city finally drained the loch and built New Town."

"Mmm."

I rattled on with my monologue while Katrina, blissfully oblivious, stared off over the rooftops and out to sea. We were both caught up in our separate worlds when a new voice suddenly jolted us back to the present.

"Tha's a big gun."

The voice belonged to a beefy man in his fifties sporting a gray crew cut and a green rugby jersey, standing beside what was undeniably a very big gun. Though it wasn't clear if he had spoken to me or was simply making an observation to the air, I determined that dialogue would be preferable to two people talking to themselves.

"Sure is," I replied astutely.

"I'd like t'see how far tha' thing could blast me wife."

Tha' thing, incidentally, was a 15$^{th}$ century siege cannon named Mons Meg. I had read about it in the guidebook, but somehow had failed to notice that it was right behind me.

"Two miles," I replied brightly, holding up the guidebook for confirmation, "so long as she doesn't weigh more than a three or four hundred pound stone."

"Aye, jus' under," he grinned, bringing a meaty hand up to scratch his chin while we both admired the cannon.

"Two miles," he considered, somewhat wistfully. "That'd buy me a few minutes o' peace, but she'd find her way back." He elbowed me confidentially, and we both laughed the laugh of two men standing next to a gun.

"I dunno," chimed in Katrina, apparently now ready to re-engage the world. "Sounds like a good head start in the other direction to me."

This pleased the man immensely. "Now tha's a cheeky one," he grinned, elbowing me again. "Ye'd better nae turn yer back on her." And he pointed and winked to make sure I knew he was talking about Katrina.

Just then the man's wife, who I saw was indeed just under the cannon's weight limit, waddled up to us, joined by a large group of people crowding around the gun. The couple was part of a tour group, and the man had wandered ahead, presumably for a few minutes o' peace. He went temporarily silent as the tour guide launched into his spiel:

"And here we have Mons Meg," the guide announced, "yet another Scottish treasure fortunate to have survived the ages."

I tuned in, excited to receive the benefit of an expert storyteller for a few moments.

"Given to James II by the Duke of Burgundy in 1457, a year when artillery development was still in its infancy, Mons Meg was a masterpiece, though a bit unwieldy," the guide informed us. "Indeed, her tremendous size inspired a legend of two lovers who managed to conceive a child in the cannon's barrel."

Here, the man in the rugby jersey elbowed me in the ribs. "Ye an' the misses going to give it a gae, mate?"

"No," came Katrina's reply, from just behind our ears. It seemed like a very general no. A no that could apply to many things for a long time. Rugby Man found this very funny.

Meanwhile the guide continued: "While convenient for illicit liaisons, the great gun proved less so for the field of battle. Weighing six tons and requiring a hundred men to handle her, Meg could only be moved three miles per day, making war campaigns a laborious process to say the least. Still, anyone unlucky enough to get in the way of a 300 pound stone blasted from her great muzzle would no doubt testify to the cannon's effectiveness."

I pictured Rugby Man's wife smacking into his stomach at the end of a two-mile flight and agreed that it would be quite effective indeed.

"Of course, blasting a stone this size requires a tremendous amount of gun powder, which in turn generates a tremendous amount of heat. So much so that these siege guns could only be fired eight to ten times per day without beginning to melt down and get finicky—and believe me, the last thing a cannon operator wanted was for a gun this size to get finicky. This was convincingly demonstrated by James II, who grew fond of his new siege guns and liked to oversee their firing on the field of battle. He was doing just that when a cannon named the Lion, similar in size and construction to Mons Meg, misfired and exploded, killing the 29-year old king and earning him distinction as the world's first monarch to be done in by artillery fire."

The guide paused to let his words sink in. A smattering of nervous laughter trickled through the group, as we all took a collective step back from the cannon.

"You might want to reconsider your plan," Katrina whispered to Rugby Man, who gave a great snort and elbowed me yet again in the ribs, all the while muttering "cheeky, cheeky" under his breath. Rugby Man's wife glared at us like a teacher about to scold a group of disruptive children, causing her husband to immediately sober up, and forcing Katrina to stifle a laugh of her own.

The guide went on to relate that, given her unwieldy size and dangerous unpredictability, Mons Meg was eventually retired from the field of battle and placed in Edinburgh Castle to be used for strictly ceremonial purposes. "But even this proved risky," he explained. "The great gun's muzzle finally burst in 1681 upon being fired to honor the visit of James VII of Scotland (James II of England) to Edinburgh. It was the last time she would be fired. Rendered thus silent, Mons Meg found herself unceremoniously dumped over the castle wall into a scrap heap near Foog's Gate..."

"Now tha's an idea," whispered Rugby Man, a comment which drew snickers from both me and Katrina and an arcing purse striking his arm from his wife.

"...where she remained for some years waiting to be melted down. Fortunately, before such a fate came to pass souvenir-hunting soldiers removed her from the pile, taking her south to England to be displayed in the Tower of London. Finally, in 1829, thanks to petitions by that great patriot Sir Walter Scott, Mons Meg returned to Scotland, and today stands as one more symbol of the kingdom's heroic past awaiting visitors to Edinburgh Castle."

While Rugby Man rubbed his arm, I took the opportunity to note to the group at large that it seemed as if visitors to the castle would have a lot less to see today if it hadn't been for Scott.

"Oh, quite right," rejoined the guide, with a touch of pride in his voice. At that, he directed the group's attention to a dark, fanciful spire towering above the rooftops in the distance.

"The Scott Monument, built to honor the great Sir Walter Scott," he explained, "who, besides ensuring preservation of national treasures, managed to revive a keen interest in Scotland's romantic history and culture through his novels and poetry. Standing over 200 feet high, the Scott Monument represents the largest monument in the world dedicated to an author, and stands as a striking example of the extent to which Scotland honors those who honor it."

"This is great," I expressed to Katrina, pleased with the interaction and feeling very much a part of the group. I was beginning to regret not joining a guide from the outset.

"And now we'll be moving on," the guide announced. "Those of you who have just joined us are welcome to follow us to our next stop: the soldiers' pet cemetery."

"And thus the advantage of going it alone," Katrina reminded me.

Rugby Man gave me one more elbow to the ribs for good measure and told me to "watch out for tha' one," pointing and winking at Katrina, as his group wandered off to hear more about various dogs buried in the castle. I followed Katrina on a determined stroll back to the main gate.

Just as we crossed the drawbridge, it dawned on me that, of all the stories we had stumbled across inside the castle, one that had not garnered a mention (hardly surprising, really) was the story of the castle's capture in 1573 by Sir Thomas Crawford. I briefly considered re-entering the complex, but was convinced otherwise by Katrina, who pointed out what a shame it would be to ruin such a positive morning seeking out a tale that could only lead to disappointment.

"Think about it," she reasoned. "I'm picturing a plaque on the wall attributing the castle's capture to an anonymous 'military captain and former friend of Darnley' or, better yet, to an act of God, or a band of trolls, or anything really, so long as it avoids putting the Crawford name in print in a prominent public venue."

She had a point.

"Besides," she warned, "I can't take any more history for at least an hour."

"Oh, you've hit your limit?" I asked innocently. "When that happens you need to let me know and we'll take a…where are you going?"

Thus, I abruptly left the castle behind and hurried after Katrina toward our next adventure: a stroll down Edinburgh's famous Royal Mile.

# Chapter 10: If It's Not Scottish It's Crap

## (A stroll down the Royal Mile)

In the 12th century, when King David founded Holyrood Abbey just down the hill from Edinburgh Castle, he unwittingly established the axis upon which Edinburgh would develop. Almost immediately a road would form, connecting the castle with the abbey just a mile away. In time, buildings would spring up along this road, forming separate communities such as the High Street and the Canongate, all of which would eventually be swallowed up by an expanding Edinburgh. Today, this stretch is known as the Royal Mile.

Surrounded by a bustling city, the Royal Mile serves as the heart of Old Town and retains most of its original structures and charm. It is without doubt one of the world's most fascinating and historic streets.

It is also one of the tackiest.

Literally millions of visitors flock to the Royal Mile every year, traversing its length to take in the sights. And indeed, nowhere else could one find such a concentration of Scottish history in a single locale. Starting at Edinburgh Castle, which anchors the upper end of the road, visitors pass such important sites as St. Giles Kirk, the cathedral from which John Knox led Scotland's Protestant Reformation, the Mercat Cross, where for centuries townspeople gathered to hear important announcements, and the Canongate Tollbooth, an infamous prison and courtroom where such important cases as the Darnley murder were tried. Visitors will also pass the old Parliament House, home to the Scottish Parliament until its merger with the English Parliament in 1707, as well as the new, architecturally controversial Parliament building, where the re-established Scottish Parliament meets today.[*] Anchoring the lower end of the stretch one finds Holyrood Palace, the royal residence built adjacent to the original abbey to

---

[*] The new Scottish Parliament, which legislates strictly on internal Scottish affairs, was established in 1999, though the new Parliament building did not open until 2005. For the previous six years, the Scottish Parliament met in temporary quarters located further up the Royal Mile while the new building was being constructed. Such was the case during the summer of 2004, when Katrina and I were there.

provide an agreeable retreat for monarchs wishing to escape the draughty castle high on the hill.

This list represents a mere sample of the historic sites awaiting visitors along the Royal Mile. It is, to say the least, a lot to take in, even for the most dedicated history buff.

Fortunately, plenty of diversions line the way. Most of these take the form of gift shops, which seem to occupy every other doorway and at times are strung out several in a row. These stores sell positively everything that could be associated with Scotland, the tackier the better. Undoubtedly, these were the stores providing inspiration for one of my favorite Saturday Night Live sketches starring Mike Myers. In this particular sketch, Myers owns a store called *All Things Scottish* in which he sells all sorts of Scottish trinkets and memorabilia while regaling his customers with his motto: "If it's not Scottish, it's crap!" At one point during the sketch, a customer comes in and says something to this effect:

"I know it's a long shot, but I was wondering if you happened to have a coaster set with a picture of Scotty from Star Trek on it?"

The owner's reply is affirmative and immediate: "Box of six or twelve?"

This is funny, of course, because it is so absurd. Who would ask for such a product, and indeed, what store would possibly stock it? But here's the thing: having visited the Royal Mile, such a scenario no longer seems the least bit far-fetched. In fact, I would venture to say that without having to look too hard I could find a coaster set with Scotty from Star Trek on it in multiple stores along the Royal Mile, probably in boxes of six and twelve and with my choice of family tartan* in the background.

One can truly find anything at these stores, so long as it is something with a family tartan on it. Enter a gift store at random anywhere along the Royal Mile and you will be confronted with a spinning rack of refrigerator

* Okay, here's where the reader learns about tartan, though there will be more on the subject to come. Tartan is a pattern woven into woolen cloth, commonly (though mistakenly) called plaid in the United States. Each clan in Scotland has a unique tartan, with a set pattern of colors and lines. Thus, when a MacGregor, for example, wears a kilt or plaid made of cloth of the MacGregor tartan, he can be identified by others as a member of the MacGregor clan. Having a clan tartan started as a strictly highland convention, but in modern times has been adopted by family groups throughout Scotland.

magnets, all sporting family tartans. They will be alphabetized by last name and contain the family crest and motto on them as well as the family tartan. Next to the spinning rack of refrigerator magnets will be a shelf full of family tartan coffee mugs. Hung on the wall behind the coffee mugs will be family crest plaques. Another set of shelves will feature family tartan ties, kilts, and caps. It is a delicious bounty for those seeking identity confirmation via merchandise.

In addition to these gift stores, establishments have arisen to educate visitors on traditional aspects of Scottish culture. Thus, walking down the Royal Mile, one can visit the Edinburgh Old Town Weaving Centre to learn about the tradition of tartan, see weaving in action, and even order a custom kilt, though the impulse buyer will find plenty ready-made on the rack. Properly outfitted in tartan, our tourist can meander across the road to the Scotch Whisky Heritage Centre, where he will receive a free dram of Scotland's national beverage, along with the chance to ride in a moving barrel while learning more about whisky history and production. On the way out, he can (and will) purchase several bottles from the many on sale. Sufficiently liquored, our kilt-wearing visitor can stroll further down the Mile to see bagpipes being made by a traditional bagpipe maker, which will immediately lead to the purchase of a set he will never learn to play, and will likely be followed by a visit to the nearby Heraldry Store, so he can surprise his neighbors back home with a wall-sized banner bearing his family Coat of Arms to hang from his porch. Thus, bedecked in his kilt, trailing his banner and blowing wildly but futilely into his pipes, our drunken hero arrives at the end of the Royal Mile ready to tour Holyrood Palace, much to the delight of the Palace security staff, I'm sure.

To be fair, most people don't go as overboard as the above scenario presents, but here's the beautiful thing: they could. The Royal Mile offers tourists unlimited opportunity to get as tacky as they wish, all while passing in and out of Scotland's most important and historic sites—which should sufficiently explain my giddiness as I exited the castle and surveyed the descending street ahead.

・　・　・　・　・

Heeding Katrina's warning about overdosing on history, I suggested a casual approach to the Royal Mile. We stopped briefly at the Old Town Weaving Centre, where I discovered that Crawford tartan is an odd pattern combining the seemingly disharmonious colors of purple, green and white. The book I had read on the plane called it a "distinguished burgundy", but I assure the reader, it is purple. Continuing further down the street, we popped in and out of a few gift stores, where I amused myself—and only myself—by murmuring "If it's not Scottish, it's crap!" in my terribly affected accent while browsing through refrigerator magnets.

At the end of the first block, just before entering a section of street called the Lawnmarket[*], we found ourselves passing a stone church whose spire stuck up higher than any other in Edinburgh. The architecture was intriguing, but what made us stop and take a closer look were the café tables set up outside the entrance. It seemed the church had traded in its pious congregation for thirsty pedestrians.

"I could certainly sit for a spell," Katrina suggested in a tone that said, "We're about to sit for a spell." This was fine with me. We had been on our feet for several hours by this point, and I had no intention of passing up the opportunity to enjoy a creamy ale at a church. We veered instinctively to the door.

The church, as it turned out, had been transformed into an arts center called simply "The Hub". The café made up just one part of this new center, which served as the year-round headquarters for the Edinburgh International Festival, of which I had never heard prior to sitting down at the table. As we enjoyed our pints, I read about the Festival in our guidebook and was—as I often am—astounded by my ignorance.

The Edinburgh Festival is huge. Started in 1947 as a way to focus people on classical music and theater after years of war and strife, the Festival was an instant hit. People from all over the United Kingdom

---

[*] Don't confuse the Lawnmarket with the Grassmarket, where our hotel was located. They are different places, though they are only two blocks apart and share strikingly similar names.

flocked to the city, enjoying the opportunity to listen to symphonies and live theater rather than the falling bombs and wailing sirens that had dominated so many of the previous years. To say that the Festival has grown since that first year is to engage in gross understatement. It has positively exploded, with half a million people from all over the world now flocking to Edinburgh each August to enjoy what has become the world's largest celebration of the arts.

"Who knew?" I thought, sipping my pint.

Today, only a fraction of the offerings visitors have to choose from are actually endorsed by the Edinburgh International Festival, the official body that started it all back in 1947. The EIF has stuck to its original mission, sponsoring classical music, theater and ballet for spectators to enjoy—and let's face it, such a festival can only get so big. To get as huge as the Edinburgh Festival has become, other performances, which are decidedly not classical and range from street buskers to punk bands and circus acts to avant-garde theater, have been added over the years, giving the streets a Mardi Gras feel during Festival time. Most of these non-classical performances fall under the umbrella of an alternative organization called the Edinburgh Festival Fringe.

The Fringe, as it is known, is actually as old as the EIF, forming accidentally when eight less orthodox theater groups showed up uninvited to the first Festival and were labeled "the fringe of the official festival" by a critic. Each year thereafter, the Fringe, which thrived on the controversy it created, grew bigger and bigger, realizing that for every person who wants to attend a symphony, there are two or three who want to see a risqué play or laugh out loud to Monty Python-style comedy; and, indeed, the Fringe today has far outstripped the original EIF, offering the lion's share of entertainment each August. At the 2005 festival alone, the Fringe presented 1,799 shows, requiring the participation of over 16,000 performers. According to the Fringe website, had a particularly avid festival guest desired to see every show back to back, it would have taken five years, three months and twenty-five days to do so. This is a big festival.

I was amazed to read the list of celebrities who have performed at the

Festival: a list that includes such figures as Dudley Moore, Jude Law, and every member of Monty Python for starters. American celebrities have also made the trip, with comics from Richard Pryor to Robin Williams performing for Edinburgh crowds. Reading through the literature, I gathered that, despite these big name attractions, the Festival owes just as much of its flavor to the no name performers who show up each year to entertain the passing crowds on the sidewalks of the Royal Mile. It is these street performers who infuse the air with so much festivity, and I'm talking about all of them: the guy on the unicycle, the woman playing "God Save the Queen" on a set of wine glasses, and even the human statue people, who cover themselves in bronze body paint or white powder and stand motionless all day on the corner.

"Now those people deserve respect," Katrina pointed out.

"Who? The statue people?" I asked.

"Heck yes. My hearty respect goes out to anyone who has figured out how to make a buck by not moving all day."

Looking at the calendar, we were missing this year's Festival by less than three weeks—a fact that at first struck me as disappointing, but on second thought seemed definitely for the best. I was reminded of something a friend of mine from Louisiana told me a few years back, when I told him I wanted to see Mardi Gras. "Everyone should see Mardi Gras at least once," he had said, "but they should also see New Orleans." That's how I felt now about Edinburgh. On a future visit, I'd love to go back and see the Festival. It would without question be a wild, thrilling experience. But right now, I was happy to just see Edinburgh. We paid for the drink and moved on.

Crossing the Lawnmarket, we took a detour off the main road to explore Lady Stair's Close, one of Edinburgh's many famous closes. With their narrow passages and hidden courtyards, the closes are a fascinating quirk of Old Town, giving the streets character and depth, and in any other city would be a haven for drug dealers, prostitutes and serial killers with names like "Max the Axe". Indeed, in days gone by they were home to

Edinburgh's seedier element, and the scene of many dark crimes, made all the more terrifying by the shadows of gargoyles and niches cast by the gothic architecture. Though today city officials keep them clean and secure as a centerpiece of the tourist district, it would still give one pause to enter a dark close alone at night.

Modern Edinburgh thrives on its gothic, haunting past of which these closes played such a part. Here and there along the Royal Mile, Katrina and I passed signs advertising "Terror Tours" or "Fright Nights" or some such catchy phrase. These tours take guests through the streets of Edinburgh after dark for the express purpose of making full-grown adults cower in a puddle of their own tears. Judging from the signs, groups are led through the closes and wynds of Old Town by a pasty-faced guide sporting a long, black cloak and top hat—the type of person that would look right at home in a B-list horror film or in a university coffee shop. Throughout the evening, the guide unveils stories of legendary ghosts, witches, and very real criminals from the city's checkered past, as carefully crafted special effects—a well-timed howl or cackle, or a shadow disappearing around a corner—cause the group to huddle a little closer together.

Katrina, who stopped for a closer look at each such sign we passed, thought this would be a fantastic way to spend an evening. I, on the other hand, who have been known to tremble nervously while passing through haunted houses created by school children, mumbled some blather about out-of-work actors doing anything to make a dime and quickened my pace.

Fortunately we were exploring the Royal Mile in broad daylight, so I was able to enjoy the character and architecture of Lady Stair's Close without trembling in a corner—a good thing as there was much to see. A stone stairway led down into the close, which opened onto a multi-leveled courtyard enclosed by Renaissance-age buildings. In the courtyard stood an intriguing edifice with a round stone tower and beckoning wooden doorway. This was Lady Stair's House, a beautiful seventeenth century residence that now houses the Edinburgh Writers' Museum.

As the reader may have noticed by now, Scotland takes great pride in its literary history. Already in our travels, we'd touched on the Robbie

Burns trail, the Edinburgh literary pub tour, the Scott Monument, and now here was a whole museum dedicated to Scotland's three most famous writers: Sir Walter Scott, Robbie Burns, and Robert Louis Stevenson.[*] Of Burns, I have related quite a bit. Of Scott, a little. Of Stevenson, to this point, nothing. But I assure you, everything you want to know about any of these three writers can be found in the Writers' Museum in Lady Stair's Close. Original letters, diaries, manuscripts, photographs, timelines, furniture, pipes, you name it, all belonging to these three lions of Scottish literature clutter the rooms. And if you need more information than the exhibits can give, just ask the little old lady sitting by the stairs. She knows the rest.

This little old lady, who greeted us with a trembling voice from a chair beside the spiral staircase as we entered, was not quite old enough to be the original Lady Stair, who lived in the 1700's, but may have dated Robert Louis Stevenson, who died in 1896. Despite her advanced years, a set of bright eyes revealed a youthful energy beneath the wispy gray hair and frame. Our visit to the Writers' Museum was made all the more pleasant by her presence. A lively conversationalist, she harbored unparalleled expertise on all three of the museum's featured authors, though she confessed partiality to Stevenson, further heightening my suspicion of a prior liaison.

Robert Louis Stevenson, incidentally, ranks as one of my favorite writers as well, so the little old lady and I hit it off right away.

"It's over a century old, but I still think *Treasure Island* is the most thrilling adventure book ever written," she confessed, citing Stevenson's famous work.

"Me too!" I exclaimed. I was very familiar with the book, as it formed the centerpiece of one of my favorite teaching units at my school in the Caribbean.

---

[*] Sir Arthur Conan Doyle, the author who created one of the most recognizable characters in all of literature, Sherlock Holmes, and defined the detective novel for generations to come, does not seem to be revered in Scotland despite having been born and raised in Edinburgh and having received his medical degree from Edinburgh University. He was not mentioned in the Writers' Museum so far as I could tell, and his name did not appear in the index of my Scottish guidebook. Perhaps this is because he did most of his writing in England and his stories tend to be set there rather than in Scotland. At any rate, I found the oversight curious.

"Oh, do tell me more," she pleaded, clapping her frail hands together.

So I told her of uninhabited Norman Island, located just a few miles away from my home, which locals claim served as a model for Stevenson's *Treasure Island*. I have great fun challenging my students to test this theory by first reading the book and researching Robert Louis Stevenson's life, and then taking them on a boat trip to Norman Island so they can compare it to the geographical descriptions of Treasure Island in the novel. It's a great project because nobody knows for sure if Norman Island really was the model for Stevenson's book or not, though enough tantalizing evidence can be found on both sides to lead to good debate.

The little old lady pondered the question herself and then professed that were she but a few years younger she'd join us on our next trip to the island. Indeed, it was probably the first time in fifty years she had heard something related to the life and times of Robert Louis Stevenson that she didn't already know. She returned the favor by regaling me with lively stories of Stevenson's travels in the South Pacific, and, fascinatingly, of another of his famous works.

"Have you read *The Strange Case of Dr. Jekyll and Mr. Hyde?*" she asked, hopefully.

Embarrassingly, I never had, though I assured her that, like most Americans, I had seen enough Bugs Bunny cartoons to have a pretty fair idea of the plot.

Eyes twinkling, she told me that, sadly, the real book featured no talking rabbits, but was, should I care to know, inspired by events occurring within a stone's throw of where we now stood.

"Brodie Close," she whispered, pointing in the direction of the Lawnmarket. "It's named for one of Edinburgh's most shadowy figures."

She then proceeded to tell us about Deacon William Brodie, a cabinetmaker and locksmith regarded as one of the city's most respected citizens of the latter 18th century—right up until he was hanged, that is.

"For almost twenty years Deacon Brodie led a secret life that fell somewhat short of upstanding," the little old lady revealed with a knowing look and a gleam in her eye, "but nobody knew until one of his henchmen spilled the beans!" She gave a chuckle before going on to explain.

Being regularly granted access as a locksmith and cabinetmaker to many of the finer homes of Edinburgh, Brodie would make copies of keys so that he or his underlings could come back later to steal the valuables and money. The considerable funds he made from such burglary went to support the rest of his secret life, which included two mistresses, five illegitimate children, and a rather substantial gambling habit. Upon being ratted out, Brodie fled the country, only to be tracked down in Amsterdam and shipped back to Edinburgh, where in a final twist of irony, he was hanged on the very gallows he had designed for the city the year before. Legend has it that he tried to cheat death by wearing an iron collar on the gallows, a rumor that gained momentum when someone supposedly spotted Brodie in Paris following the execution.

"But by most accounts he was quite dead on the gallows and even more so after being buried in his grave," the little old lady concluded with another chuckle.

Whatever the final fate of Deacon Brodie, the nature of his split personality was immortalized by Stevenson in his famous tale of Jekyll and Hyde, which I made a point of reading shortly after we returned from Scotland on strict orders from the little old lady. It proved a fascinating read, with a bit of supernatural body-changing potion thrown in, and although set in London, is exactly the kind of story that would be born in the eerie streets of Old Town Edinburgh.

After talking to the little old lady for some time, Katrina and I explored the rest of the Writers' Museum on our own, giving me the chance to try out the spiral staircase several times more than necessary. On a more literary note, I stumbled across plenty of tidbits to keep me flush with reading material upon our return from Scotland. One of these discoveries had to do with another of my favorite books: *Ivanhoe*, the great novel of chivalry and Saxon heroism written by Sir Walter Scott. I had read *Ivanhoe* several times over the years, but not until I had browsed through Edinburgh's Writers' Museum did I realize that it was just one of a series of novels, called the Waverley novels, written by Scott. Since our return, I have read several of the others, including *Rob Roy*, *The Talisman*, and *Waverley*—the first to be published and the one from which the series takes its name—and they all make exciting reading. It's easy to see how they caused a sensation and a flourishing of pride in Scottish history when they appeared in the early 19th century.

Indeed, Scott himself seems to have fallen victim to the romanticism of his own novels, living like a noble lord on his estate of Abbotsford in southern Scotland. Here, he ran up huge debts remodeling the estate with fanciful turrets, stained glass and wood paneling, while simultaneously embarking on a failed business venture. Despite all of his literary success, he died still owing considerable sums.

Exploring the museum, I was struck by the tragedy that seemed to visit not just Scott, but all three of Scotland's literary heroes. Stevenson, who battled weak lungs and poor health throughout his life, died at the tender age of 46. Burns, who developed rheumatic heart disease due to overwork in the fields—and, I suspect, overwork with the lassies—died at the even younger age of 37. By this comparison, Scott, who besides his accumulated debts also battled lingering injuries from a childhood illness, seems to have been the lucky one, living to the ripe age of 61.

This string of tragedy added a depressing pall to the otherwise fascinating experience provided by the museum, and Katrina and I decided to move on, lest we be infected by any lingering bad luck. Though I suppose the sight of the little old lady cheerfully waving goodbye as we exited should have been enough to dispel any fears.

•   •   •   •   •

Back on the main street, we continued our walk down the Royal Mile. At the end of the block, the Lawnmarket gave way to the High Street, along which we passed St. Giles Kirk, the Mercat Cross, and the Tron Kirk, this last a 17th century church now best known as the focal point of Europe's biggest New Year's Eve party.

Scots refer to New Year's Eve as Hogmanay, a celebration our guidebook described as a leftover pagan festival "with a unique mix of tradition, hedonism, sentimentality and enthusiasm." For this read "drink fest." On December 31 each year, people who have been drinking all evening gather in the square outside the Tron Kirk to cheer and sing "Auld Lang Syne" as the bells chime midnight. Then, according to tradition, each reveler tries to be the first guest of the New Year to show up at a neighbor's house with a bottle of whisky. Of course, the second guest to show up is not turned away, nor is the third, fourth, or fifth or indeed anyone so long as they are accompanied by a bottle of whisky. Perhaps the dedication to drink Scots bring to Hogmanay is best illustrated by the fact that Scotland remains the only kingdom in the U.K. where not only January 1, but also January 2 is considered a holiday for recovery purposes. Now that's a good party.

Continuing on, the High Street morphed into the Canongate, where we passed the Tollbooth with its stone tower and antiquated clock, and stopped to linger outside the Canongate Kirk, where a wedding party was just exiting through the iron gate. The groomsmen sported full dress kilts, while a small group of bagpipers, complete with black furry hats, sent out a celebratory tune from their pipes. It was fantastic. With the architecture of the kirk, the traditional dress and the haunting sound of the pipes, the scene could easily have been from two hundred years ago; at least it could have been right up until the bride and groom came out of the church, climbed into a shiny black sports car and sped away from the cheering guests. We cheered along with them before continuing on, only to find ourselves quite suddenly at the entry gate of Holyrood Palace.

We had reached the end of the Royal Mile. Turning to look back up the hill, the castle, so dominant from other angles, here was obscured by the rows of buildings and throngs of people covering the gentle slope. We had, in fact, walked only a mile since this morning, but in terms of stories and experiences, it felt like we had come infinitely further. Our feet were fine, but our minds were worn out.

As far as tacky gifts go, I had shown remarkable restraint, helped greatly by stern looks from Katrina whenever I found myself with a useless trinket, such as a tartan dog collar (we didn't own a dog), in my hand. In fact, walking towards the gates of Holyrood, my bags contained only two Crawford ties, three Crawford refrigerator magnets, one Crawford plaque, and a CD to play in the Fiat Crumb titled *The Tartan Top Twenty Great Scottish Songs*, which would prove to be as cheesy and awful as an album sold beside a gift shop cash register promises to be. Considering I could have been wearing a kilt and blowing futilely into bagpipes in between quick pulls off a whisky bottle, I was quite proud of myself.

# Chapter 11: A Royal Soap Opera

## (A tour of Holyrood Palace)

Here's a lovely story for you:

On March 9, 1566, Mary, Queen of Scots, hosted a dinner party in her chambers at Holyrood Palace. Present at the party were eight of her close friends, none closer than David Rizzio, an Italian musician who had won Mary's favor and now served as the queen's private secretary and most trusted advisor. Conspicuously absent were her husband, Darnley, and any of the Protestant nobles who were supposed to be her leading advisors.

The party, which took place in a dining closet off of Mary's bedchamber (leave it to a queen to have a closet big enough to host a dinner party), was going along merrily enough until Darnley suddenly appeared at the door of the closet, gaining entry to the Queen's chamber via a secret stair connected to the King's chamber below (leave it to a king to have a secret stair leading to his wife's bedroom). Sitting down next to Mary, he put his arm around her, upon which signal another man, a Protestant noble sporting full armor, appeared at the doorway and demanded Rizzio be handed over.

"What offence hath he done?" asked a very taken aback Queen Mary.

"Great offence!" the man replied.

Moments later, six additional armed Protestant lords appeared at the door and pushed into the closet, which may have been big enough to accommodate a dinner party, but was by this point getting a bit crowded.* In the ensuing scuffle, the table was overturned and Rizzio was dragged from the closet, while Darnley restrained his royal—and very pregnant, I might add—wife. The Protestant lords carried the unfortunate Italian secretary through the Queen's bedchamber, down the stairs to the King's bedchamber, back up the stairs to the Queen's bedchamber and finally out into her presence chamber, where, undoubtedly tired of dragging a kicking

---

* The closet measured approximately 10 feet by 12 feet.

and screaming body around, they pulled out their daggers and let loose with a fury.

Fifty-six stab wounds later, Rizzio lay dead.

His "great offence", as it turns out, was being too close to the queen. In supplanting the Protestant lords as Mary's advisor, he had effectively alienated them from the circle of power, something they did not appreciate, especially considering Rizzio was a Catholic. Also, as Mary's confidante, the young Italian spent many private hours alone with the queen, often late into the night, giving rise to the suspicion that he served as something more than an advisor. Indeed, rumors circulated that the child she carried had been sired by Rizzio rather than Darnley. In light of this, historians have speculated that the attack which led to Rizzio's death was likely intended to bring an end to Mary's pregnancy as well, as no one much fancied the idea of Scotland's next king being the spawn of a low-born Italian musician. In the midst of the melee, a dagger, a pistol and a chair had all been aimed at the queen's belly, though to no effect. On top of these overt threats, the Protestant lords and Darnley, in particular, may have hoped that the mere shock of Rizzio's violent death would cause a miscarriage in the fragile queen.

If this was the hope, then the plot only partially succeeded. When the dust cleared, Rizzio was indeed very dead. Mary's pregnancy, however, continued uninterrupted, and three months later she gave birth to James, the little boy who would eventually become King James VI of Scotland and later King James I of England.

Consider that. Not only that James, who would unite the Scottish and English thrones, very nearly ceased to exist before he ever made it out of the womb, but that, once alive, no one was ever completely sure that he was truly the son of Darnley and not the son of the queen's secretary. Fascinating.

But let us return to our tale, which, after the murder of Rizzio, degenerates into a royal soap opera. Darnley, who had hoped to gain further power by allying himself with the Protestant lords, quickly fell out with them and ran begging for mercy and forgiveness to his wife. The lords tried to keep both king and queen prisoners at Holyrood, causing Mary and Darnley to make a daring escape on horseback through the streets of the Canongate at night. Once in safety, the queen re-fortified her position, consolidated her allies, ran the Protestant nobles into hiding, made superficial amends with Darnley though still despising him, and managed to rule for almost another year before Darnley's murder stirred the political pot again. When the explosion at Kirk o' Field rocked Edinburgh and launched Darnley into the night sky, Mary was back at Holyrood, snug in bed in the very chambers that had served as the scene of her ill-fated dinner party just eleven months before.

I swear I don't know why anyone watches *Days of Our Lives* when they could just read Scottish history. Seriously. This week: Jealous husband conspires against the man who's become a little too close to his wife. Will the baby live? If so, whose eyes will it have? Tune in next week to find out. This is Emmy-winning material.

And if the Scottish royal court were a television drama, Katrina and I were about to tour what would undoubtedly be the main set: Holyrood—which, if you think about it, is a little too close to Hollywood to be accidental.

. . . . .

Like Edinburgh Castle, Holyrood is a product of many ages. The oldest part, the abbey founded in the 12th century by King David after being safely delivered from the charging stag by the tag team of God and Sir Gregan Crawford, now lies in ruins attached to the Palace of Holyroodhouse. The palace itself evolved over several centuries, starting first as a wing off the abbey, but growing into a full-blown tower house by the early 16th century. By the end of the 17th century, this tower house was itself just one wing of a much larger palace built to honor Charles II, which seems a bit of a waste as he never lived there, Scottish kings being comfortably entrenched in London by this point. Indeed, not until the 19th century, during the reign of Queen Victoria, did the expanded palace begin receiving regular visits from Britain's monarchs. Victoria, who seemed to fancy Scotland, made annual trips to Britain's northern kingdom, residing at Holyrood as a stopover point on her way to Balmoral Castle in the highlands.

Since Victoria's reign, using the palace as a sort of "home away from home" while in Scotland has become a tradition continued by British monarchs right up to the present day—a point brought home by the brochure I was handed at the gate, which called the Palace of Holyroodhouse an "Official Residence of Her Majesty The Queen." This is a bit misleading, as Queen Elizabeth II was not about to meet us at the door with a welcoming smile and a tray of tea. In fact, the current royal family spends just a few days per year in the palace. Still its designation as a royal residence made us feel quite important, like we were royal guests who had been invited for a tour of the Queen's quarters. Of course, we were royal guests who had to pay a fee to get in.

The price of admission included use of an audio tour device, which I can only describe as a magic box sending demon voices through headphones to confuse each visitor. This nifty device probably provides a very helpful service to someone competent enough to properly control the voices so that the information given is actually relevant to what is being viewed at the time. In the case of someone less competent, like myself for example, the demon voices take over and say whatever they want when they want, so that while I stand looking at a fountain in the courtyard, they rattle on about a painting in the Great Gallery. When I eventually get to the Great Gallery, I see the particular painting already described and say, "ahhh", but by this time the demons are chatting away about a particular piece of needlework done by Mary, Queen of Scots, while imprisoned in England, which of course will be viewed sometime later in the tour.

Katrina, who seemed to have no problem working the audio tour, took pity on me at several points along the way, taking my device and pushing several buttons which would temporarily align the voices with the room we were in. This would work for a room or two until I inevitably pushed some sequence of buttons that again unfettered the demons and set them off describing some nether region of the palace.

At one point, I became so exasperated with the audio tour that I took off the headphones altogether, which turned out to be an amusing, if somewhat eerie, experience that I recommend highly. Though as many as fifteen people packed the room, the only sound was an occasional shuffle of feet or creak of a floorboard. No one spoke. Instead, the crowd silently followed along as the demon voices, unheard by me, gave their instructions. In eerie silence, heads would almost simultaneously swing to the left to check out some portrait on the wall. Moments later the group would shift, shuffling a few steps in unison to the far side of the room to check out a tapestry or a piece of furniture. It was rather creepy, like watching a dance of zombies following some rhythm from beyond the grave that only they could hear.

Despite my incompetence with the audio tour, our visit to Holyrood proved every bit worthwhile. The palace is fascinating in both its architecture and the furniture and artwork contained within. We wandered through several rooms, including the Throne Room and the Royal Dining Room, but found particular reason to linger in the Great Gallery, a room big enough to host a small soccer match.

The Great Gallery, as its name suggests, houses Holyrood's main art exhibit: eighty-nine paintings by a Dutch artist named Jacob de Wet. The paintings on display were selected from a series of 110 individual portraits de Wet painted featuring every Scottish king from the legendary (though factually sketchy) Fergus I in the 5th century right up to the very real Charles II, the king who commissioned the paintings in 1684. The huge collection, which incredibly de Wet completed in a single year, has become a somewhat comical feature of the palace. One website referred to the paintings as "mass-produced", while my guidebook described them as "unintentionally hilarious, as it is clear that the artist was taxed to bursting point by the need to paint so many different facial types without having an inkling as to what the subjects actually looked like."

Besides being known for mass produced artwork, the Great Gallery also earned fame as the banquet hall of the unfortunate Prince Charles

Edward Stuart, better known as Bonnie Prince Charlie or the Young Pretender. Charlie used Holyrood Palace as his home base during his ill-fated attempt to re-claim the throne for the Stuart family in the Jacobite Uprising of 1745, of which more later. During his brief time at Holyrood, the Young Pretender lived like the king he hoped to be, hosting celebratory feasts to dazzle his followers and win over skeptics. One such feast was fictionalized by Sir Walter Scott and described in a chapter of *Waverley* simply called "The Ball". Reading *Waverley* upon my return from Scotland, I was able to picture the setting for this ball, and particularly enjoyed the thought of Bonnie Prince Charlie proudly dancing with a young lassie surrounded by so many "unintentionally hilarious" portraits of his forebears to what he considered to be his rightful throne.

But to return to our tour of the palace, the highlight for me was of course Mary's chambers. Her bedroom, scene of the horrific murder of Rizzio, was described by our guidebook as "the most famous room in Scotland," another sobering reminder of the extent to which we humans are attracted to tragedy. I must admit I felt an odd thumping of excitement to be in such a grim place. The castle caretakers, it seems, understand that we are a sick and demented race and have capitalized on these very impulses. "Until a few years ago," according to my guidebook, "visitors were shown apparently indelible bloodstains on the floor of the [presence chamber], but these are now admitted to be fakes, and have been covered up." Incredible. Yet, despite reading this and thinking how gullible thousands of visitors must have been, I found myself looking around the chamber and into the dining closet, searching for streaks of dried blood or overturned furniture from the struggle that occurred nearly 450 years ago.

Along with memories of this sensational murder, Mary's chambers did offer reminders of the more tender side of history. I particularly enjoyed a glass case filled with mementos of the tragic queen: bits of jewelry, personal effects, and, more endearingly, samples of needlework created by Mary's own hand during her twenty-year imprisonment in England. I pointed these out to Katrina.

"She was pretty talented," I remarked, genuinely impressed with the well-preserved samples, comprised of intricate, multi-colored designs.

"Yes, she was," agreed Katrina, "though I guess you would be too if you had twenty years to practice with nothing else to do but plot the assassination of the Queen of England."

A very good point, I had to concede.

Emerging from the palace, we entered a section of beautiful gardens whose flowers were presumably described by the audio tour, though my demon voices espoused the merits of Renaissance furniture at the time. A curving path twisted through the flowers, leading us toward a site I was particularly keen to see: the ruins of the original abbey.

Since its founding nearly nine hundred years ago, Holyrood Abbey has witnessed its share of significant events in Scottish history. Kings and queens have been born there, crowned there, married there, and buried there. In fact, James II, who lived and reigned in the 15th century, experienced every one of the aforementioned milestones within the abbey's walls. Mary herself was twice married at its altar: first to Darnley, and then to Darnley's likely murderer, Bothwell. Thus, it surprised me to find that after the roof collapsed in the 18th century the abbey was not restored. Today, it sits silent, a crumbling wing off the adjacent palace.

We walked through the ancient doorway to the "interior" of the main church that dominated the abbey ruins. The walls, their medieval masonry displaying carved angels and vaulted arches, stood relatively intact. The same was true of the floor, still covered in massive flagstones and monuments bearing inscriptions of long-dead Scottish nobility and clergy buried beneath. Yet, the blue sky poured in from above, exposing the whole to the elements and giving the place an ethereal feel. Katrina and I silently explored the length of the church, reading the inscriptions and feeling very much like we walked on sacred ground.

The abbey represented the end of our Holyrood tour. Throughout, I had looked in vain for a plaque giving information on the abbey's founding. I figured that here, if anywhere, the true story of King David's hunting party featuring the heroics of a fearless Sir Gregan Crawford might appear for public consumption. But such hopes went unfulfilled. The brochure we'd received at the gate repeated the legend of the vanishing stag, as did my guidebook. Nowhere throughout the palace, the abbey or the grounds did any mention surface of a Crawford having had anything to do with the founding of such a significant and sacred place in Scotland's history. And though I have no idea what the demon voices in the audio tour had to say on the matter, I think it's safe to assume that, given their unfriendliness to a current Crawford, there is little chance they went out of their way to honor Sir Gregan.

Thus, it was without too much reluctance that I handed my possessed audio device back to the gate agent and exited Holyrood Palace.

• • • • •

We walked back to the Grassmarket in the lethargic state one achieves after the brain has reached its saturation point. The journey down the Royal Mile, though fascinating, had turned our minds to mush, and I was now as content as Katrina to not have to think anymore. The time had arrived for our nightly ritual of dinner, stroll, and pub.

An Indian restaurant just off the Royal Mile provided dinner. We were the only customers in the restaurant, which may not be a ringing endorsement for the food, but did mean we enjoyed fantastic service throughout the meal from the three waiters on duty.

Our evening stroll found us following a curving street named Candlemaker Row out of the Grassmarket and up a hill to the University of Edinburgh. We explored the campus, which contained an interesting mix of beautiful old buildings and ugly new ones, and patches of green, tree-lined lawns. Everywhere college kids were doing college things: playing soccer, reclining on a bench with a book, and arguing about which pub to go to later that night.

Fortunately, we didn't hear any of them mention a pub named Sandy Bell's, our intended destination for the evening. A flyer in our hotel room had recommended Sandy Bell's as an establishment where customers could count on two things: a great selection of beer on-tap and live folk music—

the perfect itinerary for two mush-minded travelers like us. Thus, for the third time in as many nights, we ended a pleasant evening walk by crossing the threshold of a welcoming pub. And, for the third time in as many nights, the pub delivered.

We entered a long and narrow room with a wooden bar running along one side. Katrina ordered her customary cider while I picked a beer at random from the many I'd never heard of. The bartender was talking to a young man at the bar who seemed to be no stranger to the establishment. The conversation centered around a local soccer upset that had apparently ticked off a large contingent of fans, the bartender being one of them.

"It was bluidy robbery," said the bartender, referencing some perceived bit of foul play.

"Ah, I'm tired o' hearin' it," said the young man. "Every time they lose somebody goes a-runnin' for his claymore, but it doesna change a thing. They bluidy lost. I say accept it and move on."

I liked that expression very much: to go "a-runnin' for his claymore". A claymore, I understood by this point, was a Scottish sword. I had seen pictures of William Wallace's claymore, a long, two-handed broadsword quite capable of taking off limbs in a single stroke. The expression put a funny image in my mind of a stadium full of soccer fans pulling out claymores and brandishing them at the referee after every call that didn't go their way. But then it occurred to me that we were talking about Scottish soccer fans—the most rabid such breed on the planet, who are quite content to lose the match so long as they win the brawl afterwards—and that perhaps the expression wasn't just a figure of speech. We took our drinks and moved to a table across the room that seemed safely out of swinging distance.

We had the table to ourselves for a while, but this wouldn't last long. Sharing tables seems to be common practice in Scotland. At almost every pub we visited throughout our trip, we were at some point during the night joined by other patrons who pulled up next to us and readily engaged in conversation. This took us by surprise at first, given that such a thing rarely happens in America where privacy reigns supreme. In my U.S. experiences,

127

people were far more likely to take chairs from a table than to join it. In fact, in all my time in American bars—a time more considerable than I care to admit—I can't recall a single instance when random strangers joined my friends and me at a table. In Scotland, it happened almost every night.

Once Katrina and I got over the shock, we grew to enjoy sharing our table. My fear of short talk would disappear after a pint or two, and having someone new to meet and swap stories with added to the convivial atmosphere of the pub.

As Sandy Bell's filled up, three archaeologists joined our table. One was a university professor, while the other two worked as commercial archaeologists for private corporations, meaning that big companies would hire them to make sure no ancient gravesites or grown-over forts stood in the way of their next office complex. I found this somewhat disappointing, as most of my prior understanding of archaeology came from Indiana Jones films. Somehow, it didn't seem like these two spent much time fighting off Nazis or cannibals with nothing more than whips and sarcasm. Well into my second pint, I told them as much.

"Aye, yer right there," grinned the archaeologist opposite me, a bespectacled woman (let's call her Marian) in her forties with long sandy blonde hair. "Our employers would be rather put out if we turned up the Ark of the Covenant. We please them most when we find nothin' at all."

"Aye, sure" countered her partner, his pint arrested halfway to his lips, "but let's admit tha' findin' nothin' is nae such an easy task in Britain where nearly ever' inch was inhabited at one time or another. A bluidy guid challenge, findin' nothin'." He nodded at us before taking a big gulp.

Marian went on to explain that stumbling across ancient bones or relics slowed down a company's construction plans with paperwork and further excavation and could even stop a project altogether. This I understood, but there didn't seem to be much romance in it. Now done with my second pint, I gave voice to this thought. The university professor gave a big laugh, setting down his glass with a bang, and let it be known that he was of much the same mind.

"Imagine how disheartening," he bellowed, "t' spend years studying archaeology only t' land a job where yer number one goal is tae find *nuthin'.*"

"I suppose it pays well?" Katrina offered hopefully.

"Aye, it does," replied the professor, "tha's why I let them pay for the pints."

The professor, who I will call MacIndy, seemed more promising than his colleagues. He specialized in the Saxons of medieval Scotland and had long, wild hair that suggested his passion for the subject went beyond books. He may well have been swinging across a chasm to escape death in a booby-trapped castle earlier that day.

Seizing on the opportunity of having an expert at hand, I told him that I was researching my family history in Scotland and that, according to one genealogy I had seen, Crawfords were descended from Alfred the Great, a famous Saxon king.* MacIndy gave me a tolerant, but amused look and replied, "Everyone is related to Saxon kings, mate." I'm not sure what he meant by this exactly—either that Saxon kings did a lot of sleeping around or that the historic record is sketchy enough for anyone to claim descent—but the response made me hesitate before asking further questions regarding family history.

Searching for other conversation topics proved unnecessary as the music started up at this time, seemingly all of a sudden. I looked around a bit mystified, as I hadn't seen a band enter or set up. The room possessed no stage, no sound system; just a long narrow, bar with many tables. Upon closer inspection, I traced the source of the music to a group at the corner table who, besides their pints, also possessed a bagpipe, a fiddle and a flute. It was very low-key, and every bit terrific.

The experience gave me my first up close look at bagpipes, that most famous of Scottish instruments. Once in widespread use throughout Europe, bagpipes first appeared in Scotland sometime around the 15th century and have become indelibly associated with Scottish culture ever

---

* The Crawford history book I had purchased before the trip claims that Thorlongus, the grandfather of Galfridus de Crawford (mentioned in Chapter 7), was himself the great-great-grandson of Alfred the Great.

since. Over the years, several styles of pipes have evolved, the most famous being the Highland pibroch, the pipes one sees being played by kilted military men wearing fluffy hats on every other postcard in Scotland. (The rest of the postcards feature cows or sheep muttering witless expressions like "In Scotland and missing Ewe!".) The pibroch gained fame amongst the Highland clans as a military instrument, used to rally troops and send signals during battle, and afterwards to play a tune for the gathered clan, either melancholy or spirited depending on how they fared that day.

The pipes being played at Sandy Bell's were of a smaller variety than the pibroch. The piper, who wore no furry hat, sat as he played with the bag tucked under his arm. He would blow periodically into one pipe that filled the bag with air. At the same time, he would squeeze the bag between his arm and body forcing the air out of other pipes, called drones and chanters, like a bellows. I watched with fascination as the piper's fingers moved rapidly over the chanter—the pipe providing the melody—covering various holes along its stem to change the tone of the notes reaching our ears.

A night of such observation cleared up one of the long-held mysteries of bagpipes in my mind. Once a piper starts playing a song, there are almost no breaks in the music; the sound is continuous. I never understood how the piper could achieve this without breaking to take a breath, and just assumed that all pipers possessed superhuman breathing abilities, like those free-divers who plunge 400 feet underwater with no supplemental air. In fact, pipers are not such freaks. Rather they achieve the continuous notes by squeezing the bag ever so slowly, so that they get good mileage out of every breath they put in. Such art results in a beautiful, haunting sound, with sustained notes coming out of the drone pipes while a' melody simultaneously emits from the chanter, allowing a single piper to sound like many. Add to this the sound of fiddle and flute, as we now had, and the result was magic.

We sat captivated and listened for hours to the music, which varied between fast tunes that tempted me to get up and perform a knee-slapping, high kicking dance and slower melancholy tunes that spoke of tragedy and loss. The mood of the room ebbed and flowed with the wonderful music.

The only thing detracting from the evening took the form of a loud, obnoxious group of Americans standing at the bar, who insisted on including the entire pub in their conversations, as if everyone was just dying to be part of such witty banter as: "Hey, it's Joe's birthday, woo-hoo!" or "Hey, let's drink a shot for hot Scottish chics, woo-hoo!" or sometimes, when coherent thoughts escaped them, just "Hey, woo-hoo!" Not a strong statement for the homeland. With each shriek, most of which came in the middle of the music, I would offer an apologetic smile to our table of archaeologists and find myself pondering where I might find a Canadian flag to sew on my forehead.

You just never know when someone might get fed up and go a-runnin' for his claymore.

Walking back to the hotel through the streets of Old Town hours later, I basked in high spirits. I felt like we had done about as much in Edinburgh as one can possibly do in a day and a half and made a vow to return on a future trip. There remained much to see: Arthur's Seat, New Town, and the Museum of Scotland, for starters. And let me not forget the National Library, which as the repository for the country's archives holds the most complete genealogical data of any single institution in Scotland, and where interesting facts about ancient Crawford heroics are presumably kept buried in drawers and on dusty shelves, safe from the casual public eye.

But a night of bagpipe music had stirred a restless spirit, and I found myself itching to see the majestic scenery of the highlands. By car, the highlands lay just a couple of hours away. We imagined ourselves there by the next day.

This would turn out to be a bit naïve. But how could we know how much there was to see between here and there?

# Chapter 12: Air Wallace

## (A detour through Elcho)

The shape of Scotland makes it a challenge to describe. It's not like those states which—due to the particular cut of their coastlines, the path of a bordering river or the arbitrariness with which boundaries were determined by politicians with a fetish for nice straight lines—bear an uncanny resemblance to everyday objects. Michigan the oven mitt, Oklahoma the saucepan, and Colorado the floor tile stand out as obvious examples. Geographic descriptions become easy to verbalize in these states, saying such and such a landmark is located in the "panhandle" of Oklahoma or in the "thumb" of Michigan. This is not at all the case with Scotland which, with its lacerated coastline and outlying islands, resembles nothing in particular other than itself. I've tried to visualize objects that do bear a slight resemblance to Scotland—a seahorse, perhaps? a spilled bucket of paint?—but these all seem more confusing than helpful. Then again, I was never very good at making shapes out of passing clouds, either.

"I see a dog," someone would say.

"I see a blob," I would answer.

"I see a witch on a broom," would come next.

"Still a blob, here."

"I see a carousel in the forest, and leaves are falling off the trees."

"Blob."

And so the afternoon would pass.

My point is that I'm not a very trustworthy source for this sort of thing. Knowing this, I have decided not to try, and have instead provided a map of Scotland at the front of the book. The reader may wish to refer to it now as I attempt to hone in on just what exactly constitutes the highlands of Scotland.

Shapes aside, this is not an easy task, for the highlands comprise a rather abstract notion. Far beyond a physical distinction, the very term "highlands" captures a culture, history, language and tradition quite literally a world apart from the rest of the country. In strictly geographic terms, however, the issue becomes more distinct. As a physical region the highlands are set off from the rest of Scotland by a geologic phenomenon known as the Highland Line. According to the eminent highland historian Fitzroy MacLean, this ridge, which separates the jagged peaks, steep valleys and deep lochs of the highlands from the more rolling hills and forests of the lowlands, runs in a diagonal line from Stonehaven on the east coast to Helensburgh, a few miles northwest of Dumbarton, in the west.

The Highland Line is the product of a continental train wreck. It came into existence when two tectonic plates collided over 400 million years ago in an event known to geologists as the Caledonian Orogeny. The force of this collision caused the land north and west of the line to rise up, similar to the Himalayas of Asia. Unlike the Himalayas, which are relative newcomers to the planet (indeed, the Himalayas are still rising today as India continues to plow into the Asian continent), the highlands comprise one of the oldest mountain regions on Earth, having formed in the days prior to the supercontinent Pangaea. In the nearly half billion years that have elapsed since, water, ice and wind have slowly sculpted the region into the rugged and haunting landscape that gives the Scottish highlands their unique character today.

It was this very landscape that Katrina and I were so anxious to glimpse as we left Edinburgh the next morning and crossed the Firth of Forth to the north. Driving toward the town of Perth, one of the gateway towns to the highlands, we planned to stop at Scone Palace briefly before continuing into the highland interior to sleep in some yet to be determined locale. We couldn't wait. In my mind, crossing the Highland Line would resemble the drive from Phoenix to Flagstaff, Arizona in the American Southwest—minus the cactus, of course. Starting at 2,000 feet above sea level in Phoenix, the route ascends onto the Colorado Plateau, a much younger and higher area of uplift than the Scottish highlands, taking car and driver on a thrilling trip to 7,000 feet and transforming the scenery from organ pipe cactus dotting dry, flat plains to towering ponderosa pines blanketing the slopes of snowcapped peaks—a dramatic shift of scenery for a three hour drive. I expected the trip into the highlands to be similarly dramatic, albeit on a smaller scale.

As it turns out, the Highland Line would prove to be a much more formidable barrier to us than the approach to the Colorado Plateau had ever been, not because it is steeper or less accessible (it is not), but because there was simply too much to see before we left the lowlands. For two days, we would approach the Highland Line, engine whining as our Fiat Crumb prepared for the rugged climb into the mountains, only to be turned off course at the last minute by some unexpected attraction we just couldn't miss. After our second consecutive night sleeping on the border of the highlands only to get in our car the next morning and drive back toward some late-remembered destination, Katrina began to compare our travels to a pinball game, with the Highland Line a benevolent but very effective flipper batting us away in some new direction whenever we would approach. In a way, it made the highlands, already steeped in mystery and lore, more tantalizing than ever.

The first bat of the flipper came just as we prepared to enter the town of Perth. Hurtling down the highway, we whizzed past a blue sign that made me put on the brakes, much to the surprise of Katrina and the driver behind me, and pull to the side of the road. The sign announced the turn off for Elcho Castle, which I recognized as a name somehow intertwined with Crawford history. I recalled the name from one of the many tales I had read on the plane, though it hadn't landed on our list of places to explore mainly because I had no idea where Elcho was and, let's face it, one can only do so much family research on a two-week vacation and remain married. Sitting on the side of the road, however, I explained my reluctance to drive by a site of Crawford importance so close at hand. Katrina, whose patience for this sort of thing approached saintly levels, agreed, and I turned the car back toward the Elcho exit. It was a decision we would not regret.

On the way, Katrina read aloud the tale of the Crawfords of Elcho.[*]

---

[*] Like many of the tales related here, this story was originally recounted by Blind Harry, and like all of his work, should be considered accurate in every detail and not exaggerated at all.

• • • • •

Late at night in the dawning years of the 14th century, a boat was stealthily rowed ashore at the port of Perth, on the banks of the River Tay. The oarsmen took care to keep quiet, as among their passengers huddled Sir William Wallace, returning to an English-occupied Scotland after several years abroad. Disgusted with the fickleness and backstabbing of the Scottish nobility who continued to divide the country, Wallace had taken to France several years earlier to offer his help to Scotland's old ally against the English. In his time away, Edward's English soldiers had solidified their hold over Scotland and were now firmly in control of Perth when Wallace's boat docked silently in the night.

Proceeding under cover of darkness to nearby Elcho, Wallace and his men took refuge at the home of his cousin, Sir William Crawford, a younger son of the Sheriff Reginald Crawford whom Longshanks had hung at Ayr. Soldiers fresh off a ship tend to have an appetite, and it didn't take long for Wallace and his men, hiding in Crawford's barn, to consume all of his cousin's food stores, necessitating a trip to the market. Rumors of Wallace's presence in the area had spread by this point, causing English soldiers to be naturally suspicious when young Crawford arrived at the market in Perth and filled up his medieval shopping cart with enough food for twenty hungry soldiers. Perhaps it was simple intuition, perhaps it was the 800 English soldiers following him at a discreet distance, but Crawford suspected the English hadn't bought his story that he was just stocking up for a coming party. He hurried home to warn his cousin.

Wallace and his men, joined by Crawford, had just enough time to vacate the barn and take to the surrounding woods before an English captain named Butler showed up at Elcho with his 800 soldiers. Demanding entrance of Crawford's wife, who had remained behind, he and his soldiers searched the premises and soon discovered the barn, which bore traces of fresh occupation by a large group of men. Butler, displaying all the subtlety of a pitbull, paraded Crawford's wife outside where he set his men to building a pyre upon which to burn the woman alive unless she revealed where Wallace was hiding. To her infinite credit, Crawford's wife remained silent as the sticks piled up around her.

Seeing what was happening, Wallace stepped from the woods and rebuked Butler for using a woman in this manner, presumably throwing in remarks about his diminutive genitalia and overall lack of manhood. Enraged, Butler sent his English soldiers pursuing Wallace into the woods where they fell into a trap Wallace had set. After fifteen soldiers had fallen, the English retreated to regroup. A second attack was also repulsed by Wallace and his men, and the English again retreated as night fell. Surrounding the woods with his remaining soldiers, who still numbered well over 700, Butler vowed to finish Wallace off in the morning.

As luck would have it, morning brought a thick mist to the woods, and Wallace used the chance to launch a surprise offensive directly against Butler's camp, personally slaying two Englishmen for every one felled by his followers. In the process, Butler was killed, sending the remaining English into disarray and giving Wallace the chance to escape to nearby Methven Wood for sanctuary. The battle left Sir William Crawford wounded, though he would also reach the safety of the wood, carried there by the gallant Wallace who was presumably still killing two Englishmen with every stroke of his sword.

·   ·   ·   ·   ·

Hearing the tale for the second time, I was excited to explore yet another Crawford stomping ground, though as it turns out, had Crawfords never set foot at Elcho it would still have proved well worth the stop: for Elcho Castle was one of the loveliest castles we would see on the trip. Our first glance upon our approach revealed a stone tower house, nestled against the banks of the River Tay and topped by a crenellated walkway with fairyland turrets rising out of the corners. A majestic flag fluttered in the breeze above the tower. It seemed the sort of place a young girl could kiss a toad and have it turn into Brad Pitt.

Inside, the experience got even better. The castle was just the right size: big enough to be impressive, but small enough to explore every inch. It had also achieved the perfect stage of decay: intact enough to tour safely, but without furniture, decorations, or restorations of any kind—as if waiting for two people to move in, hang a painting and make themselves at home. Passing through from room to room, our imaginations filled in the details. The castle had no tour guides, meaning we could go anywhere we desired and linger for as long we desired, including out on the ramparts atop the tower. It was marvelous.

As we had the castle completely to ourselves, Elcho became our own personal play land. We climbed up and down spiral staircases made of stone, the kind some hunchbacked character might climb carrying a torch and casting eerie shadows just out of sight. We giggled over ancient privies, which were just wooden benches set into the stone with holes cut into them, resembling nothing more than a sturdier version of a national park pit toilet in the United States. Apparently, the waste could be cleaned out by opening little doors on the lower level of the castle that accessed the bottom of each shaft. We didn't explore those.

We did, however, linger for quite a while in the great hall, a large room with huge wooden beams supporting the flat ceiling. We ran our hands over the smooth plaster still covering the stone walls and stuck our heads into the enormous fireplace dominating one side of the room. The great hall contained the only furniture in the castle: a long wooden table placed in the center surrounded by several carved stools and an iron candelabra—as if company were expected at any moment. Indeed it seemed the room did still see occasional use. A sign on the table contained an article about a recent ceremony which had taken place in the great hall, transferring official ownership of the castle to its new master, the Lord Elcho. The article featured a picture of Lord Elcho. He was just a kid, no more than fourteen years old.

For centuries, according to the article, the castle has been the possession of the Earls of Wemyss, whose heirs receive the title of Lord Elcho and the castle for an estate. Presumably the Earl has a grander castle elsewhere and can afford to hand out Elcho to his heir. I wondered what the current young Lord would do with his castle, besides keep it open to tourists. I liked to think that once in a while he closed it down to play hide and seek with his friends or dressed up in medieval garb and invited them over for some jousting and a feast. Anyone who angered him would have to play the somersaulting dwarf. The possibilities for fun and games seemed endless.

Pulling ourselves away from the great hall, we climbed to the top of the tower, stepped out onto the stone ramparts, and gazed upon a view as splendid as any we'd seen. The river stretched below the castle, a thin blue line dividing the landscape. Across the river, forested hillsides, interrupted with green and gold meadows, rolled towards Perth, which remained hidden from view. Another castle peeked out through the trees several miles away. It was the closest I have ever come to traveling back in time.

I wanted to know more about the history of this place and its connection to the Crawfords. What was certain was that the Elcho Castle we now explored was not the one owned by Sir William Crawford which had harbored Wallace and his band almost exactly 700 years before. The brochure we'd been given at the door said the current structure was built in the 16th century, more than two hundred years later. Most likely it stood on or near the same site as the Crawford estate, however, and we decided to inquire at the gift shop for more information on the matter.

The gift shop, housed in a small outbuilding near the parking lot, was staffed by a member of Historic Scotland, an organization managing scores of castles, abbeys, churches, stone circles and other historic sites around the country. Katrina and I had purchased an Explorers Pass at Edinburgh Castle, another site managed by Historic Scotland, which allowed us to enter seven of their sites over the span of fourteen days for a set price. We were thrilled to have been able to use the pass at Elcho, and even more thrilled now because it meant we had a live person—an employee of Historic Scotland, no less—to give us information. I should not have gotten my hopes up.

As it turns out, having the name Historic Scotland prominently displayed on a badge is not necessarily a reflection of the wearer's expertise on the topic. The employee at Elcho had no knowledge of the lands surrounding the castle ever belonging to the Crawfords, nor did she know anything about Wallace's adventures in the area. She did, however, point out a tree on the property called the Wallace Yew.

"I dinna know why it's called tha'," she added, "but it probably has somethin' t' dae wi' William Wallace."

Hmmm.

"Thank you," I muttered, "I suspect you're right about that Wallace connection. Perhaps I'll just have a look around the shop."

I perused some books nestled between postcards of bagpipers and sheep, but they had no information on Crawfords in the area either. Sighing at the inevitable disappointment, we walked back to the car knowing there was only one place we could go to learn about the Crawfords of Elcho.

"I'll bet Perth has a library," Katrina suggested. The patience of a saint, I tell you.

Katrina was right, incidentally. Perth did have a library, and there we found what the reader should by this point expect: a helpful librarian, an excellent local history section, and confirmation of yet another heroic ancestor condemned to obscurity in Scotland's past. The librarian helped me locate two books which related the tale of Crawford and Wallace at Elcho and which, given more time, I should have photocopied and hand-delivered to the Historic Scotland employee back at the gift shop. As it was, I contented myself with the private knowledge that with each story I uncovered, the Crawfords of Scotland seemed to play an increasing role in the country's history.

The incident at Elcho represented the mere tip of the iceberg so far as William Crawford's exploits with Wallace were concerned. Crawford, who besides being Wallace's first cousin also served as one of his main captains, was knighted for his role in the victory at Stirling Bridge and accompanied Wallace on his adventures in France. Thus, it makes perfect sense that Wallace and his men would take shelter at Elcho upon their return from abroad. Far from making a surprise visit on distant kin, Wallace had taken shelter at the residence of one of his most trusted and able commanders—

not that any modern visitors to Elcho would be treated to this story.

I asked the librarian what Crawfords had done to be shunned as they were by popular Scotland.

"Well, I dinna know," she responded thoughtfully. "I've nae really heard anything about Crawfords good or bad."

Which, of course, was my point exactly.

I took some solace in the fact that, though the name Crawford had disappeared from Scotland's historic sites, at least Wallace still received public reverence. Even in cases where the details of his adventures seemed to be forgotten, like at Elcho, his name managed to survive in some way—in this case through a tree: the "Wallace Yew" the sales clerk had so astutely pointed out. And the more I learned about Wallace, the more I understood why his name was remembered above all others. The stories suggested a man with the leadership skills and patriotism of George Washington, but who could open up a can of whoop ass like Arnold Schwarzenegger.

If Blind Harry is to be believed, William Wallace was nearly superhuman—a hero closer to the mythical ranks of Achilles or Hercules than of actual mortal men. Throughout the poet's chronicle of Wallace's life, we are consistently treated to scenarios such as Elcho, in which Scotland's hero slays two Englishmen for every one felled by his men, or overpowers fifteen armed opponents single-handedly, or holds off an army of hundreds with just himself and a handful of followers. It is endearing, but just a bit funny in its outlandishness—funny that is, until one considers Michael Jordan.

How many times growing up did I watch Michael Jordan completely dominate a game of basketball, scoring fifty points in a game—double or even triple the performance of anyone else on his team—while routinely rattling his opponents on defense, stealing the ball and shutting down plays? And keep in mind, he wasn't playing against my hometown high school; he was playing in the NBA against the best basketball players in the world. Michael Jordan so thoroughly dominated the game of basketball in his prime that he became the very image of invincibility. So perhaps it's possible that Blind Harry wasn't exaggerating as much as historians suspect.

Perhaps William Wallace was simply the Michael Jordan of his time.

But here's the thing: Michael Jordan occasionally missed. Michael Jordan occasionally got beat on defense and let his man score. It didn't happen often. Yet once in a while it did. In basketball when this happened, Jordan could always come back to get his revenge the next day. I've never engaged in swordplay, but I'm guessing there is a difference here. How many times can one get beat in hand to hand combat with a broadsword the length of a kitchen broom and still come back fighting the next day with all four limbs? I would think not many. More typically someone slipping up on the battlefield would get out about three words ("Now what the..?") as he stares at his arm lying on the ground four feet away from him, and have just enough time to think "That was stupid…" as his head lands beside it.

So are we to believe that Wallace put himself into the thick of battle time and time again against incredible odds and consistently, routinely, without a single exception outfought his foes with such precision that the enemy's sword never landed a solid blow on his limbs or pierced a vital organ? Well, yes, I suppose we are. We know for a fact that Wallace engaged in many battles and that he lived through them all. Perhaps Blind Harry exaggerated the circumstances, but even if we reduce the odds by half, by three-quarters even, it still adds up to one amazing feat after another. In that sense, Wallace seems indeed to have been nearly superhuman. And let's not forget half-Crawford. Nor that he had at least one other Crawford fighting by his side.

With such thoughts in mind, I left the Perth library with quite a swagger indeed.

# Chapter 13: Kings in Big Tree Country

(Travels in Perth and Scone)

If it were a goal in life to sire a pack of illegitimate children while living off the labor of others, one could have chosen no better than to be a priest in 16th century Scotland. According to my guidebook, forty percent of the known illegitimate births at that time were the offspring of clergy members who apparently adhered to a rather loose definition of celibacy. Consider that. Two out of every five children conceived out of wedlock were sired by a priest, monk, bishop or other man of the cloth. That's incredible. Add to this unprecedented levels of economic and political corruption, and it is no wonder people were fed up with the Church in the 1500's.

Of course, it is one thing to be angry. It is quite another to overthrow a system that has been in place for well over a thousand years. The first attempts met with little success. Nearly thirty years after Martin Luther nailed his "Ninety-Five Theses" to the door of the Wittenberg Church in Germany, the powers that be in Scotland were still staunchly Catholic and not very open to change. This was amply demonstrated by a Protestant preacher named George Wishart in 1546. While preaching in Scotland, he was arrested by Cardinal Beaton, a leading Scottish clergyman of the time, and subsequently burned at the stake as a heretic. Wishart's execution sparked a riot by his followers, who stormed St. Andrew's Castle, murdered Cardinal Beaton and then settled in, waiting for help that would never arrive from Henry VIII's Protestant England. When the rioters finally surrendered the castle a year later, many were arrested and forced to serve as galley slaves on French ships. Among their number was a little known man by the name of John Knox.

Upon his release from slavery nineteen months later, Knox spent seven years in exile, refining his beliefs in the Protestant strongholds of England and, more importantly, Geneva, where he became an ardent follower of the French reformer Jean Calvin. Under Calvin, Knox cultivated ideas such as the doctrine of pre-destination, the rather depressing notion that God, being omnipotent, knows prior to each birth which souls will be saved.* Far more significant, however, was the belief that would form the underlying principle of the Presbyterian tradition dominating the Scottish Kirk today: that is, that bishops and other features of hierarchy within the church should be abolished in favor of a more democratic, direct worship by the people of the congregation based on the scriptures. Translation: Get rid of the bishops, and put the church in the hands of the people.

During this time Knox also published his most infamous written work, a treatise with the feel-good title: *The First Blast of the Trumpet Against the Monstrous Regiment of Women.* The work served as a thinly veiled attack on the women in power at the time: Mary Tudor (better known as "Bloody Mary") in England, and Mary of Guise (the mother of Mary, Queen of Scots) in Scotland for their resistance to the Protestant faith. Needless to say, the work doesn't have much of a modern following and has yet to appear on Oprah's list of selected titles.

In 1555, after being away nearly a decade, Knox returned to a Scotland much more ready to accept his Protestant views. Catholicism remained the state religion under the "Monstrous Regiment" of Mary of Guise and her daughter, but more and more leading nobles had by this time adopted the Protestant faith. On this stage, the fiery Knox, who by all accounts was a tremendous and intimidating speaker who could both convince and terrorize people into his point of view,** prepared to assume control of the Protestant Reformation in Scotland. Knox would succeed where Wishart had failed, though the transition to Protestantism would not be easily won.

Looking at my guidebook as Katrina and I left the Perth library, I was surprised to find that one of the earliest and most dramatic events of the Scottish Reformation had occurred just steps from where we now stood, in a 15th century church called St. John's Kirk. From the pulpit of St. John's in

---

* One would think this idea would be quite liberating. After all, if we are all pre-destined to our fate, everything seems rather out of our hands, doesn't it? So pop a cork and let the hedonism begin. In fact, reaction to this doctrine was quite the opposite. To prove to those around them that they were indeed one of God's Elect, pre-destined for eternal salvation, followers of this doctrine became quite righteous and stodgy—giving rise to the image of uptight, no fun at all-types wearing black Pilgrim hats and listening to sermons for hours on end.
** Indeed, no less a personage than Mary, Queen of Scots, is claimed to have said: "I fear the prayers of John Knox more than all the assembled armies of Europe."

1559, Knox whipped the congregation into a righteous uproar with a fiery speech about the sin of idolatry. Just after Knox concluded condemning Catholics for their statues of Mary and Jesus and other tangible symbols of divinity, a Catholic priest thought it might be a good idea to calm the congregation by celebrating Mass.

Bad idea.

When a "young lad" who had been particularly inspired by Knox's words protested the Catholic ritual, the priest struck him for his heresy.

Bad idea, number two.

The youth retaliated by throwing a stone that damaged the Kirk's altar and catapulted the congregation into mayhem. The seething crowd flowed out of the church and into the local monasteries, where they proceeded to loot and smash the sacred relics and statues they found in an effort to purge their town of the sin of idolatry. Now there's something that doesn't happen every Sunday.

The damage was appalling and many valuable treasures and works of art were lost forever—which of course was the whole point of the exercise, though Knox would later distance himself from such violence, saying it was not his worshippers who rioted but rather the "rascal multitude". I suspect that members of the congregation, rascals and non-rascals alike, were thankful for any distraction relieving the tedium of the famously long sermons of the 16th century. (Recall the kitchen behind the Crawford Gallery in Kilbirnie.) But I digress.

As our plans for the day had already taken an unexpected turn at Elcho, we decided we could spare a few moments more to explore St. John's Kirk, whose spire dominated Perth's town center. I always find it awe-inspiring to stand in a spot where a major historic event—whether tragic or great—occurred, as if merely being in that place and running my eyes over the same scenery and touching the same objects gives me a connection to the people, now long dead, who took part in the event. I felt this way now inside St. John's Kirk, gazing at the pulpit from which Knox gave his speech, not knowing—or maybe understanding perfectly—the effect his words would have on the ticking time-bomb that was the congregation. The ornately carved pulpit towered above the pews, offering a view the length of the nave all the way to the doors at the back of the church through which the angry crowd would have exited on its mission to loot the monasteries.

A sign beside these doors referred to the church's modern congregation as a member of the "Church of Scotland, part of the Reformed tradition", a reminder that the power of Knox's words and the momentum of the Reformation were no fleeting matters, but endure today. Nor were the riots at Perth an isolated act of violence. Not until late in the 17th century, well over a hundred years after Knox's sermon at St. John's, would religious violence end and the official Scottish Presbyterian tradition be established as the state religion once and for all.

While on the topic of religion, I should mention that it was in Perth that our second miracle of the trip occurred (the first being the pick-up truck full of strong men materializing on a deserted road just after I lodged our Fiat Crumb in a ditch). On this occasion, we had just exited St. John's Kirk and I was attempting to take a picture of its spire when my camera, which had to this point operated flawlessly, decided to retire. As I pressed the button to take the photo, the camera froze mid-picture, like a computer locking up. The shutter stuck halfway open and the viewscreen went blank. The power, however, remained on, and attempts to turn it off went completely unnoticed by the camera. After a few moments had passed during which I stood there hitting useless buttons and looking dumbly at the inert instrument in my hand (much as I had looked at the Fiat Crumb trying to will it out of the ditch), Katrina suddenly pointed over my head and said, "Maybe they can help."

I turned around to see what she was pointing at and saw—I'm not making this up—a store called "The Camera Shop". It was located directly behind me, not ten paces away. The only thing more convenient would have been a store, spontaneously erected around me where I stood, called "Scott, We Can Fix Your Broken Camera".

We entered the store, babbling an explanation ("'Twas the darndest thing…") to the middle-aged man behind the counter, who sized up our dilemma with a raised eyebrow.

"Let me guess, mate," he said, leaning toward me in a confidential manner, "she tried to take a picture of you, did she?"

He gave a wink to Katrina, who found the comment far more amusing than necessary, and held out his hand for the camera. Taking it in his hands, he turned it around, hitting buttons to no effect and staring at it quizzically (I took some satisfaction in this) before announcing that if we left it with him for a couple of days he would see what he could do, though he made no guarantees.

"On the other hand," he announced more enthusiastically, waving a hand at the rows of items on display, "perhaps you'd fancy a new camera."

Moments later, we were back on the streets of Perth, new camera in hand and a couple hundred pounds poorer. I'm not sure what this meant in U.S. dollars—I struggled with the exchange rate all trip—but based on the weakness of the dollar at the time, I think it was roughly a downpayment on a house. Still, we had salvaged the memory card from the old camera so as not to lose any of the photos taken on the first four days of the trip, and as a matter of time, the entire ordeal hadn't taken more than fifteen minutes. All in all, we felt pretty lucky.

The streets of downtown Perth have been closed off creating a pedestrian-only zone, a feature I find highly appealing and wish more towns would adopt. We saw lots of people out and about, so different from the centers of most American towns, which are deserted because everyone shops at the mall out by the highway. Katrina went to poke around the shops a bit, while I sat down on a bench to fiddle with the new camera and its dozens of features. I particularly liked the zoom, which proved far more powerful than that of our last camera.

"Stop zooming in on that window," Katrina chastised, sneaking up behind me some minutes later. I hastily put the camera away, as she handed me a pile of brochures she had picked up from an information office. "I thought we should learn what there is to do around here other than look for forgotten ancestors."

Thus, I discovered that Perthshire, the county we were now in, was "Big Tree Country", still housing remnant stands of towering pines, birch and juniper trees that once made up the great Caledonian Forest. Caledonia is the Latin name given to Scotland by the Romans, and in the days preceding their occupation a great and wild forest full of ancient, gnarled trees covered much of the highlands. The Stone Age inhabitants of this fairy woodland would have had to keep a wary eye out for the bears, wolves, and boars that lurked in the primeval forest. By late medieval times, much of this forest had disappeared, cut down to make way for sheep and cattle herding, the timber being used to develop the land to the south. Today, sadly, the once mighty Caledonian Forest remains only in isolated fragments: the Black Wood of Rannoch Forest, Weem Wood, and others. And those venturing out into these fragments need not worry about bears, wolves or boars, all long since vanished from Scotland's landscape.

Still, the region is fortunate to have the fragments it does. Sometime over the last three hundred years, the inhabitants of Scotland realized they rather liked trees, and set about preserving the few that remained. On top of this, some regions were even replanted thanks to the efforts of naturalists like David Douglas, a young man who started as a gardener at nearby Scone Palace but would take his love of plant life across the ocean to the American wilderness where he collected over 200 species to introduce to Britain—among them the majestic fir which bears his name. Douglas's trees may not have been native, but that didn't stop them from thriving on Scottish soil, growing to huge heights and dominating much of Perth's landscape today. Re-vegetation efforts were further helped by the eccentric "Planting" Dukes of Atholl, a noble family who planted some 27 million conifers between 1738 and 1830—an average of over 800 trees per day for nearly a century! To say this family liked their trees is to barely hint at their dedication.*

The result of such efforts is a Perthshire taking great pride in its

---

* This is a family that merits further mention. They continue to prove their eccentricity today by maintaining the only private army (the Atholl Highlanders) still in existence in Scotland. Visitors can see this army drill and practice to the call of pipers at Blair Castle, the ancient stronghold that has served as the family home since the 13th century and is presumably now surrounded by a whole lotta trees.

natural environment today. Indeed, the region's entire marketing strategy seems to center on it. The brochure in my hand boasted of the "record breakers" contained in the county: a hedge, said to be the world's tallest, over 90 feet high, and a Douglas fir, claimed to be Britain's tallest tree at just over 200 feet, among other examples.

"Well, what are we waiting for?" Katrina noted drily. "That seems like a full day right there."

"But wait, there's more," I pointed out, putting on my best infomercial voice. "Besides these record breakers, the lucky tourist can marvel at a host of other famous trees. These include the venerable Birnam Oak, said to be the last survivor of the wood made famous by Shakespeare's 'Macbeth', and the Neil Gow Oak, under which the famous Scottish fiddler liked to sit and compose." The brochure went on and on in such fashion.

"Oh, tell me more," Katrina said, feigning interest. "Please say that there's a Robbie Burns Birch, where the poet liked to steal away with unsuspecting lassies."

I picked up the thread. "How about a Wallace Pissing Pine, where the great warrior once stopped to relieve himself while holding off twenty Englishmen with his free hand?"

"Or the Crawford Stump," Katrina rejoined, "a tree commemorating an event no one can remember, and which was therefore cut down and turned into toilet paper."

We spent a few slaphappy minutes making up such trees that should exist in Big Tree Country but don't, though we soon found our attention wavering—much as the reader's may be now. Suffice it to say, Perthshire has some big, old, famous trees of which it is immensely proud.

Naturally, along with this focus on nature and wilderness comes the economic opportunity of outdoor recreation. A second brochure proffered by Katrina listed the numerous ways visitors to Perthshire can get out and interact with the natural environment. Many of these were to be expected—hiking, mountain biking and horseback riding, for example—but the list proved far more expansive than that, including no less than 36 categories of recreational activities. It seemed the marketing wizards of Perthshire had thought of something for every sort of traveler. There were extreme sports, such as rock climbing, hang gliding and even cliff jumping, for those who enjoy teetering on the precipice of death. For aquatic types, there were water sports of every speed, from canoeing to whitewater rafting. Then, for those who enjoy nature most when they spoil it for others, there were the loud sports: ATV rides, powerboating and other such activities involving large, powerful engines. Even those who like to hunt down and kill things were not forgotten, with archery, clay pigeon shooting and even falconry offered to would be hunters or medieval re-enactors. Then, just when it would seem the entrepreneurs of Perthshire must have exhausted ways to get out into nature, there were activities for the drunk and stupid. Two of these, sphering and aqua-sausage rides, deserve special mention.

Sphering is a sport—and I use the term loosely here—that originated in New Zealand, and from what I can tell was invented by drunken teenagers left home alone with a tire pump and an abnormal quantity of bubble-wrap. In this activity, participants experience the beauty of the countryside by strapping themselves inside a large inflatable ball and then rolling headlong down a hill. Ball and human embark on what the brochure describes as "a wild and bouncy tumble" that "will have thrill seekers and outdoor enthusiasts queuing up". Simply astounding. If you have ever dreamed of seeing the world from the perspective of a tumbleweed with the view filtered through chunks of your own vomit, this is the sport for you.

Aqua-sausage rides, on the other hand, are for a drunken hillbilly family reunion. In this activity, up to five adults sit upon what is ominously described as a "novelty inflatable" while a powerboat tows them around one of the many lochs of Perthshire. The brochure cheekily asks the question: "Can you avoid a 'dunking'?"

"I don't know about you," Katrina cautioned, "but when I hear the terms 'aqua-sausage', 'novelty inflatable' and 'dunking' all referring to a group activity, a red flag goes up. I'm picturing five fat guys sitting on an inflatable Daisy Duke doll holding up cans of Budweiser and shouting 'woo-hoo' while a powerboat drags them around a lake trying to knock them into the water."

Somehow the scene seemed more at home on the lakes of Tennessee than the lochs of Scotland, but there you have it.

Reading over the brochure, we commented on all the activities we would like to do. Sphering registered disturbingly high on Katrina's list, causing me to mumble something about all the fun we would have hiking later on the trip, check my watch fretfully to note the passage of time, and announce that really we should be heading off to Scone Palace if indeed we still wanted to see it. Fortunately, seeing the site that had for centuries been the traditional crowning place of Scottish kings ranked higher on Katrina's list than tumbling down a hillside strapped to an inflatable ball and a potentially traumatic scene was avoided.

• • • • •

Crossing the River Tay, we left the town of Perth and drove north into the countryside, arriving within minutes at Scone Palace. Scone represented one of six incredibly beautiful, turreted castles we would see in a three-day span after leaving Edinburgh, causing us to dub this segment of our journey "the fairyland tour". Though others would be just as beautiful, no castle we saw on the journey could rival Scone for its significance to Scotland's glorious past.

It was to Scone in the 9th century that Kenneth MacAlpin brought the Stone of Destiny, placing it on Moot Hill, a gentle rise just behind the current palace. Prior to this, warring factions had kept Scotland divided into four distinct regions: the Scots of the West with their Irish roots, the Picts of the Northeast, the Britons of the Southwest, and the Anglo Saxons of the Southeast. MacAlpin, a Scot who also had claims to the Pictish throne through his mother, united all the lands north of the Firth of Forth and is generally regarded as the first king of a united Scotland, though several centuries would pass before the lands south of the Firth were brought under control and the Vikings driven out of the west and north.

Following the tradition begun by MacAlpin, Scone became the place for Scottish coronations. One by one, famous Scottish monarchs, including

Macbeth, Robert the Bruce, and even Charles II, crowned almost exactly eight centuries after Kenneth MacAlpin, set their feet on Moot Hill to receive the honor of ruling over Scotland. Today, everyday folks such as Katrina and me and any other visitor willing to pay admission to enter Scone Palace are invited to set their feet on Moot Hill where they can view the small chapel adorning its crest and the place in front of the chapel where the Stone of Scone stood for centuries before being carried off by English soldiers. A supposed replica of the stone occupies the place now, though I stared at it for some time considering the possibility that it was the real stone with the replica now unwittingly on display in Edinburgh Castle. Or the possibility that both were fakes, with the real stone being somewhere else altogether, safely hidden and maybe looking quite different from these impostor stones. Who could possibly know at this point?

Besides Moot Hill, the substantial palace grounds offered plenty to explore. We had our choice of strolling through an ancient burial ground, scurrying hamster-like through a classic hedge maze, or wandering in awe through a grove of towering North American trees: redwoods, noble firs, and the first Douglas fir to be planted in Scotland, reminding visitors that Douglas the naturalist was very much a son of Scone. Overall, the layout of the grounds showed a wonderful thoughtfulness with diversions for people of all ages: a playground for young children, a pasture full of furry highland cattle, a butterfly garden, and walking paths everywhere.

Then there was the palace itself.

Scone Palace is simply beautiful. The castle, comprising a mixture of additions built from the 13th to the 16th centuries, had undergone restoration in the 19th century and looked to my eye as if it could last another half millennium at least. The red sandstone blocks that made up its exterior were made all the more striking by the green ivy climbing the walls, reaching up the square turrets that flanked the arched entryway. Inside, the beauty continued, with exquisite collections of paintings, ivories, antique furniture, porcelain, and rare books adorning each room.

Despite all this wealth and beauty, nothing caught my eye more than the simple family portraits and candid photographs stuck here and there throughout the palace. For Scone remains a family residence. A portion of it is available for tour, but the vast majority of the castle is closed to the public so that the Murrays, who have owned the land since King James VI gifted it to them four centuries ago, can go about their daily lives. I found it more than a little endearing to be standing in a room full of priceless decoration, only to have my eyes rest on a picture of a young girl hugging a dog, or a young boy dressed in quite modern clothes smiling and looking up at his grandparents.

Some rooms took the family touch even further, offering collages of pictures from significant family moments—weddings, formal dinners, a relaxing moment out of doors—with captions so that visitors knew who the subjects were. It was just like looking through my family album in Ohio—people smiling, dogs running on the grass, somebody caught in the middle of a funny expression—except that instead of my Cousin Darold, Uncle Gary, or the odd, but persistent appearance of a fellow of no relation named Bucky, captions referred to these people as the Earl and Countess of Mansfield, or Lord Freebag and Lady Hambone, or other such titles.

As we drove away from this beautiful, historic castle, I found myself thinking about these photographs, but couldn't figure out why they had left such an impression. Katrina, who had been likewise struck, shared her own perspective on the matter.

"I just can't believe those people still exist," she marveled, referring, I assume, to the British nobility. "I mean, I can't believe people still live like that."

And, yes, that did capture part of it, but it seemed that beneath this shock lay a more human revelation. I couldn't quite put my finger on it then, but time has helped clarify the experience.

So allow me now to offer my thanks to the Murrays of Scone, also known as the Earl and Countess of Mansfield, for reminding visitors like me, in a very unostentatious way, that the nobility does indeed remain very much alive and well in Scotland, but further that, beneath their possession of titles and wealthy, historically significant estates, they are really just like you and me—albeit with more expensive dogs.

# Chapter 14: A Musical Interlude

## (An evening in Dunkeld)

In 1540, a new instrument was invented in the Italian town of Cremona. Its makers called it the violin. Over the next 500 years, this stringed creation would prove exceptionally versatile and today stands as one of the few instruments to be equally at home adorning the shoulders of classically trained musicians in symphony halls or tucked under the chins of men wearing overalls and answering to names like Billy Bob and Cletus. For the former we can thank the composers of the European continent: the Germans, Austrians and others who incorporated the violin into the great compositions of classical music. For the latter, we can thank Scotland.

When the violin first appeared in Scotland a few years after its invention, it was an instant hit. Its sustained notes and haunting tones reminded Scots of the bagpipes, and its portability soon made it an essential piece of the country's folk tradition. Over the years, Scottish musicians, isolated from the methods of the continent, would experiment with new techniques for playing the instrument, ultimately developing a jauntier style that became known as "fiddling". Thus, the violin of classical musicians became the fiddle of folk musicians, and the world was all the richer for both—though America owes a particular debt to the fiddle.

In the 18th century, a wave of Scottish immigrants poured into America, fleeing religious persecution and economic hardship in an English-dominated society. These settlers, finding the coast of America already well settled (and that by Englishmen no less!), pushed westward into the wild mountains of the southern Appalachians. There a distinctive mountain culture took root: a culture which today conjures images of a hardy, independent people, simple and god fearing, with an occasional affinity for siblings and barnyard animals. But these pioneers—the original hillbillies, if you will—carried with them far more than an adventurous spirit and a recipe for homemade whisky. They also brought the rich traditions of Scottish folk music to the hills of America. And for this music,

153

the Appalachians would prove fertile ground.

Armed with their voices and fiddles, these settlers made the mountains come alive with the ballads and dance tunes of their homeland. Isolated from civilization, music became the common thread that held communities together. Individual families would pass evenings with fireside sing-alongs. Periodically, multiple families would gather at a specified barn or church for a night of music and dancing in exactly the same way communities gathered for ceilidhs* in the village halls of Scotland. Over time, the blending of the old songs with new influences (notably African) and instruments (such as banjoes, guitars and mandolins to compliment the fiddle) gave rise to a distinctive style of music: the bluegrass and country sounds which underlie the American folk tradition today. The style is unique to America, yet inextricably indebted to its Scottish roots.

This connection was brilliantly captured in the year 2000 with the release of a little-regarded Hollywood movie called *Songcatcher*. In this movie, set in the early 1900's, a professor of music from an American university visits her sister, who has started a school in the southern Appalachian Mountains. Upon her arrival, the professor discovers not only the central role music plays in mountain life, but that the songs being sung, thanks to decades of isolation, represent some of the purest forms of Scottish and English ballads still in existence. As one might expect, a movie based on centuries-old ballads and lacking considerably in special effects and fast-paced action didn't receive much attention at the box office, which is a shame because it was extremely well done and gives great insight into the music of Appalachia, and, by association, the rich Scottish legacy that spawned it. The film features many beautiful, old ballads, such as "Barbara Allen", "Geordie", "Lord Randall", and "Come All Ye Fair and Tender Ladies"—songs of love, loss, and, in some cases, a surprisingly graphic display of violence. I particularly enjoyed a song, sung by an elderly woman on her front porch, about cutting off the head of an unfaithful lover and

---

* A ceilidh, pronounced "kay-lee", is a gathering of people for a night of music and dance in Scotland. The ceilidh is especially popular in small communities and is usually held in a central location, such as a village hall.

kicking it against the wall. Those Scots sure could spin a tune.

Violent lyrics aside, the other thing that struck me about the movie was how thoroughly music seemed to permeate mountain society. Everyone seemed to sing—old people, young people, honest people, slimy people, people with strong voices, people with raw voices, people with squeaky voices, it didn't matter—and almost any occasion could merit a song: obvious moments, such as after dinner or walking along a path, but also unexpected moments, such as after a difficult childbirth or the loss of one's land, as if the music itself could offer solace at such times. I wondered if, like the songs, this thorough embracing of music had its roots in the settlers' Scottish heritage.

Little did I suspect that I would find the answer to this question on our first night out of Edinburgh at an unassuming inn called the Taybank.

• • • • •

Our reasons for choosing the Taybank were simple enough. Thumbing through the guidebook trying to figure out where we would spend the night after leaving Scone, we had stumbled across an entry for the hotel, describing it as "a real beacon for music fans with regular live sessions in the convivial, TV-free bar. The rooms are simple and inexpensive, and the rate includes a continental breakfast." What was that? Live music in lieu of bad TV, cheap rooms and breakfast to boot? I would have driven a good distance to check into a place like that. As it was, we only had to drive about fifteen minutes. The Taybank was located in the town of Dunkeld, just up the road from Perth.

Dunkeld, as it turns out, is a cradle of musical talent in Scotland, though we had no idea of this at the time. The town served as the stomping ground of Neil Gow, the famous 18th century fiddler generally regarded as the country's foremost composer of strathspeys and reels. More recently, Dunkeld has been home to one of Scotland's greatest modern folk musicians: a singer/songwriter with the wonderfully Scottish name of Dougie MacLean. MacLean is a brilliant guitarist and fiddler with a

155

mellifluous voice, who captures the spirit of Scotland through both his renditions of traditional folk songs and his own original compositions. In the spirit of folk life, these latter tend to dwell on the everyday toils of the common man, with songs about learning to work the scythe or drinking in the pub with old friends. His most famous song, a ballad titled "Caledonia" which can only be described as a love song to Scotland, has become a standard in Scottish pubs, elevating Dougie to near icon status north of the Tweed.

The town of Dunkeld—most of whose residents probably know MacLean or his family personally, as the community has only a few hundred residents—is understandably proud of its native son, and keeps the musical tradition alive at the Taybank. MacLean and his wife founded the hotel years ago as a kind of musical gathering place for the area. Though under different ownership today, the Taybank continues in this role, featuring regular live folk music, usually taking the form of spontaneous jam sessions by whatever musicians tend to be congregated that evening. To this purpose, a collection of guitars, fiddles, banjoes, and other stringed instruments hang on the walls above a piano tucked into a corner of the pub ready to be placed into the hands of any inspired customer. We looked forward to enjoying a pint over some live music that night, though it was still early evening when we reached Dunkeld. In the meantime, we had time to get our bearings.

Now, I want to forewarn the reader that my tale for the remainder of this chapter will likely be peppered with sweeping adjectives—wonderful, terrific, perfect, neat!—that might smack of insincerity in their casual claims of the grandiose. Do not be fooled; their usage is sincere and, in my mind, fully justified. I know one should not judge a town based on a single evening (a few hours, really), so I will contain my claim to my own experience. For all I know, at other times, the town of Dunkeld may be a hideous hell on earth, populated by thieves, mean old ladies and obnoxious children, and plagued by blood-thirsty insects. But for the night we passed nestled in Dunkeld's bosom, it was one of the most perfect places on earth.

For starters, consider the setting. Dunkeld straddles the Highland Line, tucked into the base of the Grampian Mountains. The approach was beautiful as we wound our way gently upwards through the trees following the River Tay. Looking at a map now, I realize that we just missed by a fraction of a mile seeing the world's tallest hedge and must have passed within a hair's breadth of the Birnam Oak, though we remained blissfully unaware of such diversions at the time. We poked along transfixed by the simple beauty of the scenery, which hit a highpoint as we left the town of Birnam and crossed the River Tay into Dunkeld. The route over the Tay took us across a seven-arched bridge, nearly two hundred years old, spanning the river sparkling below in the early evening sunlight.

We drove the length of the town, which took about thirty seconds, looking for the hotel. Quaint shops and whitewashed houses lined the street, with a large cathedral, partially in ruins, peeking out from behind the buildings. Beckoning little side streets broke off here and there but didn't promise to go far. As if to underscore this last point after a few hundred yards the town simply stopped. There was a meadow with a driveway leading to a hotel somewhere in the forest—much too grandiose to be the Taybank—and then the woods resumed. Turning around, we retraced our steps and found the Taybank, as the name suggests and as the reader likely realized several paragraphs ago, located directly by the river's edge.

Names are wonderfully descriptive in Scotland, and I needed to learn to trust their literal value. This proved difficult after years in the States, where names are often so blatantly misleading that one develops, if not a wariness, certainly an immunity to their meaning. This holds especially true for the names given by crafty developers to the new housing communities swallowing up farmland across America today. My sister's family lived for several years in a development just outside my hometown in Ohio (by the new mall, of course) that managed to contradict itself within its own name, calling itself "River Valley Highlands". Think about that.

At any rate, the Taybank was one of the first buildings we had passed, just to the right of the main road as we'd entered the town within full view of the bridge. It was a tidy, white, two and a half storey building with small paned windows and a gabled roof. Tables lined the patio outside the entrance, and a few scattered drinkers basked in the evening sunshine. We parked our car in the lot and went inside.

We entered a pub full of tables with a square wooden bar set into one side. Acoustic instruments, concert handbills and Dougie MacLean posters hung on the walls. Approaching the bar, I had a sudden fear that, like at the White Hart Inn, I had arrived several decades too late at a Taybank that now operated as just a pub. The bartender, a young woman in her twenties with dyed coal black hair, didn't seem put off, however, when I asked about a room. Rather she pushed a key at me and said in a neutral tone, "Top of the stairs. Keep going up until you can't go up anymore. It's a double, but it's the only room left."

"That's good, because there are two of us," I replied, taking the key and glad to have found a home for the night. The bartender gave me a wry smile and turned away. I soon found out what she'd meant.

The room, as the guidebook had warned us, was not about to adorn the cover of Good Housekeeping. The snug little chamber contained two small beds: one to the left of the door as we walked in, and another in a little alcove at the back of the room, which I guess qualified the room as a double. Each bed measured slightly wider than an ironing board.

"So are we going to get really cozy tonight or sleep separately?" I asked, good-naturedly.

"I'll take this one," Katrina replied, closing the discussion as she dropped her pack on the bed nearest the door.

The room, I should note, had no bathroom. There was a toilet down the hall to be shared by the two or three rooms on the top floor and a full bath on the floor below, to be shared by everyone in the hotel so far as I could tell. It was a bit like being in a fraternity house. Katrina was less than ecstatic.

"I think it's time for a pint," she announced.

Downstairs, I ordered the customary cider and ale and took them outside. I didn't see Katrina at the tables by the entryway, and for a moment it crossed my mind that perhaps she had bolted back to the fancy hotel at the other end of town, where she would undoubtedly find a roaring fireplace surrounded by Fabio-looking characters who could afford rooms with bathrooms inside them thanks to the money they made posing for romance novel covers. At second glance, I located her across the street, looking like she didn't need to go anywhere any time soon. She had claimed a spot at one of several picnic tables that had been thoughtfully placed in the grass near the river's edge. The waters of the Tay rolled smoothly by just a few yards from her feet, the view framed by the graceful arches of the stone bridge just upstream. Katrina's mood, I was pleased to note, had improved greatly.

We sat for some time sipping our pints and watching the river. Birds played in the trees at river's edge, leaving their branches to swoop low over the water's surface, only to return to their perch and add a song to the sounds of the gurgling water. Across the street, the tables in front of the hotel filled up with drinkers and, we noticed, diners, so when the time came for a second pint we placed a food order as well. The bartender, who was never rude but always very matter of fact, let us know that she had no problem with us taking our food across the street, so long as we didn't expect her to walk it to us.

"Ye'll be waiting some time fer that, I can tell ye," she said.

"No problem," I said, "and we'll bring our plates back."

"I should hope so," she said. "Otherwise I'll have tae charge ye fer them."

If we had done nothing but eat dinner and sip our pints by the Tay that evening, it would have been a night to remember. As it was, the evening just kept getting better.

After dinner we went for a walk through the town of Dunkeld. This took us down the main street we'd already driven, but it was nice to see it again at a strolling pace. Dunkeld is a very tidy town, with flowerboxes in abundance and neatly painted trim of various colors framing the windows of the whitewashed houses. We turned down a side street that looked particularly appealing, curving back from the main road. Small, neat houses lined both sides of the street, their doors opening right onto the sidewalk.

Bicycles and a ball or two lay here and there along the road, which dead-ended after a couple hundred feet. The overall impression was of a very comfortable, lived-in neighborhood, where kids would laugh and play and be perfectly safe, while their mothers watched from a window or from a neighbor's doorstep.

Katrina looked at me and said, "I could live on a street like this." A rather funny statement, considering our house in the islands—perched on a cliff with no sidewalk and no other houses in sight—could not have been in a more different setting. And yet, I knew what she meant. The neighborhood had a very comfortable feel.

Continuing on, we soon reached the outskirts of town where we turned down the driveway towards the fancy hotel. The road skirted a meadow for a while, and then plunged into the heart of the woods. The scenery was simply beautiful. We began to see first hand why Perthshire styles itself "big tree country". Thick oaks and towering pines and lots of other trees I couldn't name closed out the sky above us, filtering the light onto the needle-strewn path below. The hotel, when we reached it, consisted of a renovated country estate proving every bit as fancy as we'd suspected. Fancier, if that's possible. It looked like just the sort of place that would keep a stock of Fabio-like characters on payroll to sit brooding in chairs around the fireplace. I shuffled Katrina quickly past the entrance.

From the hotel parking lot, we discovered, much to our pleasure, a walking path following the river that led back to Dunkeld. It took us through the forest, and finally deposited us back on the other side of the meadow right at the doorstep of the cathedral.

The cathedral, and indeed the whole town of Dunkeld, was once of major importance to the pious of Scotland. In the 9th century, when Kenneth MacAlpin united the Picts and Scots and moved his capital to Scone, he made nearby Dunkeld the religious center of the entire kingdom. To make his point, he even had the bones of St. Columba, the evangelizing monk from Ireland who traveled throughout Scotland in the 6th century, brought to Dunkeld to consecrate the site. The current cathedral dated from the 13th century and was dedicated to St. Columba, though it lay now in partial ruins, having been largely destroyed by zealots during the Protestant Reformation.

Katrina and I wandered through the cathedral ruins. The scene reminded me of Holyrood Abbey, in that the walls stood relatively intact but without any roof above to give shelter. Unlike Holyrood, the floor had also disappeared, being replaced instead by a beautiful, lush covering of the greenest grass, giving one the feeling of being both inside and outside at the same time. We walked through the center of the cathedral, flanked by a series of vaulted stone arches separating the nave from the aisles on either side. The stone pillars supporting each arch seemed to grow straight out of the grass, as did the gravestones scattered here and there throughout this curious "indoor" lawn. We marveled at the sublime, sylvan nature of the ruin, with the towering trees of Perthshire peeking over the tops of the walls. It was one of the most peaceful settings I have ever experienced.

As the light started to dim, however, my thoughts returned to the Taybank with its guitars hanging on the walls and the promises of live music made by my guidebook. Pulling ourselves away from the cathedral, we made the short walk back to the hotel.

The pub, upon our return, was unexpectedly quiet. Patrons occupied a few of the tables, but no band was in sight. I wondered if we had hit the Taybank on an off night.

"There's a session going on upstairs," the bartender replied to my query about live music.

"A session?" I inquired.

"Aye, a folk session," she replied. "Different musicians bring their instruments and set up. It's very informal. Ye can take your pints and gae'n up."

The second floor contained a room apparently dedicated to these folk sessions. A large room, though small for a music venue, was cluttered with chairs in a more or less circular arrangement. A young man going prematurely bald was strumming an acoustic guitar and softly singing a tune as we poked our heads in the open doorway. A handful of others—some holding instruments, some not—occupied other chairs. It seemed more like a group of friends playing in a dorm room than live music out at a pub, and we hesitated at the door unsure if we should enter. Seeing this, one of them looked up and beckoned us into the room.

As we entered and took chairs around the circle, the young man continued playing. No one spoke. The song sounded like a traditional Irish ballad and I didn't quite catch all the words, but the melody was wonderful. When the song finished, everyone clapped and murmured words of approval: "Well done." "Beautiful, mate." "I love that one." And so on. Then, with no preamble, the man to his immediate left brought his guitar to his lap and started fingerpicking what sounded like a flamenco tune. In a strong voice, he poured out Spanish lyrics, displaying an incredible range, all the while alternating between picking and strumming a bold, syncopated rhythm. When he finished, the people in the room again shared comments of genuine enthusiasm; and then the person to his immediate left readied his guitar and began to play: this time another ballad, but sounding more Country and Western than Celtic.

I began to sense what was happening. Apparently, a folk session was similar to an open mic night in the United States, where anybody can play. But instead of having to go up on stage, musicians just take turns going around the circle. This was great, except that now only one person stood between me and the current musician. I began to get nervous, not knowing what was expected. I should note that at that time I did own a guitar and occasionally attempted to play, though no one would accuse me of being on a performance level. My audience usually consisted of Katrina, who tolerated my strumming but never actually requested me to play, and my cat, who usually slept through my playing but sometimes would acknowledge me by getting up, stretching and leaving the room to sleep elsewhere. Sitting in the room with a handful of people listening to yet another talented musician belt out a tune, I didn't know what to do. I was out of my league but didn't want to insult the group if everyone was expected to play. Fortunately, the man to my right solved the dilemma.

When the current song finished and the applause and comments had died down, he simply gave a wave and said, "I'll pass. I'm just enjoying the talents of others."

The room seemed to accept this without question, and then all eyes were on me. Following my neighbor's lead, I said something similar, as did Katrina. We didn't get off as easily as our neighbor, however. Our accents gave us away as Americans, and we found ourselves being welcomed and asked about home, how we liked Scotland and other such questions. Everyone was very nice, and then the session continued.

The middle-aged woman to Katrina's left had no instrument, so I was surprised when, rather than passing, she said, "Here's a song we'd sing at kirk when I was a wee bairn. Ye all ken the lyrics, so feel free to jyne." Then she opened her mouth and belted out the most beautiful a cappella version of "Amazing Grace" I have ever heard. It's never been a song I've particularly cared for, but sitting in the room listening to her raw voice, which carried the tune but was not particularly trained, gave the song a purity of context that made me hear it as if for the first time. Everyone let her take the first few lines alone, and then others began to join in as she had requested. The voices filled the room and I found myself singing along. ("Amazing Grace" is one of those songs everyone knows the words to whether they like it or not.) Looking to my left, I saw that Katrina, who admittedly sang worse than me or the cat, had also joined in. The room reverberated with energy.

When she finished, the singer's husband—a calloused fellow who looked like he had spent the majority of his days outside—also belted out a traditional a cappella spiritual: "Down to the River to Pray", which I recognized thanks to a recently released version by Allison Kraus for the *O Brother, Where Art Thou?* soundtrack. Allison Kraus is considered a country or bluegrass singer, and hearing the song now in this context—being sung a cappella by a salt of the earth Scotsman with eager harmonies being added by the rest of the room—brought home the strong connection that exists between the folk music of Scotland and America.

Sitting there in the session room of the Taybank, this cross-ocean connection and the extent to which music permeated folk society in Scotland—as it did in the Appalachians—was suddenly, and in a very tangible way, exposed to its core. The songs, even the ones I didn't recognize, all sounded vaguely familiar. And everyone in the room seemed to have a musical talent. After the a cappella couple, a father—who looked like a long lost brother of Gerard Depardieu—strummed and sang a ballad on guitar while his daughter accompanied him on flute, adding in harmonies on the chorus. Had a highland cow walked in and grunted out a tune at that moment, I don't think anyone in the room would have batted an eye. Rather they would have enthusiastically clapped, murmured their words of approval and then looked expectantly at the sheep next to it in the circle. The enthusiasm—the pure and simple joy of music—was contagious.

By the time my turn came around again, I was itching to play. (I had also downed a pint or two in the interval, which seemed to help.) Borrowing a guitar from Depardieu, I brought it to my lap, but after a few false starts I almost gave up and passed. I can't explain it, but in my awe of the situation, I seemed to have forgotten how to play most songs. The room, however, wouldn't hear of it, and Depardieu and Balding Guy threw out encouraging remarks, as my brain quickly scanned the list of folk songs I could play. In a bit of subconscious irony, I settled on Bob Dylan's "Don't Think Twice, It's Alright". As I started strumming and singing the first verse, the energy in the room seemed to pick up—feet were tapping, hands were clapping, and most of the room was even singing along. The effect—which may have been intentional—was reassuring and allowed me to relax and have fun with the song, feeding off the energy of others. The experience was thrilling.

Finishing, I returned the guitar to Depardieu as the listeners murmured their words of approval and a cappella lady prepared to launch into the next tune. Thus, the evening progressed. From time to time, someone new would arrive, and pretty soon almost every chair was full. Some newcomers joined in; some just sat and listened, tapping their feet. We went around the room several more times before Balding Guy finally closed the session with a Dougie MacLean song that everyone in the room knew but Katrina and me. I would make sure that never happened again by buying two Dougie CD's on our way out in the morning. These would prove to be a much better purchase than the Tartan Top Twenty disc I had bought on the Royal Mile and would serve us well for the rest of the trip and beyond.

As we left the session and walked upstairs to our room, I was soaring. The experience had heightened my curiosity of Scottish folk music, and I would spend considerable time in coming months learning more about the country's rich musical legacy. For that night, however, I was content to feel like a rock star—though I would wager Bob Dylan never had to sleep alone on an ironing board after a gig.

# Chapter 15: Holy Grail Abducted by Aliens

## (A tour of Rosslyn Chapel)

A few miles south of Edinburgh lies the tiny village of Roslin. If you are of the science-minded type, you will recognize this village as the home of the Roslin Institute, where in 1997 scientists presented the world with Dolly, the planet's first cloned sheep. If you have read Dan Brown's mega-best selling novel *The DaVinci Code*—and chances are you have, as at last count it had been read by nearly every person on earth—you will recognize the village as the home of Rosslyn* Chapel, supposed repository of the secret bloodline of Christ. Either way, you will have identified a village that has been a lightning rod for religious controversy. It seems the Christian church frowns on attempts by humans to play God (that is, by cloning a living being) and even more so on suggestions that the Son of God may have liked to play human (that is, by having sex and siring a child). But as any tabloid will attest, controversy sells, and today the little village of Roslin is one of the most popular destinations in Scotland.

The main reason for this is Rosslyn Chapel. Not many people, as it turns out, are lining up to see a sheep, cloned or not. The chapel, on the other hand, has fascinated visitors for five centuries. It can be debated whether the church contains the secrets of the Holy Grail, but no one can deny it is a place steeped in mystery.

The chapel was built in the 15th century by William St. Clair, the third and last Prince of Orkney and a member of a family deeply associated with mystic traditions. The St. Clairs, or Sinclairs as the name came to be spelled in Scotland, held title as "the hereditary grand masters of Scottish masonry" in 1601, though their role in the Scottish order** may extend all the way

---

* Although the town is spelled "Roslin", the chapel retains the ancient spelling of "Rosslyn".
** Masonry and freemasonry, in this context, refer to the quasi-secret societies that have existed over the years whose members have been supposed keepers of secret knowledge, religious or otherwise, passed down from one generation to the next. Scottish freemasonry, in particular, claims to be descended from the Knights Templar, supposed possessors of secret knowledge or treasure acquired during the Crusades to the Holy Land. In modern times, Masonic societies have become less secret, though they still pride themselves on secret handshakes, passwords, and other such cloak and dagger accoutrements. Before

back to the 15th century reign of James II. This would have coincided perfectly with the life of William St. Clair, who began constructing Rosslyn Chapel in 1446. The massive construction project, which employed stonemasons from all over Europe, spanned four decades, ending in 1486, two years after William's death. What was completed was actually only a fraction of the intended project; indeed, what we call Rosslyn Chapel today was only meant to be the choir of a much larger church. Completed or not, the chapel stands as an unparalleled masterpiece of masonry work, and it doesn't take too much of a conspiracy theorist to think some strange message may lurk within its walls.

The only wood used in the construction of the building is found in the doors and in a crest set over the baptistry arch. The rest of the chapel—the walls, the pillars and arches, even the ceiling—consists entirely of stone, and nearly every inch is intricately carved. At first glance, the casual observer to Rosslyn will see exactly what one would expect to see adorning the walls of a Christian church: angels, apostles, saints, biblical scenes such as the crucifixion of Christ or the sacrifice of Abraham, all mixed in with seemingly random decoration for flair. A closer inspection, however, reveals something more: mixed in with these pious images are carvings that seem wholly out of place with any Christian tradition.

Many of these are unquestionably pagan, such as several carvings depicting the Green Man, a Celtic nature god with vines growing out of his mouth and twisting around his face. Dragons from Norse mythology line the base of a pillar, gnawing at the roots of carved vines that twist their way up the column toward the ceiling. Other carvings present blatant allusions to freemasonry, such as a depiction of a Knight Templar, the order ostensibly formed to protect crusaders to the Holy Land, but long suspected to have rather been protecting a secret found in Jerusalem's Temple of Solomon during the first Crusade—a secret that created great wealth for the Templars before leading to their violent suppression in the

---

being dismissed as a bunch of quacks—which I understand is tempting—consider that these societies' ranks have included such historic characters as Botticelli, Leonardo DaVinci, Isaac Newton, and Benjamin Franklin, to name but a few.

14th century.

In some cases, even the carvings that seem traditional have something amiss. One such carving depicts a winged angel, standard enough until one registers that it is hanging upside down and bound with a rope. Other seemingly normal angels, winged and with cherubic faces, are found upon closer inspection to possess bodies covered in fur and contorted into grotesque postures. "What is going on here?" the visitor starts to ask.

Even the faces that adorn the walls are not what they first appear. A series of three faces, for example, which at first seem to be those of saints or revered family members, become somewhat more mysterious when it is noted that one has a gash cut into its forehead. In fact, these faces tell a story of murder associated with the very creation of the chapel itself. The story goes as follows: When plans called for the carving of a particularly elaborate pillar, the Master Mason traveled to Rome to study the original upon which the design was based. During his absence, his talented apprentice took on and completed the pillar, creating a masterpiece of unparalleled craftsmanship. Upon his return from Rome, the Master Mason was so envious of his apprentice's work, he struck the apprentice on the head with a mallet, killing him on the spot. The pillar, which thankfully was not likewise destroyed, became known as the Apprentice Pillar and continues to astound visitors today with its beauty and intricate design. To commemorate the tragedy, the faces of the Master Mason, the skilled apprentice, and the apprentice's grieving mother were carved into the church walls. Thus an episode of violence is added to the already bizarre story of Rosslyn Chapel.

But perhaps nothing stands out as stranger than the botanical carvings twisting throughout the church. Mixed in with the standard vines and flowers are several plants, such as Indian corn and cacti, found only in the New World. Keep in mind these were carved decades before Columbus set sail on his voyage to America—a fact which would seem to lend credence to the family's claim that William St. Clair's grandfather, Prince Henry of Orkney, crossed the ocean to North America a century before Columbus set sail with his three ships.

There seems to be something for every conspiracy theorist embedded in the walls of the chapel, which explains why, even before *The DaVinci Code*, Rosslyn was a sort of Mecca for armchair historians and pseudo-scientists: the type who claim to see Elvis in a shopping mall or to know who was really behind the JFK assassination. Books have been written associating Rosslyn with everything from UFO's to the Holy Grail, and, until recently, the chapel had a small but dedicated following amongst those who dabble in the occult. With the 2003 publication of *The DaVinci Code*, which postulates the caretakers of Rosslyn as the descendants of Christ and the entire chapel as a coded map leading to the Holy Grail, this following would get a lot bigger.

By bringing the mysteries of Rosslyn Chapel to the masses through his novel, Dan Brown inadvertently brought the masses to Rosslyn Chapel. The fact that the novel never claimed to be anything but a work of fiction mattered not at all. Visitation to the church increased by 79 percent the year after the book's publication in a phenomenon the media labeled "*DaVinci Code* fever". In 2004 alone, 68,000 visitors crossed the chapel's threshold.* Some of these were undoubtedly pious wanderers wishing to pay their respects at a sacred, religious site, or history buffs come to study an architectural wonder. Many more, however, were fever-afflicted pilgrims, lured by the sensationalized theories of a mass-market novel.

I know. Katrina and I were two of them.

· · · · ·

Unfortunately, we were two of them without the first clue as to where Roslin was. Katrina and I had talked about visiting Rosslyn Chapel when we first settled on Scotland as a vacation destination, but in my subsequent frenzy of genealogical research the matter had been forgotten and never discussed again until, quite unexpectedly, I woke up in Dunkeld on our

---

* Visitation in 2005 increased by more than 70 percent again to a whopping 117,000 visitors. In fairness, visitation was on the rise prior to the publication of *The DaVinci Code*. According to Stuart Beattie, director of the Rosslyn Chapel Trust, visitation in 1995 was only 9,500 and by the year 2000 it was already up to 30,000.

sixth day in Scotland with Rosslyn on my mind. I don't know why the thought occurred to me then—perhaps I had dreamt about being abducted by a UFO—but when I mentioned it to Katrina, she agreed that the chapel definitely needed to be on our list of things to see.

Pulling out my trusty guidebook, I located Roslin with an ironic laugh. It was six miles south of Edinburgh, just minutes from where we had stayed for two nights before leaving and driving north. Sighing, we realized that if we were going to see it, it would have to be now, as the rest of our travels would only take us further away. It looked like the highlands would have to wait one more day. The flipper had struck again.

This was one of those times which made us truly appreciate the small scale of the Scottish countryside. Backtracking all the way south of Edinburgh from Dunkeld looked like a considerable endeavor on the map. Once we made the decision, however, little more than an hour passed before we found ourselves edging the Fiat Crumb into a parking spot in the tiny village of Roslin. The chapel stood on the outskirts of town, and we walked down the main street toward it with great anticipation. We were prepared to be confronted with mystery. We were prepared to be confronted with history. We were not prepared to be confronted with scaffolding.

As we entered the chapel grounds, we were presented with a view of what we could only assume was the chapel, but which was hidden from base to rooftop behind a metal framework of scaffolding. This scaffolding, we would later learn, was part of a major restoration project begun in 1997. The metal framework supported a slate canopy spanning the roof of the chapel, much like a large umbrella, with the purpose of keeping the structure dry and giving the stonework a chance to rid itself of the water that had accumulated within over the past half century. In the 1950's, well-meaning caretakers had sealed the chapel's interior to protect the carvings. The sealant worked so well that it didn't let a drop of water through. Of course, this meant the water simply collected inside the walls, saturating the stonework and threatening the integrity of the entire structure. The "drying out stage" taking place during our visit was set to last for years, during which time the Rosslyn Chapel Trust, the organization responsible for managing the historic site, was researching ways to remove the 50-year old sealant so that the problem wouldn't continue after the canopy's removal. Brilliant.

The upshot of this restoration was that visitors for years[*] would not get a good view of what the exterior of the chapel actually looked like—which I'm sure gave rise to plenty of complaints from cranky visitors, afraid that perhaps a critical clue to the Grail's location had been covered up by scaffolding. In a respectable attempt to make the best of a bad situation, the Rosslyn Chapel Trust had erected a walkway near the top of the scaffolding so that visitors could get the unusual view of seeing the exterior of the building, specifically the upper reaches of its flying buttresses and spires, close up. I don't know about other visitors, but for me this succeded in taking the sting out of not being able to see the exterior of the chapel from a distance. I enjoyed strolling around the walkway—no more than a catwalk with a see-through grating for a floor (not an exercise for those afraid of heights)—peering at gargoyles and carvings which had not been seen at this close range by anyone save the occasional maintenance man since the original masons carved them over five hundred years ago. By the time I descended from the scaffolding, I felt as if we'd been given a rare privilege rather than a raw deal.

If seeing the outside was a privilege, seeing the inside was nearly heart stopping. We entered the chapel and gasped. No matter how much we had read about Rosslyn and its carvings, nothing had prepared us for that first glimpse. Every inch of the interior seemed to be carved. Texture was everywhere; flat surfaces nearly non-existent. It was completely overwhelming. One could easily spend hours examining a single wall. Conversely, if one were looking for a specific carving—a Green Man or the Knight Templar, for example—it could take a week to locate it, like looking for the proverbial needle in a haystack. Fortunately, the considerate

---

[*] The scaffolding was erected in 1997 and stayed up until 2013. I returned to Roslin in 2016 and got to enjoy the fruits of the Rosslyn Chapel Trust's good labor. The Chapel has been restored and protected for future generations to enjoy and a new visitor center has been added to help handle the crowds: a good thing since *The DaVinci Code* film was shot there in 2006 sending visitation up even higher!

members of the Rosslyn Chapel Trust understand this and offer visitors the opportunity to part with a small sum of money in return for a guidebook to the chapel's carvings—an opportunity I gratefully accepted.

Using the guide, Katrina and I toured the interior of the chapel, lingering at the more interesting carvings: a Green Man, the Apprentice Pillar, a carving of a St. Clair ancestor holding Robert the Bruce's heart, which he had attempted to take to the Holy Land for burial.[*] I particularly enjoyed a series of carvings showing angels holding various musical instruments. Some of the instruments were to be expected, such as a harp or a recorder. Others showed angels playing bagpipes and a stringed instrument that could have been a guitar or mandolin—like members of a heavenly bluegrass band: the Halleluiah Boys or some such group.

The whole of the interior was surprisingly small. The chapel measures only 35' by 70', and it didn't take us long to make our way through the entire room. We purposefully didn't linger, as we were feeling a bit awkward about the experience. Touring a church is not like visiting a museum or a roadside attraction, such as the world's largest ball of twine where the whole point is to ohh and ahh and point and laugh and otherwise make a spectacle of oneself. The whole time we were inside at Rosslyn, joined by others come to ogle the carvings, a handful of people were sitting or kneeling in the pews in the center aisle, reminding us that the chapel still serves as a working church. A formal prayer session even took place while we were there, with a man reading prayers aloud to the people occupying the pews while the rest of us went around looking excitedly for pagan symbols.

There must be a real love-hate relationship between the local congregation and the tourists filing through on a more or less constant basis. On the one hand, visitation to the church provides critical financial benefits, necessary to keep the more than 500 year-old structure maintained. On the other, it means the local worshippers almost never get the church to themselves, but rather share it with pea-brained specimens like the young

---

[*] The 14th century journey was ill-fated. St. Clair and many of his cohorts met their death in battle against Islamic Moors in Spain long before they got close to the Holy Land. Robert the Bruce's heart was returned to Scotland by those who survived the battle and interred at Melrose Abbey.

couple who pushed in front of us as we studied the Apprentice Pillar.

The man held an armload of guidebooks and gazed thoughtfully at the pillar, while the woman reached forward, as if to run her hands over the rough bumps of the carved vine twisting around the column.

"It's weird to think the Holy Grail may be inside there," the woman noted in a voice filled with awe.

"I read the head of Jesus might be in there," added the man, lifting the handful of books as if to verify his claim.

"Perhaps Jesus's head *is* the Holy Grail," Katrina added helpfully over their shoulders.

Man and woman looked at her thoughtfully as if she had said something worth considering. Katrina nodded at them solemnly to indicate she understood the gravity of the situation. A woman sitting in a nearby pew gave us a tired look that seemed to say, "Move on, pin-heads."

We moved on.

A stairway led down to the crypt, and we descended to see what secrets it might hold. The answer was very few. At least very few that we would get to enjoy. The crypt consisted of a rectangular room, enclosed with stone blocks and fairly barren of decoration. Indeed, it was the one place in the chapel that didn't feature elaborate carvings on every available surface. A gravestone for William St. Clair containing Templar markings was on display, and interesting mason's marks adorned some of the stones, but that was about it. The rest of the vault had been sealed in the 17th century and not opened since, which of course has led to all sorts of speculation as to what may be inside. I have to admit I found myself staring at the walls wondering what mysteries may lay within, what secrets I may be passing within feet of at that very moment.

The Rosslyn Chapel Trust, for its part, plays an interesting role in the perpetuation of the Rosslyn mythology. The Trust has denied all offers to open and excavate the vault, but at the same time does nothing to discourage the mysterious personality of the chapel. Indeed, a museum in the visitor center dedicated considerable attention to the subject of freemasonry and other mystical organizations. As I wandered through after leaving the chapel, I was confronted with displays relating the history of various secret orders, a detailed comparison of the floor plan of Rosslyn Chapel with the floor plan of the Temple of Solomon (on which the entire church, had it been completed, was supposedly based), and a collection of tools and symbols associated with various orders of freemasonry from around the world. This information was all very helpful to me, since my previous knowledge of Masonic orders was based on Flintstones cartoons and generally consisted of wearing funny hats and addressing the leader as the Grand Poobah.

The gift shop continued to play up the mystery theme, with a healthy collection of books and videos theorizing on Rosslyn's secrets. I noted with amusement that mixed in with these Rosslyn-specific items were other books and videos which had nothing to do with Rosslyn at all, but simply discussed various paranormal topics: UFOs, ghosts, and whatnot. The Rosslyn Chapel Trust knows its audience. The gift shop was doing a brisk business.

Katrina was helping matters. As I amused myself reading the backs of some of the books (the one I had in my hand professed to know "the truth behind extraterrestrial contact, military intelligence and the mysteries of ancient Egypt" and warned that "a conspiracy...targets and threatens us all." Ahhh!), I watched her approach the counter with an armload of books—"for the school library," she insisted. I have read some of these books since and they are almost all ridiculously far-fetched, and all very intriguing. I think the most fascinating thing for me is how so many different authors can look at the same carvings and use them to make theories which in normal circumstances would seem idiotic appear almost plausible. If nothing else, they are creative. One of my favorite theories— and the most realistic, it seems—claims that Rosslyn's carvings hold no secrets, but simply tell a story. The authors start at one wall and take the reader around the chapel, showing that the carvings are really following the journey of life from birth to death through their various symbols.* It is all

---

* This theory is put forth by Mark Oxbrow and Ian Robertson in their book *Rosslyn and the Grail*. The book was published in 2005, the year after our trip. I read about it in an article published by the Scottish

quite convincing; but then again, so are many of the other theories—though not necessarily the one about Jesus's head being in the Apprentice Pillar.

That's the whole problem—or the fun, depending on how one looks at it—with Rosslyn. There's an old saying that give 10,000 monkeys 10,000 years to type randomly on computers and eventually they'll produce Shakespeare—along with a whole lot of nonsense, I suppose. Well at Rosslyn, there are so many carvings and so many conspiracy theorists willing to put them together in various ways that just about any theory can be produced. And one of these is probably the right one—but there's a whole lot of nonsense, too. I left Rosslyn feeling like a high school freshman, unable to distinguish between Shakespeare and a load of nonsense.

As we walked back through town, I read through the literature we'd picked up in the chapel. There was quite a bit to see for such a tiny village. History or architecture buffs could explore the ruins of Rosslyn Castle, also owned by the Sinclair family and reputedly haunted (why is that not surprising?) by a black knight on horseback. Nature lovers could take a pleasant wooded walk through nearby Rosslyn Glen, and check out the rocky gorge with its swift-moving stream. And if that wasn't enough, one could always go in search of a cloned sheep.

Sadly, most visitors to Roslin don't see any of these other attractions, remaining single-mindedly focused on the chapel instead. I would like to say Katrina and I were different, but I think the reader knows better by this point. In our defense, I would offer that, having already gone quite out of our way today, we were awfully anxious to get back north. We very much wanted to see the highlands before the aliens came and took us away.

newspaper, *The Scotsman*, on October 13, 2005. The article, by Diane MacLean, is optimistically headlined: "Rosslyn Chapel's extraordinary carvings explained at last". Well, I'm glad that's settled.

# Chapter 16: Dungeons and Puffins

## (From Dunottar to Stonehaven)

The opening pages of my guidebook contained a feature, splendid in its randomness, entitled "41 Things Not To Miss", the implication being that any tourist who didn't engage in these forty-one activities was a loser who had just wasted whatever money he had spent on his Scottish holiday and would have been better off staying in Ohio, New Jersey, or wherever it was he called home. I found this a trifle unfair, as the events were often specific to a time of year, such as the Edinburgh Festival which takes place in August and the Hogmanay Festival which takes place over New Year's Eve, thus requiring a stay of at least five months in Scotland to avoid being a complete failure. And just who arrived at this "41" number anyway? Someone with a fetish for prime numbers? Why not a nice round number, such as "40" or a number that makes sense for a common length of stay, such as "7" or "14"? I found the feature annoying to say the least.

But it had color photographs...and I'm a sucker for color photographs, especially when they're of haunting Scottish scenery and offer the only visual stimulation in an 850-page book. Thus, I found myself scanning the forty-one separate photographs frequently during idle moments, such as on the plane or at night in our various hotel rooms. One picture repeatedly captured my attention: a ruined castle set dramatically on a rocky peninsula connected to the mainland by a narrow isthmus of rock. Cliffs fell abruptly to the sea on all sides of the castle, which rested precipitously on the flattop of the rocky outcropping, as if someone had shorn off the top for the express purpose of constructing a fortress there. Grass grew atop the peninsula and a beckoning path wound its way from the mainland, across the isthmus and into the heart of the castle.

I longed to walk along that path. The setting was so surreal, so perfect—the stone of the castle, the green of the grass, the brown of the cliffs, all surrounded by the deep blue of the ocean stretching out to the horizon. Number 40 on the aforementioned list, the guidebook's caption told me I was staring at Dunnottar Castle, a "memorably dramatic ruined fortress, surrounded by giddy sea cliffs." Giddy, indeed.

Katrina was likewise taken by the photograph, and we decided early on that, despite our aversion to the list, Number 40 was truly not to be missed. The only problem was that Dunnottar was nowhere close to anything else we intended to see. Perched on the east coast of Scotland just a few miles south of Stonehaven, Dunnottar sat quite literally on the eastern extremity of the Highland Line. Had we continued driving into the highlands from Perth, as had been our original plan, we would have had to take an abrupt right turn and drive back out of the highlands to see the castle. Given the size of Scotland, this would have entailed a side trip of no more than an hour, hardly a daunting prospect; but after our detour that morning, we decided to drive straight from Roslin to Dunnottar, following the coast well to the east of Perth and putting off the highlands yet another day until we had seen the castle. We would sleep in Stonehaven that night.

This bears a look at the map: if you've been following events carefully, you will note that we drove from Dunkeld south to Roslin, toured Rosslyn Chapel, got back in the car and drove north to Stonehaven, toured Dunnottar Castle, and still had time for a leisurely dinner and pleasant stroll in town before calling it a day. And at no point did we feel rushed. Rather, we had just enough time to listen to our two new Dougie MacLean CDs from beginning to end during the two hours it took to get from Roslin to Dunnottar, which would prove to be the longest single driving stretch of our trip. Scotland is not a big country.

The route, incidentally, took us through Fife, the county just north of Edinburgh across the Firth of Forth. Fife is famous for being the home of St. Andrews, which itself earned fame as the birthplace of golf. It was there, or somewhere in the vicinity, that Scots adapted the sport in the 15th century from a similar French game requiring players to hit a target with a ball. Some enterprising Scotsman, realizing with incredible prescience that over 500 years later out-of-shape doctors, lawyers and politicians would need some excuse to spend four hours of their day not working, replaced the target with a hole, and golf as we know it was born. To say the game caught on in Scotland is to engage in gross understatement. James II, who reigned in the 15th century, had to ban the game as his soldiers developed a rather all-consuming preference for golf at the expense of other more necessary pursuits, namely archery practice. The ban may have worked temporarily, but it did nothing to dampen the long-term enthusiasm Scots showed for the sport. Today, the country boasts over 400 golf courses. In the immediate vicinity of St. Andrew's alone, golfers can choose from no less than seven courses to play. Of these, the most famous by far is the Old Course of St. Andrew's Royal and Ancient Golf Club, that venerable institution which now serves as the international governing body for golf. The Old Course hosted the British Open as far back as 1873, and is generally regarded as the most historic golf course in the world. Its popularity is such that tourists wishing to play on its hallowed fairways must enter a daily lottery for a chance at securing a tee time.

Not wishing to spend our holiday surrounded by old men in frightening trousers whose sole purpose for being in Scotland was to chase after a little ball, swearing and banging their clubs against the turf, we bypassed St. Andrew's and kept heading north toward Stonehaven. I've learned since that this was a mistake. By all accounts, St. Andrew's is a beautifully preserved town, a tad on the snooty side, perhaps, but with far more to it than we had suspected. It is home, rather obviously I suppose, to St. Andrew's University, Scotland's oldest such institution, having been founded in 1410 during the reign of James I—making higher learning in Scotland roughly the same age as golf. Visitors can also explore St. Andrew's Castle, where the reader will recall George Wishart, the protestant reformer, met his end at a fiery stake, soon to be followed to the grave by Cardinal Beaton—the man who had ordered Wishart's execution. Beaton was seized by a mob, stabbed to death and thrown into a deep pit called the "bottle dungeon", which still features on the castle tour. And what's this? Looking at my map now, I see that St. Andrew's is also home to something called the Crawford Arts Centre. However did I miss that?

As the reader may suspect, St. Andrew's now ranks high on the list for my next trip to Scotland. I should note that it features also as Number 28 on the "41 Things Not To Miss" list, so it seems that by visiting St. Andrew's I will be one step closer to not being a complete loser.

But I digress.

· · · · ·

The approach to Dunnottar proved every bit as dramatic as I'd hoped, but what else would one expect from a locale so incredibly scenic it was used as the setting for the 1990 movie version of Hamlet.[*] Leaving the car in a parking lot just off the main road, a path—yes, *the* path from the photograph—took us across a grassy meadow, which rolled in low, undulating hills for a couple of hundred yards and then abruptly stopped. Beyond the edge of land, an expanse of blue sea stretched to the horizon. What we could not see from the parking lot, but could only sense, was that between that edge of land and that expanse of sea rose a set of wondrously formidable cliffs, which, though quite invisible now, would hardly fail to escape notice when one was about to step over the edge and plummet more than a hundred feet to the rocks and crashing waves below.

The optical illusion was such that from the beginning of the path, the ruins of Dunnottar Castle looked as if they were sitting comfortably on the mainland, easily accessible to any passerby. It was only as we approached nearer that the land began to fall away on each side, ultimately revealing the castle to be perched on a quite separate landmass altogether, joined to the one we were on only by a narrow neck of easily defensible land—where a handful of soldiers could seemingly hold off an army. Walking the path to Dunnottar Castle was one of those rare moments when the word "breathtaking" was entirely apropos and could be used without any sense of hyperbole or cliché. Thus, I will use it now without guilt. The view was breathtaking.

The ruins, on the other hand, proved less so. They consisted of a complex of generally roofless (and in some cases, wall-less) buildings and

---

[*] This was the version starring Mel Gibson, who, despite being Australian, seemed to spend much of his time shooting movies on Scottish soil before he self-destructed.

required a fairly creative imagination to get any sense as to what the castle may have looked like in its heyday. For those lacking such an imagination, I highly recommend purchasing the excellent guidebook, as Katrina and I did at the gate. It combined beautiful photography of the castle complex with a detailed, section-by-section explanation of its various features. Thus, when Katrina and I stood near, say, the 14th century tower house or the 16th century storerooms, we were able to recognize them as such. I assure you that, with the possible exception of the tower house, I wouldn't have otherwise.

"Hey look, a pile of rocks," Katrina would say.

Glancing at the guidebook, I would elaborate: "Says here it's the stable."

"Uh-huh."

Then a moment later: "Look, another pile of rocks."

"Says here it's the smithy's forge."

"Uh-huh." And so on throughout the castle ruins.

As we walked, I read colorful anecdotes included in the guidebook relating Dunottar's surprisingly brutal and bloody history. Occupying such a formidable site, it would be easy to suppose, as I had, that the castle had stayed relatively free of conflict over the centuries. One would expect an army to take one look at the fortress, spread around some murmurings peppered with phrases like "bloody lunacy" and "you've got to be kidding me", and simply march on by. But alas, no. Rather, Dunnottar has been so central to events in Scotland that the guidebook put forth the claim that "this rock and the buildings on it have reflected in miniature much of the rich and tragic story of Scottish history." A grand claim, but one not without merit.

Indeed, each phase of Scottish history seems to have played out a significant chapter on the rocks of Dunnottar. In the 5th century, the time when the Celtic Picts controlled northeastern Scotland and a full century before St. Columba would appear on the scene, a Christian named Ninian, who would become Scotland's first saint, established a religious center on Dunnottar to serve as headquarters for his evangelizing missions in the area. By the end of the 9th century, this religious center had become a full-fledged fort just in time to be sacked and burned by the Vikings, who so enjoyed raiding Scotland in those days—this being over three centuries before a meteorologically-attuned Crawford at Largs helped end such nonsense forever.

Another ancestor, however, arrived just in time to affect events at Dunnottar. In 1297, William Wallace approached a Dunnottar then in the hands of the English, having been captured by Longshanks's troops and now providing a staging ground for English domination of northeast Scotland. Wallace, as he was wont to do, successfully stormed the castle and then, in a move reminiscent of the Barns of Ayr (which had just occurred earlier that year), set fire to the timber castle and even the one stone building that occupied the rock at the time, the chapel, in which most of the English garrison had taken refuge. This particular episode shows Blind Harry's penchant for hyperbole at its best, as he claims no less than 4,000 English perished that day, either by burning, by the sword, or by falling over the cliffs to the rocks below in their effort to escape the wrath of Wallace…who we can assume was accompanied by just a handful of men.

Wallace's liberation (if that's what it's called) of the castle, came during an era of back and forth, when Dunnottar seems to have been fought over like the prize possession it was, occupying such a strategic location. Following the death of Robert the Bruce three decades later, Dunnottar again fell into English hands, only to be swiftly retaken and—why is this so inevitable?—burned by Sir Andrew Moray, the regent for Robert the Bruce's young son, David II. It was after this third burning that the castle finally landed in the hands of the Keiths, an influential Scottish family who would hold it for the next three hundred years. The Keiths took the wise and rather obvious step of reconstructing the castle out of stone this time around, keeping it safer from the burning brands of attackers. Thus, most of the ruins seen today date from the 14th century forward, the one exception being a section of the stone chapel which somehow survived, as the English soldiers within did not, Wallace's earlier attempt to burn it to the ground.

Of course, the fact that the castle was now built of stone did not mean the end of conflict at Dunnottar. It just meant that would-be attackers had to work a lot harder to get inside. This is amply demonstrated by one of the most famous events from the castle's history: the defense of the Honours of Scotland, those sacred symbols of monarchy that narrowly escaped destruction by Oliver Cromwell in the 17th century.* Once Cromwell's troops got word that the Honours had been taken to Dunnottar, they quickly converged on the castle and began to lay siege. Defended by just sixty-nine men, the castle held out for eight long months, and would have held out for longer but for the arrival of English artillery reinforcements which began a heavy bombardment of the castle in the spring of 1652. When Dunnottar finally succumbed that May, it stood as the last place in Scotland still flying the royal flag.

With the surrender of the castle, Cromwell's minions poured into Dunnottar to claim their spoils. History does not tell us what they found, though we may assume it contained the usual items left behind by soldiers after an eight-month siege: a deck of playing cards, some leftover artillery and a stack of magazines under the mattress. But three things Cromwell's men certainly did not find were a royal crown, sword and scepter. The Honours were long gone. Thanks to Dunnottar's strength, the Scots had had plenty of time to form a back-up plan to protect the sacred relics, and at some point during the long siege the Honours had been secreted out of the castle and transported to the kirk in the nearby town of Kinneff, where they would be kept buried beneath the floor until the restoration of the monarchy eight years later.**

Thus, the Honours were saved, but Dunnottar Castle appeared a little worse for the wear. The battered castle complex was left exposed to the

---

* For those needing a reminder, recall that this was the time when Cromwell had overthrown and beheaded Charles I in an attempt to end what was perceived as the tyranny of the monarchy. Scotland became a target of Cromwell's wrath when its nobles shortly thereafter crowned Charles II at Scone, and the Honours had to be rushed into hiding to avoid being melted down at Cromwell's hands.
** How the Honours were transported to Kinneff from Dunnottar is unknown to this day, though both leading theories point to the same heroine: a Mrs. Grainger, the wife of the minister at Kinneff Kirk. The first and most probable story is that Mrs. Grainger arranged to have the sacred relics lowered over the cliff at the back of the castle where one of her servants was gathering seaweed. The second, and more entertaining, is that Mrs. Grainger personally secreted the crown, scepter, and 1.3 meter-long sword beneath her clothing and walked (rather stiffly, I suppose) straight out of the castle.

elements, ushering in a long period of decline and dereliction that continued well into the 20th century, before preservation and restoration efforts finally kicked in to save what was left. As I mentioned earlier, this wasn't much.

Still, this dereliction didn't mean the end of tragedy at Dunnottar. Perhaps the most tragic chapter of all occurred just three decades after Cromwell's siege, at a time when the once mighty fortress served as a makeshift prison for 167 unfortunate souls. For this story, the reader will require a little background.

As we have already established, Scotland, like much of Europe, entered a period of religious turmoil in the 16th century. In the early days of this struggle—that is, in the days of Mary, Queen of Scots, and John Knox—the struggle raged between Catholics and Protestants; in the next century, after Protestantism had been well-established in Scotland, the struggle would center around the question: "What kind of Protestants do we want to be?" The 17th century kings and their supporters favored an Episcopalian form of religion, such as that established in England, featuring bishops and a hierarchy resembling that of the Catholic Church—except substituting the king for the pope. (You can see why the king liked this.) These kings, who the reader will remember ruled from London (the English and Scottish crowns having been unified in 1603), proved to be just a tad out of touch with their Scottish constituents, who favored a Presbyterian style of worship without hierarchy. Scottish leaders who adhered to this latter school of thought signed a covenant in 1638 to protect what they considered to be "the true religion", and thus the Presbyterians became known as Covenanters. This Presbyterian style would eventually prevail and become the Scottish church of today, but in the late 17th century the matter was by no means settled.

Thus, we come to the unhappy story of the Covenanters in the Whig's Vault at Dunnottar. The Whig's Vault, as it is known today, is really just a cellar—damp, gloomy, and not overly large—situated at the far back side of the castle rock; yet, for two months in 1685 it served as prison for 167 men and women whose only crime was that they would not subscribe to the

Episcopalian prayer book and recognize the spiritual supremacy of the newly crowned King James VII. For nine weeks, these 167 Covenanters shared this cellar in what can only be described as the most squalid of conditions. A book titled *The History of the Sufferings of the Church of Scotland* (not a book recommended for someone looking for a pick-me-up) describes the floor as "full of mire, ankle deep", and notes the room was so crowded that the men and women "could not sit without leaning one upon another"—and then in the mire, it would seem. And as the Covenanters "had no access to ease nature", modesty was apparently out of the question. As for food and water, the Covenanters received only what they could pay for, which was not much. Apparently, when they all left their respective houses the morning of their capture, they hadn't thought to stock their pockets with enough money for a two-month prison stay. How foolish of them.

Under such conditions, matters of religion began to take on a new light for some. Thirty-seven prisoners eventually relented and took an oath of allegiance to the crown to gain their release. This is not remarkable. I would have done so after the first five minutes. What *is* remarkable is that the other 130 did not. Instead many attempted escape—an act requiring a squeeze out the tiny cellar window followed by a harrowing walk along a narrow ledge 160 feet above the crashing waves. Of the twenty-five who attempted this, only eight were successful. Two fell to their deaths on the sharp rocks below, and fifteen were recaptured and tortured for their efforts. Then again, not attempting to escape also proved dangerous. Five Covenanters simply died in the vault from the squalid conditions. It is amazing that the number wasn't higher.

When, after two months of suffering, the more than a hundred remaining prisoners were finally removed from the cellar, it was to be deported to the West Indies to serve as laborers. Seventy of them would die of fever on that journey or shortly after their arrival in the islands. It was a tragic ending to a tragic story, and as I stood in the ill-lit Whig's Vault staring at the damp moss clinging to the walls and trying to imagine what it must have been like to share the room with 166 other people, I had a sudden and very strong urge to be out of that place.

Unlike the Covenanters, I fortunately had that choice and within seconds—though no matter how quickly I walked, it didn't seem fast enough—I was back out in the daylight and standing amongst the grass and the castle ruins atop the rocky peninsula.

And the view was once again breathtaking.

This dichotomy reveals one of the strange truths about Scotland: one would be hard pressed to find another country in the world where so much brutal tragedy is juxtaposed against so much marvelous beauty. I stood for some time on top of the peninsula at Dunnottar, looking at the landscape and the sea. From this angle, the grassy meadows of the mainland could be seen atop the dramatic cliffs, which fell quite perpendicularly to the water. Below, where the cliffs met the sea, the waves had been hard at work over the last several million years, sculpting the rocks and even carving out sea caves: dark openings that instantly drew my curiosity. I found myself thinking what a fascinating place to snorkel it would be, so long as one didn't mind a little hypothermia. Chilled with the thought, I turned my focus to the sky, where scores of birds circled above the cliffs.

Dunnottar may be a difficult place to be a human, but it is a splendid place to be a bird. According to our guidebook, the peninsula serves as quite a hangout for a variety of our feathered friends, including herring gulls, fulmars, kittiwakes, guillemots, razorbills, and the occasional peregrine falcon. It was another bird, however, that captured my curiosity and had me peering over the cliffsides hoping for a glimpse: the strange and lovable puffin. The guidebook contained a picture of the odd-looking birds sunning themselves on a rock. Puffins rank as one of nature's most humorous creations, looking like a cross between a penguin, a parrot and a stuffed animal one might win at a county fair (the kind where the head pops off after five minutes). Rather squat birds with black plumage, white bellies and colorful beaks, they are unmistakable in their goofiness, and I desperately wanted to see one. Unfortunately, the puffins frequent the rock in the spring and early summer, so they were long gone by the time we peered over the cliffs in late July—though they (and every other bird species, it seems) had left plenty of evidence of their presence behind on the rocks. Resembling nothing more than a Jackson Pollock painting, almost every inch of cliff was splattered with droppings.

I wandered back to the car disappointed at missing the puffins but in much better spirits than I had been in the Whig's Vault. There is nothing like a little nature, splendidly reflecting the earth's immutable processes of 400 million years, to make humans and their endeavors fade into insignificance. Though I would hardly try to convince a Covenanter of that sentiment.

•   •   •   •   •

Just over the hill from Dunnottar, we descended into Stonehaven, a pretty coastal town which, over the course of the year, takes on an array of interesting personalities. On New Year's Eve, inhabitants celebrate the ancient ceremony of Fireballs, parading through the streets swinging cages of burning debris to ward off evil spirits. In mid-July, Scots flocking to its pretty beaches are entertained with an annual Folk Festival—which, like the puffins, Katrina and I had just missed. Instead, we arrived just in time for Techno-Rave-Club Night.

Techno-Rave-Club Night was not an official town festival; don't look for it in the guidebook. No, this activity was quite confined to our hotel just off the town square. Actually, it was confined to the room directly beneath ours in the hotel. This we learned upon check-in from the sympathetic clerk at the desk.

"I'm 'fraid there's only one room left," she informed us, looking apologetic. "It's right above the dining room where the kids'll be dancin' tonight." She poked her finger in the direction of a sign which read, "Dancing Tonight, loudest music you've ever heard, 11pm to crack of dawn" or something to that effect.

"Ye can hav it a' half price," she said.

Warily, Katrina held out her hand to receive the key.

We took our bags upstairs to the room, which proved small but tidy enough, and silent for the moment. It was only late afternoon, and we probably should have tried to sneak in a nap then and there, knowing what lay ahead, but we had a town to explore—starting with the pub next door. It was in this pub, after we had ordered up our customary ale and cider and sat sipping them cheerily upon our barstools, that I witnessed a strange and mildly disturbing event.

A young man who looked to be in his early twenties walked in the door, approached the bar, and, in a Scottish accent as thick as any I'd heard, ordered a Budweiser. I paused mid-drink, my lip suspended in creamy ale, and stared in disbelief. The man in question leaned on the counter inches away from tap after tap of flavorful Scottish beer, yet his voice had held no hint of irony as he ordered the biggest mass-market beer in America. I studied his face closely, but it showed no signs of insanity or dimwittedness. I looked to the bartender, but instead of laughing in the young man's face and having him escorted out of the pub, he simply leaned down to a tiny refrigerator beneath the bar, opened it and produced a bottle of Budweiser. I choked, sending a spray of ale onto the bar.

From where I sat, I could see the refrigerator, one of those under-the-counter types with a glass door so that the contents could be seen from the outside. As the condensation on the door cleared, it revealed not just Budweiser, but row after row of cheap, watered-down American beers: Michelob, Miller Lite, even Coors Light. Apparently, this young man was not alone in his tastes. I thought of the heckler from the White Hart Inn in Edinburgh holding his pint up to the light: "Try that wi' Coors Light and ye'll gae blind." What was going on here?

After the young man left with his bottle, I called the bartender over. "I couldn't help notice that that young man ordered a Budweiser," I said, striking a confidential tone as if the absurdity of such an action spoke for itself. The bartender looked at me blankly.

"Doesn't that seem a bit odd," I continued, "when there are so many better beers on tap?"

The bartender just shrugged. "Every lad has his tastes, I s'pose. Dinnae care for the stuff mysel', but a lot of lads order it. 'Specially the young ones."

I pondered this as I sipped my pint. Somehow a trend—if, indeed, it was a trend—of young Scots drinking watered-down American beer just didn't sit well with me. The only rationale I could summon for such a fad was that, by drinking such beer, the youth of Scotland could stay better hydrated and less drunk, allowing them to dance longer at all night techno-rave-clubs. Of course, this rationale only worked at this particular pub in this particular town on this particular night, and didn't begin to explain why this pub, and many others I began to notice over the rest of our stay in Scotland, stocked bottle after bottle of cheap American beer in tiny under-the-counter fridges with glass doors. It was as if it was a secret that only the truly hip knew about: where to get the special, lower-quality product. The thought so depressed me, I put down my unfinished ale and announced the desire to go for a walk. I wanted to see if the rest of Stonehaven was as strange as our hotel and its pub.

I am pleased to say the evening got better from that point. Stonehaven proved a delightful town for walking, and was, we would discover, actually like two towns in one. The regular town, which housed our hotel, featured a main square surrounded by a commercial district and residential houses all bounded by a beautiful, pebble strewn beach; but tucked away just to the south of this stood a separate harbor town, feeling like a tiny, secluded fishing village. A seaside road wound its way around the harbor lined with attractive two-storey buildings, all with gabled roofs, and housing restaurants, shops, and a local history museum. We stopped for dinner at one of the waterfront restaurants, sitting for a pint outside while we waited for our table, enjoying the view of the boats anchored in the harbor. Colorful sailboats with yellow, green and blue hulls reflected in the calm water alongside little motorboats with covered pilothouses perfect for trolling off the coast. It was like being back in the Caribbean, except cooler and with better beer.

After dinner we returned to the main town for an amble along the beach. We were not alone. Local families walked together, children played; some brave soul even swam in the cold water, but the beach was large and everyone felt like they had it to themselves—or at least we did. We walked along fascinated by the pebbles, which were of every color, but particularly of deep pinks and reds.

"Oohh, look at this one," Katrina remarked stooping down to examine a particular stone. She stood up and handed me her prize: a brownish-red rock speckled with hundreds of white, gold and silver flecks. It was the size of my hand.

"Wouldn't that be perfect for the wall I'm building around the patio back home?"

Over the last few years, Katrina had taught herself to build stone walls, and in the process had become something of a rock connoisseur. She would spend hours exploring the beach at home, looking for interesting specimens: a rare color or a unique pattern. She was like a kid in a candy store at Stonehaven, which proved to be a rather aptly named town.

"Yeah, it would stand out. We don't have anything like it at home," I replied, and then made as if to toss the rock back onto the beach.

"Don't do that," Katrina exclaimed, snatching the rock out of my hand. "We're taking it home."

"We're taking a rock home from Scotland?" It seemed there might be more convenient souvenirs to pack in a suitcase.

"Rocks," she said, as she continued scouting the beach, bending over every two or three steps for a closer look. "But just three or four. They'll serve as great reminders of our trip."

"Why can't we just buy postcards like everyone else?"

"Don't worry, I'll put them in *my* bag if they're too heavy for you."

"Ouch."

Thus I found myself stooping on the ground looking for unique specimens to add to Katrina's growing horde. And though I may not have been overly excited about the five hand-sized rocks that ended up in my backpack for the trip home, I had to admit later they did look good in the patio wall and evoked fond memories of a beautiful place.*

---

* Now that I write this, I'm not sure taking stones off a beach in a foreign country and transporting them back to your house is permitted—actually, I'm quite sure it is not. So let's just say that I am not

Those memories, by the way, will selectively end with the walk on the beach, as there is no need to relive the events upon our return to the hotel that evening. We returned to a quiet room, and began to rejoice in our luck, thinking the dance night had been cancelled and wondering if our room discount would still be honored. Then, just as we crawled into bed, it began.

Thump, thump, thump. All bass. The kind you can actually feel coursing through your body when a low-rider, having swapped out its backseat for a sound system, drives by. "Great," said Katrina. "I've been wondering what music we'd get to fall asleep to. I was hoping for a seventies mix, heavy on Abba. But techno works, too."

I looked at my watch. It was just now 11:00. Katrina and I had nearly gone to sleep before the youth of Stonehaven even began their night. Thus, on top of lying in bed with my head bouncing uncontrollably, though rhythmically off my pillow (thump, thump, thump), I got to lie awake pondering just how un-cool I had become. Burying my head in my pillow, I closed my eyes and pictured the youth downstairs, gyrating on the dance floor while holding their Budweisers and Miller Lites. Suddenly, being un-cool seemed just fine. I settled into the night with a smile on my face—and was slowly thumped to sleep.

advocating this at all, and that the whole patio nonsense is just something I thought would have been nice at the time, before we threw the rocks back onto the beach and went back to our hotel room empty-handed.

# Chapter 17: Haunting with Shakespeare

## (Tours of Glamis, Balmoral and Cawdor Castles)

The year 1040 marked a turbulent time in Scotland. The reign of King Duncan I, which to that point had proved unremarkable at best, took a turn for the worse with a disastrous battle against the English at Durham. Later that year, two of Duncan's restless subjects, a high-ranking noble named Macbeth and another named Thorfinn, took matters into their own hands, leading an army against the king near Elgin just off the coast of the Moray Firth. In the course of the ensuing battle, Duncan was slain (some sources say by his own disgruntled men), and Macbeth was shortly thereafter crowned at Scone as the new king of Scotland.

This was not as traitorous as it may seem. Bear in mind that Scotland as a united kingdom had existed for just two centuries at this point—Kenneth MacAlpin having been crowned at Scone in the mid-800s. A hereditary monarchy had not yet been definitively established; indeed, practice at the time followed the old Gaelic tradition of electing each new king via a council made up of the descendants of past kings. The king-elect received the title of "tanist", and was crowned upon the death of the current king. In the 11th century, however, the move toward a hereditary system was catching on and often led to treachery as a way of keeping the monarchy within family bloodlines. Duncan, for example, had been elected tanist only after his grandfather, King Malcolm II, had had Duncan's main rival killed, thereby ensuring the kingship for his grandson. Thus, when Macbeth became king, he did so with the support of many in Scotland, as he had been elected by the council following Duncan's death, and furthermore had as strong a claim to the throne through bloodlines as had the previous king.

Macbeth reigned for seventeen years, and seems to have been a welcome improvement over his predecessor. Indeed, he is styled as "Mac Bethad the renowned" and "the generous king" by two contemporary sources. Fitzroy MacLean, the eminent highland historian, refers to

Macbeth as "an able and reasonably benevolent ruler." One person who most certainly did not share these opinions, however, was another Malcolm, this one the son of the slain Duncan who went by the endearing nickname of Canmore, which means "bighead". In 1057, Malcolm Canmore (or Malcolm Bighead, if you like) successfully overthrew Macbeth, killing the king, and was subsequently crowned himself at Scone as Malcolm III. And thus the wheel of revenge turns.

Five and a half centuries later, the above events were loosely chronicled in what has arguably become the best known literary work of all time set in Scotland: Shakespeare's tragic play *Macbeth*. To say the play has made its mark in the sphere of literature is to not even hint at the position of elevated status it holds. Consider: *Macbeth* is required reading at almost every high school throughout the English speaking world. It has been made into no less than four Hollywood movies, and that's not counting the numerous adaptations spawned by the story, wherein the plot remains similar, but the setting changes to another time or locale. Thus, we have film versions based on *Macbeth* taking place in modern-day Scotland, medieval Japan, gangland Chicago, a hamburger stand in Pennsylvania, mafia-ridden New York, southern Australia, and, my personal favorite, Mumbai, India in a Hindi adaptation called *Maqbool*. The story has been made into two operas, a musical, an animated film, and even a comic book. Finally, to show that no one, not even the sexually depraved, lurk beyond the reach of Shakespeare's power, *Macbeth* was made into a porn film called *In the Flesh* in 1998. And now I think my point is made.

Still, for all its stature, *Macbeth* as a historical source is absolute rubbish. Never mind that the facts and circumstances of events are completely contrived, the very character of Macbeth in Shakespeare's play bears no resemblance to the historical king referenced above. In the play, Macbeth represents a character of moral depravity, a scheming, power-hungry man who goes on a killing spree to overthrow the rightful and good King Duncan and silence any would be opposition (including the wife and children of a leading noble) to his own new role as king. Macbeth is accompanied in his murderous plotting by his wife, Lady Macbeth, whose guilt-ridden bouts of sleepwalking give us some of the most famous lines of literature, to wit: "Out, damned spot, out, I say!" as she tries futilely to wash the indelible blood of her conscience off her hands.* This may be good literature, but as historical commentary it borders on character defamation. Still, we shouldn't be too hard on Shakespeare here. It would seem he came about this "revised" version of events honestly, and further, that this revision would have proved infinitely more pleasing than the truth to Shakespeare's ultimate patron: King James I of England (James VI of Scotland), king at the time of the play's publication.

Let me explain.

Shakespeare took his version of events of Macbeth's life from a work called *Chronicles of England, Scotland and Ireland*, written by Raphael Holinshed and published in the 16th century. Holinshed, for his part, took his version of events from a work called *Historia Gentis Scotorum* (History of the Scottish People) written by Hector Boece and published just a few years before. Boece, as it turns out, was a Scotsman whose major goal in writing his book was to flatter his patron, King James V. James V, claiming kinship with both Duncan and Malcolm Canmore, would have much preferred to think of his ancestors as the righteous men portrayed by Boece than as the truth may otherwise bear out: that is, as borderline incompetent in Duncan's place, and as a vengeful murderer in Malcolm Canmore's. For that matter, this version of events glorifying Duncan and Malcolm and maligning Macbeth appealed equally to Shakespeare, whose patron James I (and VI) was the grandson of James V and, thus, hailed from the same ancestral stock.

All this serves as a very roundabout way of making two points. First, Shakespeare, despite being one of the greatest and most influential writers of all time, was not above sucking up to his royal audience and should not be relied upon as a historical source. Second, it provides a handy—if rather circuitous—way of introducing two of our destinations for the day: the castles of Glamis and Cawdor.

For those needing further help making the connection, I refer you to

---

* The quote is from Act V, Scene 1.

Act I, Scene 3 of *Macbeth*: "All hail, Macbeth! Hail to thee, Thane of Glamis! All hail, Macbeth! Hail to thee, Thane of Cawdor! All hail, Macbeth, that shalt be king hereafter!"

Hey, I said it was circuitous.

•   •   •   •   •

After our day at Dunnottar, Katrina and I felt in the mood to take in a few more castles, and northeastern Scotland offers plenty from which to choose. Castle sightseeing qualifies as big business in northeastern Scotland, where tourists can actually sign up for pre-packaged tours to shuttle them from one ancient specimen to the next upon a route known as the Castle Trail. This works out splendidly for those who like to spend their holidays traveling in groups full of people they have never met—and apparently this is a common breed, as visitors to Scotland can sign up for pre-packaged tours focused on any number of singular interests. Besides castle tours, one finds whisky tours, which go from one distillery to the next (sampling as they go), golf tours, literary tours, pub tours, and probably a dozen more I simply haven't seen the signs for yet.

Katrina and I, shying away from group travel, devised our own plan for the day, inspired nonetheless by the itinerary of a combined literary and castle tour. (Genius!) We would visit two castles associated with Shakespeare's *Macbeth*, Glamis* and Cawdor, and in between, would swing by the castle of Balmoral, which serves as a royal residence each summer when Britain's monarchs flock north for some cool air and woodland scenery. This itinerary carried an added bonus: as Balmoral and Cawdor lay nestled deep in the highlands, we would finally cross that seemingly impassable barrier, the Highland Line, which had kept us at bay for the last two days. Of course, Glamis lay below the Highland Line, and well to the south of Stonehaven where we woke up that morning. Thus, after a hearty breakfast we found ourselves pointing the Fiat Crumb once again to the

---

* A pronunciation tip is in order here. Glamis, despite looking like it wants to be pronounced "Glam-iss", is actually just one syllable: "Glahms", as I was informed by several amused Scots on my visit.

south, backtracking across much of the ground we had traveled the day before. It would prove to be the last bat of the highland flipper.

At the start of Shakespeare's play, Macbeth holds the title Thane of Glamis, and much of the major action, including the treacherous murder of the visiting King Duncan, takes place inside Macbeth's Glamis Castle. Understandably, much is made of this by the caretakers of the real Glamis Castle today. During our tour, Katrina and I were treated to a view of Duncan's Hall, where the murder supposedly took place, and quotes from the play figured prominently in the castle's brochure, and why not? Ok, Macbeth never actually held the title Thane of Glamis, and sure, Duncan actually met his death near Elgin, miles to the north, but I tell you this: if Shakespeare featured my home as the setting of one of his plays, I wouldn't be too bothered about the details while bragging to the neighbors. But all of this is quite beside the point, because here's the thing: regardless of one's stance on historical accuracy and even if you care not a lick for Shakespearean brilliance, Glamis is every bit worth a visit.

First off, there is the approach. A narrow lane serving as the castle's driveway winds its way through acre after acre of woodland. For a time we saw nothing but trees. Then, as the road straightened, distant hills came into view, followed by the flying turrets and pointed roofs of the castle nestled in the valley below. As we drew near, more and more of the castle, from the top down, came into view, until finally the whole of its massive, pink-stone grandeur was revealed. And it was massive. I don't know how many rooms the castle has, but in a photograph I took of it, I can count over a hundred windows—and that's just looking at one side! There is something humbling about approaching such a structure in a Fiat Crumb, though I imagine it would be just as humbling in a Bentley or stretch limousine. Glamis is the kind of castle that should only be approached on horseback.

It has not always been so grand. The castle that now comprises Glamis started as a hunting lodge used by kings in the 11$^{th}$ century.[*] In 1372, it was

---

[*] As such, it is likely that the real Macbeth actually did visit on occasion. Rather ironically, Malcolm II— Duncan's grandfather—did die there.

given to the Earl of Strathmore and Kinghorne by King Robert II, and since that time the estate has been in the hands of the Earl's descendants, the Bowes-Lyon family, who greatly expanded the structure over the centuries, making it into the fairytale castle one sees today. Though you may not recognize the Bowes-Lyon name, I'd bet my house you're familiar with the castle's most famous resident: Lady Elizabeth Bowes-Lyon, better known for the latter half of the 20th century as the Queen Mother. If you need more help still, she's the kindly looking elderly woman wearing a hat (always) that appeared near the center of any photograph of the royal family prior to her death in 2002.

The Queen Mum, to use her endearing nickname, was the daughter of the 14th Earl of Strathmore, and as such, spent much of her childhood running through the halls of Glamis Castle—an appropriate beginning for a life which turned out to be something of a fairytale itself. In 1923, she married Prince Albert, the younger son of King George V, after turning him down on four previous occasions. Thirteen years later, she became Queen of England when her husband's older brother, who was by this time King Edward VIII, unexpectedly abdicated the throne to pursue a love affair with a married American woman. Is it any wonder the royal family just can't stay out of the tabloids?

Lady Elizabeth served as queen until her husband's death in 1952, at which point her daughter was crowned as Queen Elizabeth II. Her reign may have been over, but Lady Elizabeth still had plenty of life ahead. As Queen Mum, she lived to the ripe age of 101, winning the enduring love of the British people—but nowhere does she remain closer to the heart today than at Glamis. Her memory abounds throughout the castle. On the tour, Katrina and I were treated to a viewing of her bed, her dolls, her photographs, and even wonderful tales from her childhood, such as the time she and her brother dumped cold water on approaching guests to simulate the dumping of boiling oil onto invaders at the castle gate. Now there's an image to try to rectify with the elderly woman in the hat.

All of this may be fine for those fascinated by the royal family (and this includes many), but, for me, the real charm of Glamis lay in other quarters.

Some of these qualified as simply amusing, such as the paintings in the castle's chapel by Jacob de Wet. The reader will recall de Wet as the painter who churned out portrait after portrait of comical-looking kings hanging in Holyrood Palace. At Glamis, de Wet again leaves his audience scratching their heads as they view depictions of biblical scenes which look relatively normal until one notes St. Peter wearing a pair of spectacles and Christ sporting a rather dapper hat. Keeping with the theme, I half expected to see St. Luke wearing a Lakers jersey and listening to an iPod. Where did de Wet come up with these things?

More intriguing still are the stories of the castle's many ghosts. Glamis ranks as one of Scotland's most haunted castles, being frequented by no less than five spirits, though some sources claim even more. This spectral cast includes a knight in armor who tends to enter rooms and loom over beds of rather startled guests; a woman with no tongue who wanders the grounds pointing at her mutilated face and presumably saying, "mmmph, mmph, mmmmmmmph!"; a young black boy, the ghost of an ill-treated 18th century servant who inhabits a chair outside the Queen Mother's bedroom; and, most famously, a specter known as the "Grey Lady", thought to be the ghost of Janet Douglas, wife of the 6th Earl, who was burned as a witch in 1537 and since then has been known to loiter in the castle's chapel.

These sightings aren't reported by just the occasional nutcase after too many drams of whisky. No, these ghosts are reportedly seen frequently and by a number of different (and quite sober) witnesses. Indeed, on one occasion, over a hundred people claimed to simultaneously see the Grey Lady. The way the ghosts are talked about on the tour and in the castle literature, it would appear that their presence, far from doubted, has gained acceptance as a fact of life in the castle by the residing family—all of which quite guarantees I will never be found within five miles of Glamis after sunset.

Still, that doesn't mean I can't appreciate a good ghost story or two, and one in particular caught my interest as we wandered the castle halls. We had toured a number of formal rooms, rife with paintings, fine furniture and other delicate relics when suddenly we descended a staircase and entered a room called the crypt. The change in atmosphere was dramatic: the walls and ceiling had been left bare stone, decorated with the mounted antlers and heads of various animals, and cluttered with arms and armor. The decor alone would have made it my favorite room in the castle—the sort of place one might stumble across Shaggy and Scooby Doo cowering behind a shield—but it got even more interesting when we learned about the secret it supposedly contained. The crypt's two windows stood recessed many feet back from the interior of the room, giving the impression that the walls are impressively thick. Our guide informed us that this is deceiving, however, and that the space between the windows actually houses a lost room, sealed hundreds of years ago.

Legends abound regarding the discovery of this room. My favorite claims that guests hung towels from every window and then went outside for a look only to find that one window had no towel, even though they were sure they hadn't missed any. This tale begged the following question, which I asked our guide: why not just fetch a ladder and investigate the window from the outside? The answer, predictably, centered around a supposed curse which would mean death to anyone entering the room.

"Ah, of course," Katrina responded to this news. "A curse."

A more pragmatic explanation might suggest the family is simply not all that interested in finding out (or revealing, as the case may be) what's inside—the assumption being that the truth qualifies as either too horrible to behold (the room contains the bones of dead puppies) or too boring to make a good story (the room contains the hot water heater). Naturally, in the absence of certainty a tantalizing legend has emerged to explain the existence of the room and the strange noises many guests have heard coming out of it.

Legend has it that sometime in the 15th century a visiting Earl was playing cards with the then current Lord Glamis and losing quite badly, to the point that Lord Glamis put away his cards and advised his guest to quit. Offended, the visiting Earl, who had had quite a lot to drink, stood up and bellowed through the castle that somebody—a family member, a servant, anybody—had better play cards with him. There were no takers, it being a

Sunday, and thus the Earl, in a wonderfully pouty moment, stated that he would then play cards with the Devil himself—at which point a tall, dark stranger appeared at the door (suspiciously adorned with horns and pitchfork?) and agreed to play cards. They went into the now secret room, which was instantly and magically sealed, and the pair was never seen again, though castle guests to this day report hearing the sounds of dice and swearing coming from the room from time to time.

This makes a fun story, though it likely would not have stuck with me were it not for one detail I have left out to this point: the cranky Earl was known as Beardie Crawford.

How about that for an unexpected twist? There I stood enjoying a little ghost story, when all of a sudden the Crawford name (attached to the wonderfully descriptive moniker "Beardie", no less) suddenly appeared front and center in a public forum.

"Are you kidding me?" I whispered to Katrina as we walked to the next room. "Crawfords storm castles, drive away Vikings, save the lives of kings, and get strung up to die by traitorous English soldiers, yet can't get a public acknowledgment; but here a belligerent drunk who sells his soul *to the devil* to support a *gambling habit* is suddenly a man worth talking about."

"Oh, go easy on ol' Uncle Beardie," Katrina said. "At least someone is keeping the name alive. Is it too late to add a pitchfork and a Jack of Diamonds to the family crest?"

Of course, this Beardie Crawford doesn't really qualify as a Crawford at all, as I quickly pointed out to Katrina. He was a Lindsay, Alexander Lindsay, the 4th Earl of Crawford to be exact, of the line that took over the original Crawford barony after the male heirs died out and the surviving daughter married a Lindsay (see chapter 7 for a refresher course, if you must).

"Well, that explains why he got a mention at all," Katrina whispered back. "If he was a real Crawford, the poor Earl would be stuck in that room swearing away and going further into debt to the devil, and not a single person in Scotland would notice."

A very sensible, if unfortunate point.

And with that, perhaps we should just leave Glamis behind, noting that it was wonderful and well worth the stop, though I highly recommend going in broad daylight and with company.

· · · · ·

Leaving Glamis, we finally accomplished the seemingly impossible: we traveled north and within five miles crossed the Highland Line. This is, of course, a rather notional concept. It's not as if a yellow line chalked across the countryside delineates the border (though it did appear so on our map), but other indications do serve to let travelers know they have left Lowland Scotland. For starters, the road took our protesting Fiat Crumb on a steady climb into the Grampian Mountains, and before too long we passed signs for towns with names like Glen Isla and Glen Shee, suggesting our proximity to those quintessential highland features: glens, the steep-sided valleys so common in the highlands. We passed an increasing number of peaks, rising higher and higher, and saw signs for ski resorts, though the slopes were devoid of snow and deserted in the last days of July.

The mountains here hardly qualified as imposing. Most stood comfortably under 3,000 feet in height and were rounded with centuries of wind and rain, much like the mountains of Pennsylvania. The change of scenery proved nonetheless refreshing, and promised to get even better with each passing mile.

Indeed, the route took us through the town of Braemar, a tourist headquarters that hosts the most famous highland games in Scotland, the Braemar Gathering (though we were sadly a full month early for the event), and sits within the borders of the recently established Cairngorms National Park. Here the scenery was undoubtedly highland, with steep mountainsides covered in purple heather and pale green grass. Our Fiat Crumb took on a noticeably meandering pattern, as I spent more and more time looking at the scenery and less and less looking at the road.

The Cairngorms, which received national park status the year of our visit, arguably constitute Britain's most impressive mountain range with fifty-two peaks rising over 2,700 feet within the park's borders. Ecologically, they represent a hugely important and diverse area, with vegetation ranging from one of the largest remaining tracts of ancient Caledonian forest in its northern and central valleys to sub-arctic tundra on the high plateau. The preservation of these beautiful, but sensitive areas must be balanced with the fact that the region also ranks as one of the most popular tourist destinations in Scotland, with outdoor enthusiasts flocking to its many ski resorts and hiking trails. But it is the exploration of a trail of a very different sort that lures even more people into the region each year. I speak of the Malt Whisky Trail, a route winding its way through the more than fifty distilleries populating the Spey Valley just to the north of the park.

Whisky means serious business in this part of Scotland. For centuries homemade stills took advantage of the clear waters of the River Spey until finally, in 1823, Parliament gave in and began issuing licenses to the illicit distilleries, many of which promptly evolved into multi-million dollar businesses and spearheaded what today comprises one of Scotland's most profitable industries. Some of these distilleries are instantly recognizable to even non-whisky drinkers (Glenfiddich and Glenlivet, for example), but most remain more obscure, though with strong local followings, and almost all of them offer tours, bringing in visitors by the droves. Our guidebook noted that most people travel the Malt Whisky Trail by car, though it is possible to walk or even cycle parts of the route. Traveling a route that cleverly combined large quantities of alcohol consumption with weaving pedestrians, cyclists, and automobiles all sharing the same road space did seem like a diverting way to spend a day, but in the end, we decided to stick to our less risky castle tour. Thus a few miles to the east of Braemar, we arrived at Balmoral.

If you are one of the millions of people who have visited Walt Disneyland or Walt Disneyworld in recent decades, you have a pretty good idea of what Balmoral Castle looks like. For Balmoral strikes the very image of a fairytale castle. It may be a bit more squarish than the Disney version, but its crenellated, white-stone tower house with pointed turrets in each corner certainly arise from the same fanciful architectural spirit. Not to mention Balmoral has one very important edge over its Disney counterpart: Balmoral serves as a real and quite inhabited castle.

Originally a product of the 16th century, Balmoral Castle was razed and rebuilt in a similar but larger fashion in the mid-1800s after being purchased by Queen Victoria and her husband, Prince Albert. Modern artillery and weaponry having by this time rendered castle warfare obsolete, the Queen ordered Balmoral rebuilt more for comfortable living than defense. Attached to its impressive tower house—which despite the preceding sentence does offer the appearance of strength—sprawls an equally impressive manor house, quite unburdened by defensive walls and surrounded by beautiful gardens. The whole resides in a clearing of some of the most beautiful forest imaginable, full of towering pines intermixed with birches, oaks and other deciduous trees, so that the castle remains quite hidden until one enters the clearing. From the highway, Katrina and I were just able to glimpse the pointed roofs of its tower and a fluttering flag or two sticking up beyond the tops of the pine forest.

It is this combination of seclusion and beauty that so impressed Queen Victoria when she first visited the highlands in 1842. The trip would reverse the trend of the previous 250 years, in which the highlands were all but forgotten, other than as a source of trouble, by Britain's monarchs. Indeed, Victoria was so taken with the highlands that, six years later, she leased Balmoral, having never actually seen the castle. She clearly was not disappointed with her choice, as, four years into the lease, the family jumped at the chance to purchase the castle outright, along with 50,000 acres of surrounding woodland on the River Dee. Balmoral, described by Victoria as her "dear paradise in the highlands", has served as the official summer retreat for the royal family ever since.

As a royal residence treasured for its seclusion, the castle does not go out of its way to encourage visitation. Despite warnings in our guidebook, Katrina and I paid for the guided tour through the castle, which took us through just two rooms—the ballroom and an exhibition room—and proved every bit as unimpressive as had been suggested. Still, it's hard to blame the royal family. Had I discovered such a phenomenal spot and had the wherewithal to purchase it, I would hardly have rushed to invite the general public to come hang out with me. The fact that we had the option to stroll through the gardens (which we did) or tour the grounds on horseback (which we did not) or be pulled around the grounds in a trailer by a farm tractor (which, most unfortunately, we did not) seemed quite generous, all things considered. For an American comparison, just try strolling through the Rose Garden at the White House or going horseback riding through Camp David and see how far you get before a burly man in a cheap suit and Burt Reynolds sunglasses gently escorts you to the nearest correctional facility.

Still, without much to see, we didn't linger long at Balmoral—which suggests that the royal family's plan is working—and were soon in the car driving yet further north.

Cawdor, by comparison, would be much more diverting. It was the second of the two "Macbeth" castles on our itinerary, and like Glamis, its actual connections to the historical Macbeth proved somewhat of a sham. In the play, Macbeth receives the title Thane of Cawdor after the previous Thane is stripped of his title and executed for, ironically, treason. The real life Macbeth, however, would have been quite bewildered upon receiving such a title, as it would have meant he was now lord over an empty field. Almost three hundred years would pass before Cawdor Castle finally materialized in the early 14th century.*

Like at Glamis, we did not regret our visit to Cawdor. It ranked as one of my favorite castles of the trip, mainly because it had all the features that a castle was supposed to have according to my childhood training on castle stereotypes: a drawbridge that lowered down over a moat (now just a dry ditch), a trap door that dropped unsuspecting visitors into a tiny dungeon below (neat!), and a beautiful tower house, not quite as impressive as

---

* The name of Cawdor itself is not recorded in any form prior to the Norman invasion of 1066. Malcolm III, who succeeded Macbeth, was king of Scotland by this point, and Macbeth was dead, making it all the more difficult for the latter to have received the title of Thane of Cawdor.

Glamis or Balmoral, but full of crenellated parapets and round turrets nonetheless.

We took the tour, which proved much more revealing than that of Balmoral. The current owners, the Campbell family, still reside in the castle for part of the year, but that doesn't keep them from sharing it with guests, who are treated to a thorough inspection of stairwells and ancient rooms full of tapestries, paintings, furniture, rusted tools, and—reminiscent of Scone and Glamis—a touching selection of family photographs, which I continue to assert adds a nice, homey touch to any castle. The tour also took visitors into Cawdor's underground vaults where, besides the aforementioned dungeon, one can marvel at the Thorn Room, which boasts a preserved holly tree, carbon-dated to 1372,* growing out of the floor in the center of the room. The tree, a left-over symbol from pagan times and likely the reason the castle was built on this particular spot, supposedly wards off fairies and evil spirits—implying that besides a drawbridge and trap door, Cawdor also has a little touch of magic. Can a castle get more perfect than that?

Outside, we explored the grounds, which also conformed nicely to childhood expectations. In addition to the moat, they featured a hedge maze, a beautiful garden bursting with flowers of every color, and beckoning paths to take visitors through the surrounding woodlands. On a whim, we picked one that looked inviting.

The path followed a little creek—known as a "burn" in Scotland— away from the castle, and very quickly we found ourselves in deep forest. The trees closed in, giving the impression that we ambled miles from anywhere, rather than just a few hundred yards from the castle. The size of the trees added to this effect. They were huge. Mixed in with the native oaks, pines and beeches stood imported specimens of redwoods, sequoias and Douglas firs: the biggest trees North America has to offer. Katrina posed in front of a redwood with her arms outstretched at her sides, but the tree extended beyond her reach by another foot in either direction. We felt

---

* This date, entirely coincidentally, is the same date that Glamis was given to the 1st Earl of Strathmore and Kinghorne. There is no apparent connection, though it is tempting to try to make one.

like dwarves in a magical forest and lingered far longer than we had intended, overcome with the simple thrill of being outdoors.

We had seen eight castles and two churches in the last four days. It had been wonderful, but we now felt the draw of nature that inevitably overtakes one in a place as beautiful as Scotland. The country demands an interactive outdoor experience, and, as we reluctantly pulled ourselves away from the forest and headed back to the car, we knew the focus of our trip was about to change once more. We had delved into family roots. We had ambled through the man-made halls of the Scottish nobility.

The time had come to embrace the highlands.

# Part Three

## Into the Highlands

# Chapter 18: The Fall and Rise of Tartan

## (From Culloden to Inverness)

Historian Fitzroy MacLean begins his book, *Highlanders: A History of the Scottish Clans*, with the following quote:

> *"To the southern inhabitants of Scotland, the state of the mountains and the islands is equally known with that of Borneo and Sumatra: of both they have heard little and guess the rest."*

The quote comes from Dr. Samuel Johnson, a British writer who lived his entire life within a few hundred miles of the highlands, yet took what MacLean calls a "voyage of discovery" to the region in 1773. I use Dr. Johnson's quote again now because it sums up better than anything I have heard the simple truth about the Scottish highlands: they are a world apart from the rest of Britain.

Until very recent times, and indeed, continuing today by some, highlanders have spoken a different language (Gaelic), worn different clothes (plaids, for example), and in general led a completely different way of life from their lowland counterparts. Thus, when Dr. Johnson visited the highlands just over two hundred years ago, he could without exaggeration compare the experience to visiting a foreign country half way around the globe.

One may ask how this is possible on an island the size of Britain, a landmass smaller than the state of Michigan, which had been inhabited for no less than 6,000 years by the time of Johnson's journey—plenty of time to venture out and meet the neighbors, so to speak. The answer stems from the region's topography. As the reader will recall from chapter 12, the highlands arose, quite literally, over 400 million years ago, when a collision of tectonic plates pushed a chunk of land several thousand feet higher than the low-lying areas adjacent to it. At first, the highlands would have consisted of an immense plateau, fairly uniform in height across the region, but over the course of millions of years running streams, freezing and thawing ice, and fierce winds would slowly carve that plateau into the steep mountains and narrow valleys characterizing the region today. The result of this rugged landscape was isolation: not just from the rest of Britain, but even from one valley to the next.

Thus, human history in the highlands came to be dominated by the clan system, with clans being defined as family groups, such as the MacLeans, the Camerons, or the Grahams, whose members shared a common ancestry and occupied defined regions within the highlands. Major clans, such as the MacDonalds, were further broken down into sub-clans, such as the MacDonalds of Glencoe, which though still part of the overall Clan MacDonald would go about their daily lives in a smaller group, only coming together with the larger clan in times of need or periodic celebration. It was not unusual for these sub-clans to be contained to just a single valley, and, thus, members knew every inch of their territory and became quite attached to it as a result.

Of course, topography only helped to perpetuate what was already inherent in the culture of the region's original settlers. The highlands were settled from Ireland, rather than from mainland Europe as was the rest of Britain, excepting Wales and Cornwall. Thus, highland culture has its roots in Celtic traditions, which explains not only the strong emphasis on clan structure, but also the fact that the first language of the highlands for all but very recent history has been Gaelic.* Still, it is the isolation caused by the rugged landscape that helped this Celtic-based highland culture to resist the same Anglicization which permeated life in lowland Scotland. Indeed, life in the steep, secluded valleys likely even helped to strengthen the clan system over the years, rather than allow it to fade out.

Naturally, this isolation acted in two directions. Just as highlanders were able to maintain their own culture relatively free of English influences, so were their southern neighbors able to remain astoundingly ignorant of highland culture. As tends to happen, societies compensate for ignorance by

---

* As of the 2001 census, at least 60,000 Scots were still speaking fluent Gaelic, though the number of people who have varying levels of proficiency in the language may be as high as 250,000.

applying sweeping stereotypes that cater to their worst fears or reinforce their own feelings of superiority. Thus, the English and even lowland Scots came to view highlanders as a barbarous race, or in the words of an Ayrshire resident: "a host of savages… more terrible than Turks or Tartars." No offense to Turks or Tartars, I'm sure. Further to the point, our guidebook told of a lowland poet, writing in the 17th century, who "suggested that God had created the first Highlander out of horseshit. When God asked his creation what he would do, the reply was 'I will doun to the Lowland, Lord, and thair steill a kow.'"

History shows that highlanders themselves did not always help dispel beliefs of this perceived barbarity. For example, in 1654, when the chief of Clan Cameron, a man known as the Great Lochiel, ripped out an English soldier's throat with his teeth—an action he later referred to as "the sweetest bite I ever had"—it probably didn't help to persuade the rest of Britain of highland civility. Nor did the actions of Clan MacFarlane's chief, upon learning that his wife had slept with the chief of a rival clan. In a response that left little doubt as to how MacFarlane felt about the matter, he promptly killed the rival chief, set fire to his house, and served the man's genitals to his wife for supper. But perhaps nothing did more to strike fear into the hearts of lowlanders than the practice of the famed "highland charge". This battle technique entailed highlanders sweeping down the steep side of a valley toward the enemy accompanied by bloodcurdling screams. Such methods reinforced the highlanders' image as barbarians in the minds of the English, who preferred killing their enemies in nice straight lines, though I think any of us could be forgiven for not wanting to be in the path of a large body of men in kilts, screaming at the top of their lungs and bearing down at a full sprint brandishing claymores.

In the end, most highlanders wouldn't have minded being branded as barbarians by lowland Scots, the English, or anyone else for that matter if that had only meant they would be left alone. Unfortunately, this was not to be, as any study of highland history will reveal. And nowhere would this sad truth become more apparent or more tragic than at our first stop after leaving Cawdor: the battlefield of Culloden.

• • • • •

On the morning of April 16, 1746, five thousand weary highlanders lined up at the southwest end of Culloden Moor, a bleak expanse of heather, bog, and coarse grass some five miles east of the highland city of Inverness. Many of them had been up all night, engaged in a fruitless attempt to raid an enemy camp never found in the darkness. The previous day, each man had received a single biscuit for sustenance. Across the field, ten thousand British soldiers, led by the king's son, the Duke of Cumberland, stared back at the highlanders through well-rested eyes. Between the two armies lay the open moor, offering little shelter and no high ground from which to sweep down on an enemy in a terror-inspiring highland charge. Needless to say, it was not an opportune time or place for a battle, if you were a highlander.

The battle was being waged to settle once and for all who should rule as the rightful king of Britain. The British troops supported the reigning king, George II, who stemmed from the Hanover line, a German family related to the Stuarts through marriage. George II's father, George I, had ascended to the throne following the death of his cousin, Queen Anne, who had ruled as the last Stuart monarch, a proud line that had begun with King Robert II nearly 400 years earlier.

The highlanders, for their part, didn't think much of a German king, especially one who hadn't shown the least interest in Scotland. Instead, they championed James Edward Stuart, the son of James II (VII of Scotland), the latter of whom had been forced off the throne and replaced with his half-sister Mary and her husband, William of Orange, during the Glorious Revolution of 1689. Supporters of James Edward, or the Old Pretender, as he was known, called themselves Jacobites, stemming from Jacobus, the Latin name for James. The Old Pretender had been living in exile in France and Italy since a few weeks after his birth and, with the aid of his Jacobite followers, had tried before—most notably in an ill-fated 1715 revolt—to capture the throne he believed to be rightfully his. Now, three decades later, the aging and still exiled king was giving it another shot, this time championed by his charismatic and ambitious son, Charles Edward Stuart, inevitably referred to as the Young Pretender, though I much prefer his highland nickname: Bonnie Prince Charlie.

Despite having no knowledge of Gaelic, a tenuous grasp of English, and no military training, the Bonnie Prince had landed on the west coast of Scotland in the summer of 1745, his first time on British soil, and boldly raised the Royal Standard. Since that time, thousands of loyal Jacobites had rallied to his side, most of them highlanders, and had helped the Young Pretender to victory after victory on the battlefield. Indeed, his army had captured Perth and Edinburgh, and even invaded England, marching all the way to Derby, 130 miles north of London, before deciding they shouldn't press their luck much further. Returning to Scotland, the Prince consolidated his forces at Inverness, deep in the highlands whose inhabitants made up the bulk of his support. It was now seven months into his revolution, and his army had yet to lose a battle.

Thus, when word came that the British forces had been reinforced under the Duke of Cumberland and were marching toward Inverness, Bonnie Prince Charlie and his followers confidently went out to meet them—and so found themselves gathered on Culloden Moor under the conditions previously described.

The battle went as the reader has probably guessed. The British troops opened with a barrage of artillery which lasted an hour, thinning the ranks of highlanders who had almost no artillery of their own with which to respond. As the guns paused, the highlanders charged—as they had done so successfully time and again in recent months—but on the open ground of Culloden Moor, they had no chance. Many died from British bullets. Those who made it all the way across the field met their fate at the end of a bayonet. Less than half an hour later, the battle was over—though the carnage was not. The British soldiers, on orders from the Duke of Cumberland, finished off any wounded highlanders found on the battlefield, slaughtering them mercilessly with their swords and muskets, and even with fire: thirty were burnt alive near a cottage on the moor. All in all 1,500 highlanders died that day, though many more would be hunted down and executed in the following weeks. British losses numbered less than sixty.

The Battle of Culloden marked a turning point in British history. Most immediately, it represented the end of Jacobite hopes to reclaim the throne for the Stuarts. Bonnie Prince Charlie did survive the battle, only to embark on a five-month flight from house to house to avoid capture, an action often requiring the use of disguises—such as the time he dressed up as an Irish kitchen maid, answering to the name of Betty Burke, to be rowed from one island to another. He eventually found his way onto a French ship and returned to the safety of continental Europe where he was able to finish out his days in a drunken stupor, but never again would he pose a threat to the British throne.

Much more tragically, Culloden marked the end of highland life as it once was. Following the battle, Parliament passed a Disarming Act, aimed at breaking the power of the clans and suppressing the highland lifestyle. Through this Act, weapons were banned, as one might expect, but so too were such activities as the wearing of tartan and the playing of bagpipes. English-only schools were established to root out the Gaelic language—a tactic used quite effectively more than a century later by the U.S. government in its bid to eradicate the various American Indian cultures. Most crushingly, many clans who had supported the rebellion lost the title to their land—their most vital link to economic support.

On top of these changes, there were simply less people left in the highlands to cause trouble. Many of those who survived the revolution were transported to the English colonies in North America and the West Indies as punishment. With much of the land now in government hands and the military function of the clan system suppressed, an economic upheaval occurred in the highlands, which led to the eviction of thousands of families from their land, a phenomenon now known as the Highland Clearances. Given such harsh times, many more chose to emigrate of their own accord, sailing to the colonies or moving to the cities. As a result, the population of the highlands—and therefore the power of the clans—declined rapidly.

Today, the Scottish highlands have a population density less than that of Sweden, Norway or even Papua New Guinea. Consider that.

Katrina and I knew very little about Culloden prior to visiting the battlefield. We had added it to our itinerary on the advice of a friend, who had simply referred to it as a tragic battle. Tragic, indeed. We walked around the visitor center and attempted to take it all in. The center was exceptionally well done, with an introductory film about the battle, a museum containing swords, muskets, clothing and other relics of the period, and displays on key figures involved, such as Bonnie Prince Charlie and the Duke of Cumberland—the latter of whom, following the battle, sported the well-earned nickname, the "butcher". The center was fascinating and depressing all at once, but it did give us a very good sense of the context surrounding the battle.

Thus informed, we went outside and walked around the battlefield which still looks very much as it would have on that fateful day two and a half centuries ago, except that now a series of paths winds its way through to take visitors past key points of interest. One of the most evocative modifications the battlefield's caretakers have made is to place stone markers here and there on the moor, engraved with clan names, to mark where members of each clan lined up at the start of the battle, and then, where many of them fell. This seems a simple gesture, but the effect, as we walked past marker after marker engraved with names—MacLean, Cameron, Mackintosh, etc.—was incredibly moving. I found myself standing next to particular stones and gazing across the open moor to where the English soldiers would have been standing, trying to imagine what it would feel like. Needless to say, I could not.

What I could do, however, was look at the moor and get a sense for just what a terrible spot it seemed to have a battle. Tangled heather grew everywhere—not big enough to offer shelter, but plenty big enough to trip up a man trying to run. Bogs of standing water and marshy ground only complicated things further. Had I tried to run across it—even empty-handed and with nothing to do but watch where I put my feet—I would have been face down within three steps, soaked from head to toe and looking like someone on the losing end of a mud wrestling match. How anyone charged across brandishing a revolver and sword while trying to evade oncoming bullets simply defied my comprehension.

We wandered for close to an hour on the moor, but soon felt compelled to head back to the car and move on. My state of mind reminded me of the time I'd toured the Holocaust Museum in Washington, D.C. It had been a hugely interesting and informative experience, though one that was completely heart wrenching. After the tour, I had walked away from the museum glad I had visited, but not able to claim I had enjoyed it. I felt that way now as we left Culloden.

• • • • •

Now some brighter news.

Something as sturdy and rooted as highland culture couldn't stay down forever, and, indeed, within a few decades of Culloden, a revival of sorts had already begun. Ironically, much of this revival can be attributed to the efforts of an Englishman and two lowland Scots, all of whom helped romanticize the highlands through their writings. As the end of the 18th century neared, people all over Britain were reading Dr. Samuel Johnson's account of his journey to the highlands, mentioned at the beginning of this chapter. Likewise, they were enthralled by the poetry, written in hearty Scots dialect, of Robbie Burns and, as the 19th century dawned, the romantic novels of Sir Walter Scott.

Scott's efforts, as we have seen, went beyond his writings. I have shared already the story of his search for the Honours of Scotland and of his petitions to bring Mons Meg back to Scottish soil, but perhaps nothing did more to revive an interest in Scottish—and specifically highland—culture than the role he played in King George IV's visit to Scotland in 1822.

To mark the king's visit, the first of any reigning monarch since 1650, Scott somehow convinced George IV to dress in full highland regalia. To fully appreciate this requires a mental image. So, imagine, if you will, a 280-pound man of rather short stature (if you have trouble with this, Dom Deloise will serve), dressed fully and completely in bright red tartan. The king's plaid was fashioned in vestments for his upper body and, below, formed into a pleated kilt, though a rather short one at that. To try to slim his fat legs, the monarch had donned flesh-colored tights, much to the amusement of his Scottish subjects. If you have successfully developed this image in your mind, you will have some idea of what a tremendously good sport the king must have been. British caricaturists had a heyday with the visit, lampooning the king so relentlessly that, by comparison, today's politicians seem to get off rather easily. Regardless of how ridiculous he looked, however, the king's efforts were appreciated and sparked off a full-scale revival in tartan.*

This revival received an additional boost from the well-timed efforts of a few individuals, some with very dubious credentials, to research and catalogue the various clan tartans—an effort which has resulted in the scores of tartan guides, featuring names like *Hey, What's My Tartan?* or *Your Family Tartan Explained*, available for purchase in gift shops across Scotland today. This concept of specific patterns of tartan being associated with specific families was quite a new one in the early 19th century—indeed, it was essentially invented at that time.** Prior to this, some highland clans may have been more prone to certain patterns than others, but, historically, most wore whatever material they could get, and then the cloth was almost always dyed such that it blended in with the natural environment to offer the wearer a degree of camouflage. Consider this in regards to the garish red worn by George IV, whose only hope of avoiding notice would have been to stand in front of a parked fire truck.

To be fair, the tartan researchers did base some of the patterns on historical evidence and consultation with actual clan members, but they

---

* The Disarming Act, banning the wearing of tartan, had been repealed in 1782.
** According to MacLean, the generally accepted tartans assigned to each clan today were presented by two brothers, known as the Sobieski Stewart brothers (but about whom little is known), in their book *Vestiarium Scoticum*, published in the early 19th century. Another book, called *Scottish Gael*, was published by James Logan in 1831 on the same subject.

undoubtedly took huge liberties to fill in the gaps—a fact that becomes rather evident when one considers that lowland families, who just a half century before would have looked upon anything remotely associated with the highlands as deserving of disdain, were suddenly assigned clan tartans. Thus it is that the Crawfords, a family entirely associated with lowland Scotland, received a tartan, and—no matter how ridiculous this seems—I couldn't be happier for it.

In fact, most people reacted this way to the new tartans. The numerous clan societies that had sprouted at the turn of the 19th century as a way to maintain clan pride and identity readily endorsed the patterns. These clan societies continue today, uniting members from around the world and keeping them in touch with their Scottish roots, and clan tartans remain central to their identity. I suppose the effect compares to wearing a team uniform: it makes each individual feel like a part of the whole. But there exists this crucial difference: as a fan, one can don the jersey of any team he so chooses—and even change tastes once in a while depending on a team's success (though I know the reader would never go in for such shameless bandwagoning)—but one has to be a member of the family to wear its clan tartan. It is not something one chooses; it is a privilege into which one is born. With this comes a sense of belonging, a source of pride in one's roots. No matter how suspect their origins, clan tartans have played a valuable role in keeping highland culture alive.

Another crucial change that came out of George IV's visit was the notion of tartan as formal wear, rather than something merely practical. Traditionally, tartan came as one huge piece of cloth, which folded over a belt and then wrapped around the wearer, very much like a shorter version of a toga—a "mini-toga", if you will. This style, called a "belted plaid", posed challenges when dressing; indeed, the process usually required the help of a patient wife. Once on, however, it gave a highland kilt great versatility. Typically, the extra material was bunched up with a clasp and looped over the shoulder. On exceptionally warm days, however, the material could be hung down off the belt, much as people tie their jackets around their waists today. Conversely, on cold days the material could be un-clasped and wrapped around both shoulders. At night, it provided a blanket when sleeping in the open air.

Starting around the time of the king's visit, however, ready-made pleated versions of kilts appeared. They lacked the versatility of the belted plaid, but were much simpler to wear—all of which was preferable to the landed gentry who, following the king's visit, began to wear the kilt to mark formal occasions. These are the kilts one sees people in today, and I suppose it is the simplicity that allowed the garment to survive. After all, in an era of TV dinners and thirty-second commercials, how many people would take the time to wear an article of clothing that requires another person's assistance to put on? Still, I think it a shame that the traditional belted plaid has gone out of style altogether. I much prefer its rugged look, and, no matter how many Scots lecture me on the subject, I simply can't find enough to differentiate a modern kilt from a Catholic girl's school uniform.

Nonetheless, the aforementioned changes regarding tartan in the early 19th century added up to one of the greatest marketing schemes of all time. Whether or not Sir Walter Scott, King George IV, or the tartan researchers were aware of what they were doing can be debated, but the net effect of their efforts stands clear: tartan has gone from being an outlawed symbol of barbarians to the unofficial national symbol of Scotland—highland and lowland alike. As such, tartan is big business, as we have already had cause to observe along Edinburgh's Royal Mile; and nowhere has tartan become more central to the economy than in the de facto capital of the highlands: Inverness.

Shortly after arriving in Inverness I decided to do my part for the local economy and make a purchase. I'm not sure what compelled me to do this—spite for the English following our visit to Culloden, my enthusiasm at finally being in the highlands, some swelling of Crawford pride, or a combination of the above?—but I followed my impulse into a store called the Scottish Kiltmaker Centre, Inverness's premier store for foolhardy visitors like me, and declared I wasn't leaving without a kilt of my family tartan. Of course, things are never that simple.

"What tartan would you like?" sniffed the man behind the desk, who I shall call MacKrab, as he had all the patience one would expect of someone who deals with three hundred people a day claiming they want a kilt and one or two who actually buy one.

"Crawford," I repeated, thinking this should suffice. It didn't.

"Ancient or modern?" he asked.

"Uhhh, what's the difference?"

At this, MacKrab looked down his nose at me dubiously, probably recognizing this as the moment the sale would fall apart. Shoving a pattern book in front of me, he advised me to flip through and choose which tartan I preferred.

Turning page after page, I quickly realized that this was all further part of the tartan sham. Almost all family tartans contain an ancient version and a modern version, which of course is rubbish because as of two hundred years ago Crawford tartan, to take one example, didn't exist at all. The only difference I could tell between the two versions constituted a slight variation of color. The ancient featured a pattern made up of three colors: purple, green and white, while the modern consisted of the exact same pattern, but substituted burgundy for purple. The only explanation I could come up with for having two so similar was that the purple one hadn't been selling well, so they came up with the burgundy one with the hope that it would appeal to the contemporary Crawford. For this reason alone, I would have picked the ancient one, but to be honest, I liked it better anyway. It reminded me of the colors of the highland hillsides that we'd passed, with their combinations of purple heather and green grass.

"Oh great, camouflage," Katrina quipped, "Hope I don't lose you when we go hiking."

MacKrab looked at us tiredly, waiting for us to get the jokes out of the way and move on so he could continue his life in peace.

Having decided on the ancient, I figured the sale could proceed. I was mistaken.

"What type of cloth would you prefer?" MacKrab sniffed.

"Iridescent silk sounds comfortable," I replied.

"Kilts are made of wool," MacKrab replied with no smile whatsoever. "Lightweight, regular, or heavy are the choices."

I decided we should just get this over with.

"Lightweight," I replied.

"Yes, I see. That is the cheapest," MacKrab muttered. See, he did have a sense of humor.

At that point, I thought we must be done, but again I was wrong. "I don't suppose you know your measurements," MacKrab asked.

When I looked at him quizzically, he sighed and began advancing around the counter with a measuring tape in hand.

"No, no, that's okay," I stammered. "I don't want a pleated kilt. I just want the cloth. I plan to wear it in the traditional style."

This stopped MacKrab in his tracks and had him eyeing me suspiciously. Not many people—in fact, no one that he had helped in his time working there, he explained—had ordered cloth for a traditional kilt. I think he suspected I might use his fine cloth to make curtains for my house or seat covers for my car. I assured him that I really just preferred the old style, at which point he quite suddenly and most unexpectedly smiled. I think he was genuinely intrigued by the novelty of someone preferring the traditional style, but more importantly, I think he finally believed a sale was imminent. Whatever the reason, he warmed up considerably and even pulled out a roll of cloth to instruct Katrina how to wrap me up in it. After the first attempt, I bore a striking resemblance to a plaid potato, but the second attempt showed significant progress. I was amazed at how much cloth wearing tartan in this style required: 16 feet, as it turns out—nearly three times my own height. I was even more amazed at how much it cost, which proved something very near £300. Fortunately, I had no idea what that meant in American dollars, though I suspected it was roughly the price of a new car.

Nonetheless, I was ecstatic and probably would have worn the kilt straight out of the store had the cloth been available. Unfortunately MacKrab said the store would have to mail it to me, as they didn't have lightweight Crawford tartan in stock at the moment—which if you think about it, stands to reason. How could any store possibly keep cloth representing six versions (both ancient and modern in all three thicknesses) of every Scottish last name in stock? At that point, they would have no space left for their jovial employees.

Despite this minor setback, we paid for the tartan, provided our address and, in short order, re-emerged onto the streets of Inverness in much better spirits than we had been since leaving Culloden.

• • • • •

As the biggest town in the highlands and one well positioned just to the northeast of Loch Ness, Inverness provides a natural gathering point for tourists. This is very good, as it offers lots of shops and services, and very bad, well, for the same reason. Our guidebook referred to Inverness as "Britain's most northerly chain-store centre." Not exactly the motto local planners would like adorning the town brochure. Still, for all its commercialism, Inverness manages to not be wholly ugly. Indeed, much remains really quite attractive.

To begin with there is the River Ness, which flows through the heart of the city and creates a scenic backdrop for downtown. We had taken a room at a B&B found among a row of old and prosperous homes facing the river. From there, a pretty walk along the bank led to the shops, restaurants and pubs of downtown. It was this walk that had taken us across a bridge to the other side of the river and into the Scottish Kiltmaker Centre shortly after checking in.

Having spent more than I had anticipated on tartan, we decided to go cheap on dinner that night—as if saving ten bucks on food would somehow compensate for dropping several hundred on cloth I had no occasion to wear. Thus, we dined at an Italian restaurant, which proved rather unremarkable apart from the fact that everyone else in Inverness had also chosen to eat there that night. (I assumed they had all purchased kilts that day as well.) By the time we got seated, placed our order, received our food, ate, and paid the check, several weeks had passed and we were more than ready for a pub.

We had passed one earlier, on our way to the kilt store, which looked promising. Called the Glenalbyn, its sign had announced live music playing that night. We re-crossed the river and entered a cozy pub, full of polished wood and, of course, a bar with many taps. The band was just setting up when we entered, so we ordered a pint each and settled into a booth. We had come just in time. Over the next half hour a steady stream of people arrived, and by the time the music started halfway through our second pint, the place was heaving. It was a lively crowd, which fit the music. The band, consisting of bagpipes, accordion, guitar and some kind of a hand drum, worked its way through a fantastic set of traditional Scottish standards while the crowd joined in, singing along and swinging their pints in the air. By this point, I recognized many of the songs, and could sing along to the most obvious lyrics. At one point during *Loch Lomond*—the song with the classic lines "Ye tak the high road, I'll tak the low and I'll be in Scotland afore ye"—so many people joined in I could barely hear the band.

This patriotic display created an exhilarating atmosphere which made the presence of the middle-aged couple sharing our table all the more alarming. They were an English couple—no, worse, they were English soccer fans—who had just returned victorious from a soccer match and planned to settle in for a celebratory night. This seemed ill advised in a country detesting all things English, especially as when it comes to soccer this emotion multiplies by a factor of ten. Diehard soccer fans in Scotland comprise a fan club dubbed the "Tartan Army", a group which has helped set the standard for soccer hooliganism across Europe.

With a heightening sense of anxiety, I looked across the table to read the Englishwoman's t-shirt which said "England rules; Scotland sucks", or something similarly un-witty and every bit inflammatory. My anxiety increased dramatically when both husband and wife started shouting out pro-English jibes to the pub in general. Katrina and I tried to fade into the booth, not wanting anyone to associate us with this couple. Anytime I accidentally made eye contact with anyone, I found myself mouthing,

"We're not with them," as clearly as I could while nonchalantly searching for blunt objects with which to defend myself. Fortunately, everyone in the pub seemed in a rather good mood, and the music drowned out most of the shouting. All the same, I kept looking for the flash of a claymore out of the corner of my eye.

The only redeeming quality of the couple was that the Englishman, rather ironically, introduced me to my first Scottish whisky. Appalled that I had not yet sampled the national drink, he immediately ordered up a round for the table. Glad to have him focused on something other than English soccer, I thanked him profusely and lifted the glass to my lips for a sip. I had expected a bit of a kick—something to burn my throat and make my face pucker up like someone who had accidentally bitten into an onion thinking it was an apple. Instead I tasted nothing but smoothness. I took a bigger drink thinking maybe the hard stuff had settled to the bottom, but got more of the same: smooth and flavorful.

I started to understand why people who drink whisky use terms like smoky and peaty, rather than ass-kicking or hellfire, when discussing the quality of competing brands. I also began to understand why Scottish whisky, commonly referred to as Scotch (but only outside of Scotland, obviously), is so popular around the world. Consider: In America, a bottle of Scotch is consumed every tenth of a second. France, a country most associated with its vineyards, imports even more than the United States, ranking as the world's single largest importer of Scotch whisky year after year. I find this staggering, though it does go a long way towards explaining how whisky has become a multi-billion dollar industry in Scotland.

All the same, upon finishing the whisky, I decided to revert back to my creamy ale for the remainder of the evening. I didn't know what alcohol content the whisky contained, and with the English couple still across from us I thought it best to keep my wits about me in case need arose to make a break for the door. After all, there were sixteen feet of ancient Crawford lightweight wool tartan in the mail that I really wanted to wear at least once.

# Chapter 19: Ciao, Monster!

## (Exploring the Great Glen)

Northern Scotland is being ripped apart, but don't panic. It will likely hold together for another few million years.

The process began some 400 million years ago when the two sides of a fault line decided to march off in opposite directions. They managed to travel about sixty miles in such fashion, tearing the landscape apart as they went, before finally running out of steam and settling down. Had they continued much further, the landmass of Great Britain would have been effectively beheaded, with the northernmost region of Scotland forming a separate island altogether. As it is, the movement created a huge gash—a rift valley, to the technically minded—in the landscape, running from Fort William on the west coast to Inverness, some seventy miles to the northeast. Consider it a botched beheading, if you will, where the head remains on the shoulders—though, Picasso-style, now faces in a slightly different direction—and a long and quite noticeable scar remains as evidence of the executioner's lack of skill. Now that the reader has this salient image in mind, let me point out one very important difference: unlike the ugly scar of a botched beheading, the gash across Scotland is astonishingly beautiful to behold.

The Great Glen, as this gash is known, continued to be sculpted by glaciers long after the fault line settled down, leaving a landscape today comprised of mile after mile of steep valley surrounded by beautiful wooded hillsides. The depressions of this valley harbor a string of three fresh water lochs, connected by rivers and effectively linking the salt water Loch Linnhe, which opens to the Atlantic Ocean in the west, with the Moray Firth, opening to the North Sea in the east. Though the rivers themselves are not navigable, a system of canals constructed in the early 19th century links one loch to another forming the great Caledonian Canal, a scenic waterway that provides one of the easiest passageways through the heart of the imposing highlands.

For much of its path, this waterway travels across one of the great natural wonders of Scotland: a twenty-three mile loch reaching depths of more than seven hundred feet—so deep that if the Statue of Liberty went for a stroll on the loch's floor while balancing the Washington Monument on the tip of her torch, no one from the shore would notice as the top of the Monument would still be some thirty feet below the water's surface. Here's another statistic for you: this one very long, very deep loch contains more fresh water than is found in all of England and Wales combined. It is a big loch.

On top of its massive scale, the loch also ranks as one of the most scenic places in Scotland. The steep wooded sides of the valley slope down to the loch's waters, while a picturesque castle ruin overlooks its western shore. Here and there, cascading streams rush down the hillsides to spill into the loch, while frequent mists hang low over the water. Postcards and guidebooks in countless numbers describe the loch and its environs as moody, haunting, and poignant. It is, without doubt, a place of timeless beauty.

So, what is this magnificent and singular location? I have purposefully withheld the name, as I wanted the reader to be able to fully focus on and appreciate the loch's beauty and scale—two points frequently overshadowed by another of its interesting features. This trick was necessary, as will soon be clear, for once I reveal the loch's name all images of beauty and grandeur will disappear, and the reader will be able to think of little else but a legendary beast of dubious existence.

I speak, of course, of Loch Ness.

And now, having said that, I will succumb to the inevitable and address the topic the reader really wants to hear about.

•   •   •   •   •

The first hint that the deep, murky waters of Loch Ness might be home to something larger and stranger than the average fish appeared over 1,400 years ago. The reference appears in St. Adamnan's 6th century biography of St. Columba, chronicling the latter's adventures in Scotland converting Celtic Picts to Christianity. In one such adventure, according to the biography, St. Columba was wandering along the shores of Loch Ness when he spied a sea monster about to attack a helpless Pict in the water. Thinking fast, the great saint made the sign of the cross, at which point the sea monster instantly retreated, sparing the Pict—who we can assume converted rather quickly to Christianity after that.

This story would be compelling except for two points: First, St. Columba seems to have encountered many monsters—dragons, giant boar, and whatnot—during his travels throughout Scotland, so the mention of a monster at Loch Ness qualifies as nothing very extraordinary. Indeed, next to St. Adamnan's biography of Columba, Blind Harry seems suddenly a stickler for realism. Second, and more bewilderingly, reported sightings of this Loch Ness monster over the course of the next thirteen centuries number exactly zero.[*] Apparently, St. Columba's sign of the cross had made a lasting impression.

All of this would change in the early 20th century, when the monster finally appears to have gotten over his encounter with St. Columba—and in a big way at that. The first monster sighting by a non-saint occurred in 1933, and ever since then, the beast seems to have become something of a people person, making scores of claimed appearances over the last seven decades and even posing for photographs on occasion. Of course, it is worth noting that the first modern sighting was reported by a Mr. and Mrs. Mackay who just so happened to own a hotel in the area. We might also consider that the Mackays' hotel was located along a new road being constructed that same year to make the loch more accessible to the public. We should further note that the person the Mackays chose to share their tale with worked as a newspaper reporter. Finally, to round out the story, we should note that the Mackays supposedly asked the reporter to keep the news quiet, as they didn't want people to think they had made the story up just for publicity.

---

[*] There have been claims of sightings from the late 19th century, but evidence for these is scant. Rather, they seem to have been invented after the fact to add support to 20th century claims.

Hmmm. Why would people think that?

Obviously, the reporter did not keep the news quiet, and the supposed existence of a Loch Ness "monster" was soon being talked about around the globe, which must have just vexed the hell out of ol' Mr. and Mrs. Mackay. Soon thereafter, monster hunters flocked to the area—staying at the Mackays' hotel, darn it all—each hoping to be the first to produce tangible evidence of the legendary beast. Those honors would go to R.K. Wilson, a London surgeon, whose sensational photograph of a long neck and tiny head sticking out of the water was published in the *Daily Mail* in 1934. The photograph, which seemed to confirm the existence of the Loch Ness Monster, or Nessie as she came to be affectionately known, caused an international sensation.

Not until 1994 was the photograph finally exposed as a hoax by the deathbed confession of Chris Spurling, one of four men responsible for staging the picture six decades earlier. It seems the monster in Dr. Wilson's photograph was nothing more than a clay head and neck attached to a child's toy submarine.* By this time, of course, it hardly mattered. The Nessie movement had built up so much steam in the intervening years the monster had even acquired a scientific name: *Nessiteras rhombopteryx*—and no, I'm not joking.** Generally believed to resemble a plesiosaur or some other holdover from the age of dinosaurs, Nessie's existence had been independently confirmed by many other sources, including photographs and films—no matter that they had, without exception, proved to be either blatant hoaxes or too fuzzy or ambiguous to take seriously. What's more, legitimate scientists had also converged on Loch Ness by this point, making

---

* The mastermind behind the hoax was a man named Marmaduke Wetherell, who concocted the scheme to get back at the *Daily Mail*. The publication had ridiculed him relentlessly the previous year, when Wetherell's claim that he had actually found tracks from the Loch Ness Monster imprinted on the shoreline had proved to be—you guessed it—a hoax. Wetherell had made the tracks himself using an umbrella stand made out of a hippopotamus foot. Brilliant.
** The name *Nessiteras rhombopteryx* is Greek for "The Ness monster with the diamond shaped fin." The name was chosen by a British naturalist named Sir Peter Scott after viewing underwater photographs which supposedly revealed one of the monster's fins as it swam past. Intriguingly, journalists have discovered that the letters of the Greek name can be reshuffled to spell: *Monster hoax by Sir Peter S.* To show that anagrams don't necessarily prove anything more than coincidence, Dr. Robert Rines, who helped obtain the photographs of the fin, noted that the same letters could also spell *Yes, both pix are monsters*—R.

226

several comprehensive attempts to prove Nessie's existence using combinations of sonar and underwater imaging. So far they have not obtained any hard proof of her existence, but—as they are all quick to point out—neither have they turned up any definitive evidence that she *does not* exist. Other than the fact that they can't find her, that is. How's that for optimism?

As funny as this last line of reasoning seems, the Nessie scientists do have a point. With a body of water as deep and as murky as the peaty waters of Loch Ness, much remains unknown. Just recently, for example, sonar evidence suggests the loch may contain a sizable underwater cave near its bottom—a discovery met with great excitement amongst the ranks of monster hunters who have already dubbed the cave "Nessie's Lair". And then, of course, there are all those people—a whole lot of people—who have stared out at the water over the last seven decades and claimed to see… something. In the face of such unknowns, speculation remains tantalizing.

These days, whether the monster does or does not exist is quite beside the point. The fact is—and on this, even skeptics have to agree—the legend itself has had a very real effect on Loch Ness, turning much of it, particularly the western shore, into a sideshow spectacle. Not one, but two major exhibition centers specializing in monster lore rank among the most visited destinations in the valley. At Urquhart Castle, a 14th century fortress overlooking the loch, tourists hardly notice the beauty of the ruins as they anxiously scan the water, ready to snap a picture of what they will swear could have been the monster, but what, upon closer inspection, looks astonishingly similar to an otter, or a drifting tree branch, or anything else that is decidedly not a prehistoric dinosaur. Gift stores along the loch sell Nessie postcards by the hundreds; hotels advertise their excellent "monster viewing" locations, and at one café, patrons can even cap off their meal with a "Loch Ness Monster" sundae.

For this reason, many Scots have grown a bit disenchanted with the loch, viewing it as nothing more than a depot for busloads of gullible tourists with fistfuls of dollars. I have to admit, I was a bit skeptical myself.

From what I had found, researching Loch Ness is like entering a world of nutcases—inhabited, seemingly, by the same people who frequent the bookshop at Rosslyn Chapel. One website I stumbled upon even warned readers of secret government plans to explode a hydrogen bomb in the loch.

"Is this something we really want to see?" I asked Katrina as we set out from Inverness the morning after our experience at the Glenalbyn Pub.

"We have to see it," said Katrina. "We can't come to Scotland and not see Loch Ness."

"We went to the Black Hills and didn't see Mount Rushmore," I replied. I had, in fact, done this twice.

"That's different," said Katrina. "Mount Rushmore is full of lazy people in RVs and is offensive to Native Americans. The Loch Ness Monster isn't offensive to anyone. It's just fun."

"Try telling that to a 6th century Pict," I muttered, giving the Fiat Crumb a little nudge on the gas. But, of course, she was right.

•    •    •    •    •

Taking our guidebook's advice, we decided to begin our Loch Ness excursion with a drive along the loch's eastern—and much less commercialized—shore. The tiny road had almost no traffic and, other than a town or two consisting of just a handful of buildings each, passed through hardly any signs of civilization. For much of its length, the road tucked into the hillside, so that the only views we got of the loch consisted of fleeting peeks—beautiful, nonetheless—between occasional gaps in the trees. After a while, however, the road descended toward the loch, and for a stretch of several miles our Fiat Crumb cruised within mere feet of the loch's shore, offering stunning prospects across the water. At one point, we simply had to pull over and take a closer look.

Lowering ourselves over the side of the road, we balanced on a cluster of rocks at the water's edge. Tiny ripples lapped against the rocks as we gazed across the loch. The day was perfectly clear—as had nearly every day been for us in Scotland (beautiful weather, that country)—and the opposite shore stood out crisp against the sparkling waters. Words like haunting and moody hardly sprung to mind. In fact, the scene was so tranquil Katrina felt compelled to reach down and dip her hand in the water—fearlessly disregarding the chance that it could be separated from her arm by the jaws of a lurking sea monster.

Almost immediately, she jerked her hand back.

"What?" I cried, leaping forward with concern, my right hand poised in the air to make a defensive sign of the cross.

"It's freezing!" she exclaimed, flicking a little water in my direction.

And it was. I don't know what the surface temperature registered that day, but below the surface the water remains in the low forties (Fahrenheit) year round—which, monster's aside, doesn't exactly invite swimming.

We lingered for a few moments on shore before continuing our drive. I was struck by the surrounding beauty, so unexpected in the shadow of the monster hype. I had heretofore associated Loch Ness with such ridiculous sideshows as the "World's Largest Prairie Dog" exhibit, which I had detoured to see years ago during a drive across the seemingly infinite plains of the American Midwest. After finally arriving and paying the entry fee, I was indeed treated to a viewing of the world's largest prairie dog. It was over ten feet high and made of cement. The brown paint of its fur was chipped and peeling. Once the show had been revealed as a hoax, I looked around to find myself standing in the middle of a trackless prairie—dry and dusty and miles from anywhere of remote interest. In the wake of such experiences, Loch Ness proved refreshing indeed. Regardless of what our day would reveal about the elusive monster, the loch itself made the trip worthwhile.

Back in the car, we followed the road, which now climbed further away from the loch, to the tiny village of Foyers, a few miles further on. After our forest walk at Cawdor Castle the day before, we were anxious to get out and stretch our legs a bit, and a signpost pointing to the Falls of Foyers seemed like the perfect diversion. The trail descended from the road toward the loch, taking us into the forest. It made for pleasant hiking, with rocky outcroppings protruding beneath a mixed canopy of deciduous and evergreen trees. As we descended, we became aware of the sound of the waterfall and shortly found ourselves at an overlook offering a most picturesque view. A stream, cascading through a gap in the rocks, plunged into a deep stone grotto, hollowed out by millennia of rushing water passing through. Exiting the grotto through high walls of rock, the stream continued on, descending rapidly toward the loch.

The tranquil scene before us had proved an attraction to no less a romantic than Robbie Burns, who penned a poem here with the informative title: "Written with a pencil, standing by the Fall of Fyers, near Loch Ness". A bit of a mouthful, but the poem itself is short enough to include here:

*Among the heathy hills and ragged woods*
*The roaring Fyers pours his mossy floods;*
*Till full he dashes on the rocky mounds,*
*Where, thro' a shapeless breach, his stream resounds.*
*As high in air the bursting torrents flow,*
*As deep recoiling surges foam below,*
*Prone down the rock the whitening sheet descends,*
*And viewless Echo's ear, astonished, rends.*
*Dim-seen, thro' rising mists and ceaseless show'rs,*
*The hoary cavern, wide-surrounding, lours,*
*Still thro' the gap the struggling river toils,*
*And still, below, the horrid cauldron boils—*

Today, part of the stream that feeds the Falls of Foyers diverts to a nearby power plant, so the volume of water rushing past us fell a bit short of the "mossy floods" and "bursting torrents" that Burns observed, though the scene was spectacular nonetheless. Other than this detail, little seemed to have changed in the two centuries since the poet penned his tribute.

The hike to the falls had taken only a matter of minutes, and neither of us was in a hurry to return to the car. Instead, we continued along the trail, hoping it would eventually loop back to the trailhead in the town of Foyers. This proved a bad assumption, as it was soon hopelessly obvious that the trail led nowhere near the town, though that was about all we could ascertain of its direction. Pushing on past all common sense (I had somehow convinced Katrina that turning around represented the less sensible option), we ended up near a little cluster of vacation houses by the loch—with the trail ending quite literally in someone's backyard. We sheepishly crossed the property to where a rough road led away from the houses, eventually connecting with the main road a couple of miles outside Foyers. By the time we made it back to the village, we were tired, famished, and—for the first time in Scotland—drenched in sweat.

"Well, that was an adventure," I muttered, as we sat outside the Foyers general store recuperating over a sandwich.

"Brilliant navigation," Katrina retorted taking a big gulp from her water bottle.

"Anyway, it felt great to be outdoors," I defended, "and the scenery was beautiful."

"True," Katrina granted, "though I suspect we might find equally beautiful hikes in the highlands that don't include cutting through people's yards or backtracking along highways."

I admitted this was probably the case. Without too much reluctance, we finished our sandwiches and squeezed back into the car to continue our drive around Loch Ness.

Foyers stood roughly half way down the loch, but between there and our arrival at Fort Augustus at the far southern end we passed nary a shred of civilization. The route comprised one of the most deserted stretches of road I have seen, which made me like it all the more.

Passing through Fort Augustus, we continued on around the loch to the western shore, where the atmosphere almost immediately changed. The road here was considerably wider and infinitely busier, playing host to everything from motorcycle convoys to oversized tour buses. Also, the roadside vegetation had been cleared to offer sweeping views of the loch, which I found a bit misguided as my natural tendency was then to stare at the beauty of the water, rather than the rapidly closing distance between our front bumper and the two motorcycles in front of us. This probably would have upset the riders considerably had they noticed. As it were, they too were having trouble paying attention to anything but the view, as I gathered from the meandering patterns they scribed in their lane.

We passed the village of Invermoriston, which our guidebook noted had wonderful trails to nearby waterfalls (I accelerated smartly on by), and continued on to the village of Drumnadrochit, further up the loch. Drumnadrochit first gained fame in 1933, as the location of the hotel owned by the Mackays. Its popularity (and population) soared in the frenzy of monster hunting that ensued, and the village has become the de facto headquarters for all Nessie-related pursuits in the years since. Thus, it seemed an appropriate first stop for our tour of Loch Ness's western shore.

Immediately, however, we faced a decision of the utmost import: whether to tour the Original Loch Ness Monster Exhibition or the newer and zippier Loch Ness 2000 Exhibition. The former, as the name implies, ranked as the more venerable of the two choices, having been catering to monster-crazed tourists for decades by that point. Besides the Nessie exhibition, it contained a 50-room hotel, which tells you something about the volume of business these places do, and a Scottish history museum called the "Braveheart Centre", which would have been quite a selling point to me, had it not been lodged in a cheesy-looking castle that appeared to be constructed of papier mache and chicken wire. On the other hand, the Loch Ness 2000 Exhibition, despite being newer, was housed in the original Drumnadrochit Hotel (of Mackay fame), a very respectable and sturdy looking Victorian building, and yet managed to offer a "hi-tech multi-media presentation" utilizing everything from special sound effects to laser beams while educating visitors on the Nessie phenomenon. Essentially, our choice was tacky vs. tackier still, and we ultimately had to resort to the guidebook to decide. It recommended the 2000 Exhibition as the better bet, noting a more equitable balance of evidence on the case for Nessie along with an actual discussion on the basic scientific principles at hand.

"Hopefully, that won't take all the fun out of it," Katrina muttered as we pulled the car into the parking lot.

It didn't. The 2000 Exhibition proved fantastic. Somehow, it managed to discuss a topic as wacky as Nessie, and still maintain, even acquire in a way, integrity throughout. The exhibition is undoubtedly slanted in favor of the monster's existence, of course. It has to be when you think about it, as skeptics don't tend to be the breed frequenting these places. Still, by acknowledging the very strong points the skeptics make, the exhibition manages to gain credibility for its own cause. I know this is an old trick used by politicians and lawyers around the world—a trick, I'd like to say, to which I am immune—but as we walked from room to room, being awed by light projections and video screens and high tech experiments like Operation DeepScan, which for two days in 1987 assembled nineteen boats side by side to cruise the length of the loch taking simultaneous sonar readings of activity in the water, I found myself starting to think, "Maybe there is something out there." Not a prehistoric dinosaur, certainly, but maybe an oversized sturgeon that swims up the River Ness from the sea (one theory) or maybe something else altogether. Goodness knows scientists have found enough weird stuff in the deep waters of the loch: white eels and arctic char and other rare species one wouldn't expect to find there. By the time we finished the tour, I wouldn't say I was a believer, but I did catch myself thinking, "Well, they haven't proved that Nessie *doesn't* exist...", and, somehow, saw nothing wrong with this line of reasoning.

If I had started to waver in my conviction, I was quickly jolted back to reality when we passed through the exit of the exhibition only to find ourselves in the gift shop. Thus, I was reminded of the world of pseudo-science I had entered. It is decreed by law that all pseudo-science exhibitions must terminate in a gift shop. This held true at the World's Largest Prairie Dog exhibit, it held true at Rosslyn Chapel, and it had now held true at the Loch Ness 2000 Exhibition. I suppose at the competing Original Exhibition, which by most accounts really puts the pseudo in pseudo-science, visitors actually drop into the gift shop via a trap door at the end of the exhibition and can only leave after making a purchase.

Fortunately, in this case, the gift shop provided a wonderfully diverting experience, nearly as enjoyable as the tour itself. This had everything to do with the hysterical line of products offered for sale. Imagine, if you can, taking all the tackiness of a regular Scottish gift shop and adding to it a wonder of pseudo-science like the Loch Ness Monster. The result is a selection of spectacularly useless products featuring an almost limitless combination of Scottish stereotypes, all anchored in the consistent theme of Nessie.

"Hey, look at this!" Katrina called to me, standing beside an enormous stuffed Nessie clothed in a kilt and playing the bagpipes.

"My dad would love this," I called back, holding up a Nessie figurine sporting a tartan cap and playing golf.

"Or how about this selection of 'monster' malt whisky?" Katrina pointed to a line of bottles featuring tartan labels with a picture of Nessie on the bottle.

Thus we progressed around the entire room—a big room—full of splendid products. I have seldom spent a more fascinating fifteen minutes.

Sadly, the clock—along with a stern look from the store clerk, who seemed unimpressed with our ability to pose for photographs with various products while not making a single purchase—suggested the time had come to move on, and we dragged ourselves back to the car. It seemed only natural to follow up the exhibition experience with a visit to the one site which had logged more monster sightings than anywhere else in the loch: Urquhart Castle.

Though, unlike most visitors, we were actually interested in the castle.

Urquhart ranks as perhaps the most photographed castle in Scotland. Partly, this stems from the beauty of the castle itself. The ruins of its encircling walls and relatively intact tower house provide striking examples of 14th century architecture. More striking still, however, is the castle's location on the western shore of Loch Ness. Perched on a bluff of the greenest grass, the castle lords over the blue-gray waters of the loch, visible from almost any angle. We had passed the ruins on our way to Drumnadrochit and looked forward to exploring them now.

Pulling into the parking lot, the first thing to draw our attention was the crowd. The sprawling lot included a many-leveled garage, and almost every spot contained a vehicle. A line of shiny tour buses, glaring in the sun, snaked across the lot as well, belching out a stream of tourists from around the world, speaking a variety of languages. The scene struck me as rather chaotic, but what one should expect when the most photographed castle in Scotland happens to reside in the heart of Nessie country.

The castle was run by Historic Scotland, which had spruced up the facilities to accommodate the constant crowds. Whereas Elcho, another castle managed by Historic Scotland, had contained only a small shack that doubled as both gift shop and ticket counter, Urquhart boasted a state of the art visitor center, complete with a museum, cinema, and café to compliment its huge gift shop. The whole is loaded with so much information and so many things to do, one could spend all day there and never see the actual castle. Impressively, this multi-leveled complex was built into the hillside so as to minimize its impact on the castle site—a fact which heightened my respect for Historic Scotland considerably.

After showing our Explorers Pass, which by this point had more than paid for itself, we were ushered into the cinema for an introductory movie. The relatively high-budget documentary did an admirable job of presenting the castle's fascinating and often violent history, but the best part by far was the film's surprise ending: as the room went dark, the screen suddenly retracted, as did a set of curtains behind it which had heretofore completely escaped my notice. There, revealed through a wall of plate glass windows, stood the very real ruins of Urquhart Castle, framed by all the beauty of Loch Ness behind it. The scene was so strikingly beautiful, and so unexpected, it elicited a collective gasp from the audience, peppered with genuine ohhs and ahhs. The effect stood out as one of the most pleasant surprises of the trip and nearly made up for what happened next.

Streaming out of the theater, we approached the castle ruins, joined by what felt like several hundred fellow tourists. Inside the castle complex, accessed by crossing a bridge over a moat—another dry ditch, but cool nonetheless—we spent the whole of our time shuffling from one ruin to the next, sandwiched at every turn between other groups of people. Every time we stopped to take a closer look or read about a castle feature, somebody would step on our heels. We consistently stumbled into other people's pictures, and found ourselves offering up apologies in a more or less steady stream. It was all quite depressing, but the final straw came in the ruins of the castle tower.

The tower, which stands relatively intact, can still be ascended by a stone spiral staircase, or turnpike staircase, as they were known. The views from atop the tower rank as some of the best in the area, offering stunning prospects up, down and across the loch; and so, naturally, climbing the tower has become a "must do" activity for those visiting the castle. The problem, however, is that the staircase is only wide enough for one person to pass. And as people going up use the same staircase as those going down, one party constantly has to give way, stepping aside into the occasional alcove or at the start of a new level to let the oncoming party pass. Given the volume of people using the stairs, human traffic jams have become a more or less constant feature of the tower—or so it seemed while we were there.

Katrina and I kept an eye on the tower for our chance, and when we sensed the crowd had lessened, made a break for it. Just behind us marched a group of forty or so late middle-aged Italians, obviously off one of the tour buses, who seemed to have the same idea. They spoke to one another in loud voices, and seemed oblivious to the idea of sharing space with anyone besides members of their group. We reached the turnpike stair just ahead of them and started to ascend, but as we neared the top of the first flight we met a family coming down. The family waited patiently for us to get to the top stair, and, once there, Katrina and I stepped aside to let them pass. This idea was lost on the Italian group behind us, however, who immediately pushed past us when we stepped aside, causing the family— which consisted of a couple and two small children—to have to huddle with us in an alcove while every member of the group filed by, their loud voices echoing off the stonework of the stair. As the last person passed, the family took its chance to dash down the stairs, while we continued to ascend.

We had not climbed far before we met other people, who had obviously been forced to the side of the wall or to take refuge in alcoves as the Italian group, whose members apparently never gave way, pushed by. This pattern continued all the way up, with us offering apologetic looks and giving way to person after person, all of whom, without fail, we found standing to the side of the stair with annoyed looks on their faces as they waited for their chance to descend.

All of this meant that by the time Katrina and I made it to the top we had the privilege of sharing one of the greatest views in Scotland with a busload of Italian tourists. There must have been fifty people in total atop the tower, all packed in like sardines and trying to enjoy the view. Adding to the challenge was the natural inclination for all of them to want to take photographs of their groups of friends with the loch in the background, which proved a rather difficult task requiring a constant jostling of people, as no one really had any room to get out of the way.

Katrina and I had finally had enough and tried to descend the staircase, but only made it half way down the first flight before we met—and I'm not kidding—some stragglers in the Italian group coming up. I tried to explain that if they let us go down there would be more room for them on top, even adding helpful hand gestures for effect, but the message didn't register. They kept coming and we were forced back up to the top of the tower. As the reader might expect, by the time we did get to the bottom we had had quite enough of the castle and crossed back over the bridge to return to the visitor center.

On our way, we noticed other interesting items placed here and there around the grounds. One in particular caught my attention: a fully reconstructed trebuchet, a type of medieval catapult used to fling boulders and fiery objects toward castles. The trebuchet was huge, and the members of Historic Scotland had cleverly positioned it to be aimed at the tower of Urquhart Castle. I briefly pondered the idea of launching a flaming fireball at a busload of tourists, but decided such action was probably frowned upon.

Thus, we continued back through the museum, which looked to be extremely well done and probably was, though we had run out of energy to linger. Instead, we made a beeline for the car and were soon driving back down the western shore toward Fort Augustus, where we said goodbye to beautiful Loch Ness and its tour buses.

•   •   •   •   •

That night we stayed in Fort William, an unremarkable town which seemed to have little to recommend it other than its location at the far southwestern end of the Great Glen. The mere fact that the town had begun as a fort built by William of Orange in his effort to break the power of the highland clans had already predisposed me against it, and our experiences there did little to mend the image. We had a mediocre meal served by an awful waitress who somehow managed to compliment her inefficiency with surliness, after which we strolled next to the busy, noisy highway along the concrete-lined banks of Loch Linnhe. Suffice it to say, the absolute highlight of our stay in Fort William was our trip to the laundromat, desperately needed on this, our eighth day in Scotland. That is about all I need tell you about our experience in Fort William.

On a positive note, we had quite a bit of time on our hands in the laundromat, a portion of which we used to reflect on a topic much on our minds that day.

"How is it that so many people, even seemingly rational and educated people, can believe in something as absurd as the Loch Ness Monster?" Katrina mused, as the clothes spun round and round in the machine before us.

"I've been wondering about that all day," I admitted, contemplating how much I could reveal without losing all of my remaining credibility. "But then I started thinking about my own feelings on the matter, from the first time I heard of the legend as a child and stared wide-eyed at a picture in some kids' magazine to my own wavering feelings today while walking through the exhibition."

238

"Oh no," Katrina looked at me warily. "You're not going to become one of those freak monster hunters are you?"

"Not hardly, but I did start to think that maybe all those freaks out there believe in Nessie for the same reason I found myself wanting to believe in Nessie, despite all the hoaxes and the lack of a shred of scientific evidence."

"And why's that?" Katrina asked, looking like she was already considering ways to check me into the nearest mental institution.

"I think it comes down to this: in an age when there aren't many mysteries left on our planet, a world with Nessie—or at least with the *possibility* of Nessie—is just a lot more interesting than a world without."

Katrina pondered this for a moment, leaning against the washing machine. "I can see that," she responded finally, nodding her head in a mixture of surprise and understanding. "You may be on to something there."

By the time we left the laundromat, we had determined that the same line of reasoning also applied to Bigfoot and the Abominable Snowman, though we both felt the world could probably do without the giant prairie dog.

# Chapter 20: Bagging the Munro Sisters

## (Hiking in Glen Nevis and Glencoe)

On the evening of February 12, 1692, the men, women and children who made up the MacDonalds of Glencoe tucked into bed for a well-deserved night's rest. For ten days they had played host to a party of government soldiers seeking shelter in their valley from the punishing winter weather. Highlanders pride themselves on a strict code of hospitality, and the MacDonalds of Glencoe were no exception, providing food, shelter and a plethora of entertainment day after day and night after night. One can imagine what a relief, what an absolute haven the warmth and festivity must have seemed to the soldiers in the otherwise cold, snow-swept valleys of the western highlands.

To show their gratitude, the soldiers rose extra early the morning of February 13 and, with startling efficiency, slaughtered their hosts in their beds. Thirty-eight MacDonalds—women and children included—were slain, though at least forty others perished in the cold as they fled from their homes, barefoot and half-naked, into the surrounding snow-covered hills. By the time the sun rose in the valley, the MacDonalds of Glencoe were effectively no more.

This massacre, which has gone down as one of the most heinous examples of treachery in Scottish history, was led by Captain Robert Campbell of Glenlyon, commander of the government troops sheltering in Glencoe, many of whom themselves were Campbells of Glenlyon and Argyll. Such "murder under trust" constituted such an affront to the highland code of honor that, to this day, the mere mention of the Campbell name will be met with a look of disdain by many a highland resident.[*] Indeed, I overheard one highlander claim—without a shred of irony—that he refuses to eat Campbell's Soup.

---

[*] It must be pointed out that this was just one sect of Clan Campbell. Other sects of Campbells were just as horrified by these actions as other highlanders and even sided with the Jacobite cause—which, after all, is what this little demonstration was all about, as will be seen momentarily.

In fairness, placing the blame entirely on Campbell shoulders misses the important fact that responsibility for this bloody act went significantly further up the chain of command—all the way to the crown itself, it would seem. The orders Campbell carried instructed him: "*...to fall upon the Rebels, the MacDonalds of Glencoe, and put all to the sword under seventy. You are to have especial care that the Old Fox [clan chief MacIan MacDonald] and his Sons do not escape your hands... This is by the king's special commands for the good and safety of the country.*" Officially, ultimate blame for the events was never established, as the two separate inquiries ordered by King William—and these only after enormous public outcry once word of the massacre leaked out—failed to arrive at any conclusion whatsoever. Not one government official or soldier was ever formally accused, let alone convicted, of any wrongdoing. Indeed, Robert Campbell of Glenlyon received a promotion.

All of this sat just fine with the king, I suppose. After all, in William's eyes, the man responsible for the bloodshed at Glencoe had already been identified and justly punished: this being none other than the "Old Fox" himself, MacIan MacDonald, clan chief and one of the first of the MacDonalds to die on the government swords. It seems that the Old Fox had missed a deadline, you see—not an advisable thing to do in 17th century Scotland, particularly when that deadline had been set by a new king still insecure of his power and acceptance.

Recall that William (of William and Mary fame) had come to the English and Scottish thrones in 1689 after James VII (II of England) had been deposed for his Catholic beliefs. This move met staunch resistance in the highlands where support for the Stuart monarchs remained strong, and skirmishes had erupted almost immediately across the region in support of the Jacobite cause.* After effectively suppressing the first round of these uprisings, King William had sent out a mandate that all clan chiefs must take an oath of allegiance to the crown or else have their clans labeled as traitors. As extra incentive, those that took the oath would receive

---

* Recall that Jacobites were in favor of restoring the Stuarts to the throne. Their cause would continue in various phases of intensity until 1746 when the disastrous Battle of Culloden, under the Stuart banner of Bonnie Prince Charlie, ended any hope of Jacobite success.

forgiveness for any past acts of rebellion. The deadline for taking the oath was January 1, 1692.

Many highland chiefs rushed to comply. Whether they intended to honor the oath was doubtful, but at least it bought them a free pass for any role they had played in the last two years of fighting. MacIan MacDonald of Glencoe, however, proved reluctant to follow suit. Clan MacDonald remained one of the proudest clans in the western highlands, and, in centuries gone by, had been one of the most powerful. Throughout the 14th and 15th centuries, the MacDonalds had been known as "Lords of the Isles", presiding over the western highlands and islands as a virtually independent kingdom from the rest of Scotland. For the last two hundred years, however, they had shown particular loyalty to the Stuart monarchs, and, most recently, under clan chief MacIan MacDonald, had openly supported the Jacobite cause in the face of King William's coronation.

Still, as the January 1 deadline approached, the Old Fox reconsidered his obstinancy in light of the safety of his clan, and at the last minute set out to nearby Fort William to take the oath, though the journey would entail a bit more than he bargained for. Arriving in Fort William on December 31, he was informed that the oath could not be administered there and that he would have to travel instead to Inveraray, over forty miles away—which meant that, given the distance, a spell of bad weather, and the fact that he had to wait three days for the absent minister to arrive from a neighboring town, it was January 6, comfortably after the deadline, by the time he finally took the oath. Nonetheless, having done so, he returned to Glencoe with assurances that he had fulfilled his obligation to the crown. Thus it was that, when government troops arrived a month later seeking shelter in his valley, MacIan welcomed them in with no suspicion and even personally invited the captain, Robert Campbell, an old rival of the MacDonalds, to dine in his home—all of which makes the tragic events that followed even harder to swallow.

I would love to say this story provides a lesson somehow, some message we can take away from even the most sober of circumstances— and in that light, I suppose the events do serve as a helpful reminder to not underestimate an insecure tyrant's capacity for evil. Not a very uplifting thought, but sadly, there isn't much else we can take away from the tragic story of the MacDonalds of Glencoe. On that note, I think it's time to turn our attention to lighter topics.

·  ·  ·  ·  ·

Glencoe, like Dunnottar, qualifies as one of those places where the scenery, beautiful beyond imagination, seems completely out of sorts with the tragic events to which it played host. In a region like the Scottish highlands, already known for striking and awe-inspiring landscape, Glencoe and its surrounding peaks and valleys manage to stand out. Its singular features—the jagged eminence of Buachaille Etive Mòr, the cluster of waterfall strewn peaks known as the Three Sisters, nearby Ben Nevis, the highest peak in all of Britain—stand as some of the most recognizable natural wonders of Scotland, adorning calendars, postcards and picture books in every gift shop. When Hollywood producers need to film a scene of quintessential highland scenery for blockbuster films like *Rob Roy* and *Braveheart*, they head to the pristine valleys, lushly clad in green grass and purple heather, of nearby Glen Nevis. It is, by any measure, a fetching location.

The secret of all this beauty, so far as I can tell, is that Mother Nature, when fashioning the region, employed the Bob Ross strategy of landscape art.

Allow me to explain.

Bob Ross, for any unenlightened readers out there, ranks as one of the great artists of the 20th century.* You will recognize him as the bearded man in a flare-collared seventies shirt sporting an impressively large brown afro who, for years, created one thirty-minute masterpiece after another on the PBS show *The Joy of Painting*. His appearance alone would have made him my favorite artist of all time, as would his personality. He was the happiest

---

* This may be yet to be acknowledged by the art world, but mark my word, in fifty years collectors will be trading in their Picassos and Warhols for a Ross over the mantelpiece.

man to ever live, and transferred this joy to viewers as he painted, chatting away about the "happy little tree" or "happy little cabin" he was adding with his brush to the landscape, while saying things like "Let's give the squirrels a tree to play in" or asking viewers "Who do you think lives in that cabin?" This is all wonderfully endearing and made the entire show absolutely worth watching, especially by comatose college students sitting on couches with half-smoked joints clutched between their fingers. But what set Bob Ross apart from every other artist in my mind was the fact that week after week he would churn out, before all those very bloodshot eyes, a masterpiece of landscape art in the time it takes most people to drive across town.

These masterpieces always followed the same formula. At the beginning of the show, Bob would appear next to a blank canvas. Quickly adding a few broad strokes as reference points—a horizon line, a shoreline, or what have you—he would then spend most of the next half hour sketching in details of a landscape so alluring you wanted nothing more at that moment than to be inside the painting. It didn't matter what it depicted—a mountain scene, a clearing in the forest, waves crashing on the seashore—it was perfect and exactly where you wanted to be. Then just as it would seem the painting had reached a point of perfection, you notice that the show still has five minutes left. At this point, Bob would dig into his palette, load a brush up with paint, and begin to cover an entire third of the painting with a giant tree, saying "I'll tell you what, we've got time. Let's add one more happy little tree close up here for perspective." And from your couch you scream "Nooooo!" because at first it seems like he has just ruined that perfect landscape, but somehow Bob fleshes it out in the last two minutes of the show and suddenly the whole looks wonderful and inviting again, except even more perfect than before. And as the credits prepare to roll, Bob turns to the camera with a big smile and wishes his viewers: "Happy painting and God bless."

The creation of Glencoe followed much the same pattern, except that instead of thirty minutes Mother Nature stretched her show out for 450 million years. The Caledonian Orogeny, which pushed the land up into the original highland plateau, provided the blank canvas. Within the next twenty million years or so (the first few minutes of the show), broad strokes were added by a huge series of volcanoes, erupting in the region and pushing the land up further into a tremendous caldera at least four times the height of Glencoe's mountains today. Over the course of the next 400 million years (that is, the bulk of the show), Mother Nature employed wind and water to carve up this caldera and the surrounding plateau, forming happy little peaks here and deep little valleys there, until the landscape must have approached a point of beauteous perfection. Then, noticing she still had a bit of time left (2.5 million years, in this case), she dug into her palette, loaded up her brush with a sheet of ice and dumped it over most of the painting. And keep in mind this was no happy little sheet of ice, but a towering mass three times as high as the Empire State Building. Imagine the universal scream of "Noooo!" coming from the couch. But somehow, over the course of the next couple million years (the last few seconds of the show, really), that sheet of ice shifted and dug and advanced and receded, until finally, less than 12,000 years ago (the last split second before the credits rolled), the ice melted to reveal a landscape even more perfect than before: full of rocky peaks and green, sweeping valleys lined with trickling streams, cascading waterfalls, and tumbled boulders, all interspersed with purplish heather. And you can just imagine Mother Nature, outfitted in a flare-collared shirt and a towering afro turning to the camera with a big smile and saying: "Happy painting and God bless."

Since 1935, the curator of much of this masterpiece has been the National Trust of Scotland, the organization that looks after more than 14,000 acres of landscape containing Glencoe and the surrounding area, including the hundreds of happy little deer, mountain hare, pine martens, wildcats and glorious golden eagles that call the valleys home. Such wildlife is joined by the slightly less wild but equally appealing sheep that free range graze on the hillsides throughout much of the park, and, inevitably, by the thousands of tourists and adventure seekers who flock to the region each year. As one might expect, the need to balance the welfare of this striking but fragile natural environment with the interests of human activity creates one of the great challenges of the National Trust, and one they handle, so far as I can tell, with the utmost acuity—which is fortunate, as the crowds show no signs of abating anytime soon.

It is only natural that such a beautiful area would become a veritable Mecca for tourists. Indeed, as early as 1873, none other than Queen Victoria herself visited Glencoe to sketch the Three Sisters, afterwards noting in her journal the crowds of onlookers who disrupted her endeavors. One such onlooker, in a move that would do any modern paparazzi proud, turned his telescope away from the view and onto the monarch, before being chased off by the Queen's henchmen. Of course, such a scene would seem like relative solitude compared to a visit today, when Victoria would have to sit with her sketch book in a parking lot opposite the peaks, surrounded by fleets of shiny tour buses, all belching out families and silver-haired couples who spend thirty seconds ogling the view and the next ten minutes browsing for postcards and posing for pictures with an ever-present bagpiper, employed by the bus companies to add authenticity and mood to the scene, as if the beauty of the peaks were not enough.

Naturally, the tour bus crowd represents only one breed of visitor to the valley. The other, more serious breed consists of the hikers and climbers who avoid these parking lot overlooks like the plague and instead lose themselves deep in the 14,000 acres of wilderness, where it is still possible to feel like one has the entire region to oneself.

Glencoe and its neighboring valleys are, after all, a climber's paradise. Though members of highland clans had likely been challenging themselves for centuries on the surrounding peaks, not until 1868 when a local shepherd made a daring climb to a site named Ossian's Cave do we get our first recorded ascent in the region. For the next two decades, a trickle of others would follow suit, recording first ascents of various peaks, but what ultimately opened the floodgates of Scottish mountain climbing had nothing to do with a death-defying feat of bravado; it was instead a simple work published by an avid hillwalker named Sir Hugh Munro.

In 1891, Munro, who had helped found the Scottish Mountaineering Club two years earlier, compiled and published a list of all the peaks in Scotland over 3,000 feet in height. This seemingly innocent list, which includes 284 peaks in all, would forever change the sport of climbing in Scotland, giving rise to the inevitable activity of "Munro-bagging", which, despite sounding like a challenge issued to fraternity brothers regarding a set of particularly fun-loving triplets, refers instead to the somewhat loftier—though equally testosterone-inspired—pursuit of summiting each peak on Sir Hugh's list.

To those familiar with higher mountain ranges—the Rockies or the Alps, for instance—climbing a series of 3,000 foot peaks may not seem like such an impressive feat. Having lived in Colorado myself, I rather laughed at the notion of the Scottish highlands as a destination for serious mountain climbing, considering anything under 10,000 feet to be something of an amble up a friendly slope, such as one might find among the rolling mountains of the Appalachians. This opinion would change shortly after Katrina and I left Fort William.

Driving south toward Glencoe, we were treated to a view of formidable looking peaks, their steep sides and stony faces resembling more the jagged eminence of the Rockies than the rounded tops of the Appalachians. Though some Munros require nothing more than a hillwalk to reach their summit, many more provide a somewhat stiffer challenge—a steep scramble up near vertical slopes, followed by technical climbing, supported by ropes and an array of specialty equipment, to reach the summit. And given that most of these mountains start near sea level and rise abruptly to their full heights, 3,000 feet above the valley floors, the weather near the summits is as unpredictable as mountains many times their height, with dangerous storms and blinding mist capable of appearing at any moment, even on the sunniest of days. Thus, it is no surprise that, since the publication of Munro's list in 1891, only 3,300 climbers—an average of less than twenty-nine per year—have become "compleationists", the term (archaic spelling included) given to those who bag every Munro in Scotland.*
I suspect the number would have been higher for the fun-loving triplets.

---

* Don't worry. Once you finish bagging the Munros, the fun is not over. You can then tackle the 219 "Corbetts" (peaks between 2,500 and 2,999 feet) and even the 224 "Grahams" (peaks between 2,000 and 2,499 feet), though the 89 Grahams located in the Scottish lowlands are also known as "Donalds".

・ ・ ・ ・ ・

Leaving Fort William behind, Katrina and I were now heading into the heart of Munro country. No less than sixty Munros—that is, over twenty percent of the total—are located within a twenty-five mile radius of Glencoe. On our way to the valley, which would serve as our home for the next two days, the road from Fort William took us into the shadow of the granddaddy of all Munros: Ben Nevis, reaching 4,406 feet into the Scottish sky.

We had no intention of climbing it. Ben Nevis, despite being the highest mountain in all of Britain—and claiming more lives annually than Everest—is by no means the toughest to summit. Indeed, our guidebook warned that in mid-summer queues can even form to get to the top, the route has become so popular. But we had woken to our first dreary day in Scotland, driving in a light mist all the way from Fort William, and could only make out the base of Ben Nevis as we approached, the upper reaches disappearing in a blanket of clouds.

"Standing in line in a cold rain waiting to summit a peak with zero visibility sounds like something I could miss," Katrina pointed out.

I agreed. We would have needed a line just to find the summit. Instead, we pulled into the Glen Nevis Visitor Centre to see what opportunities the adjacent valley offered. The answer was quite a lot.

A brochure listed an abundance of trails offering a full range of features: from easy strolls through valleys and woods to more difficult routes encompassing high ridges with stunning views—or, as the case would be today, views of an ominous wall of white promising a wondrous plunge to certain death just an invisible step away. We picked a trail that offered a little bit of everything (minus the plummet), including a waterfall, an old cottage ruin and an intriguingly mysterious item appearing on the map as a "wire bridge". Then, for good measure, we purchased Ordnance Survey #41, a map showing specific details and contour lines of the surrounding terrain in 1:50,000 scale. We figured this might come in handy over the next two days should we find ourselves scratching our heads in a mist wondering how we ended up wedged between the edge of a rocky precipice and a free-range sheep with a nasty disposition—a scenario well within our abilities.

As we drove to the trailhead, the sky, much to our pleasure, began to clear. By the time we parked the car and started down the trail, the mist had almost stopped and blue patches of sky poked through. I say again: beautiful weather, that country.

The trail, incidentally, was wonderful. The first part took us through a stretch of trees, which our brochure identified as a mixture of birch, hazel, oak, willow, and Scot's pine. Little streams lined with ferns trickled down the hillsides, passing over the path in places, adding a bit of adventure as we picked our way over the rocks. The path was not crowded per se, but we were by no means alone. Every few minutes, we'd pass a group of people, with the range of ages being worthy of note. Going for a "hillwalk", as they call hiking in Scotland, serves as a popular pastime in the country, and is apparently practiced by people of all ages—much like going for fast food is in America. Ten minutes into the hike, we had passed elderly people with walking sticks, families with small children, and even a group of teenagers, who I assume had been unable to locate the food court at the local mall. The trail was slick and a bit of chill still hung in the air, but everyone we passed wore t-shirts and shorts. Katrina and I trudged on in our rain jackets and fleeces, not ready to shed them yet, but immensely happy to be outside.

After a few minutes, the trail curved and followed the banks of a small river, which our map, in a tip of the hat to literal nomenclature, referred to as the Water of Nevis. We strolled along the banks of the swift-moving river, which jumped and cascaded over boulders in a beguiling fashion for perhaps a quarter mile further before the trail emerged from the trees into the open splendor of a U-shaped valley. The woods continued on the hillside to our right, though the steep slope to our left was virtually treeless, being clad instead in a lush covering of green grass speckled with the white and gray of tumbled boulders. The Water of Nevis snaked across the valley floor, its gravelly banks spreading out to the hills on either side. Of course, it took a moment for these details to register, as my attention—from the moment I stepped out of the cover of the woods—was pulled to the far end of the valley, where a cascade of white, lacy water slipped gracefully between two promontories of rock to plunge nearly four hundred feet to the river below. Bob Ross would have been proud.

Continuing along the valley floor toward the waterfall, we became aware of a cluster of people gathered not at the base of the falls, as one might expect, but slightly to the side, their attention captured by another spectacle in the valley. This was the mysterious wire bridge marked on our map, and the crowd had gathered to watch those brave enough, or foolhardy enough, as the case may be, to attempt its crossing. The bridge, which appeared to have been lifted from a Barnum & Bailey tent, consisted of just three wire cables, each less than two inches round, spanning the river. Crossing the bridge required a shuffling of feet along the lowest wire, some ten feet or so above the water's surface, while maintaining balance by grasping with outstretched arms the two higher wires passing to either side of the crosser's head—much like a tightrope with training wheels. The crowd looked on in great anticipation as each person left the safety of the bank and edged out over the water's surface. You could almost sense the collective desire to see someone fall.

Such sadism in this case can be excused, as there was no need to cross the bridge. The trail continued past the waterfall on the same side of the river it had followed all along, and so those who attempted the bridge did so for the sole purpose of saying they had. Being in Scotland, this included almost everyone: fit-looking men and women in the prime of life, small children straining to reach the upper wires, a grandmother with her walker, and so on. Not wanting to appear wimpy, we took our place in line.

Because the wires were so shaky only one person could cross at a time without bouncing the person ahead of them into the water. When my turn finally came, I edged out over the river, which instantly seemed much wider than it had a moment before. There's nothing like looking down at air beneath your feet to distort perspective and begin playing tricks on the mind. Ten feet—the height of a basketball rim I can still jump up and touch—suddenly seems dangerously high. Balance becomes a thing not to be taken for granted, and the simple task of holding on to two wires seems a lot to ask. I clung to them for dear life, shuffling one foot in front of the other along the lowest wire for what seemed to be a very long time. I imagined spectators on the bank torn between boredom and the escalating thrill that I just might be the one to take the plunge. Finally, seemingly much later that day, I reached the far bank and gratefully stepped off the swinging wires onto solid ground.

Katrina, who has no natural fear of heights, arrived a split second later, apparently having done back handsprings across the lower wire.

"Did you see the fish swimming beneath your feet?" she asked.

"No, I missed that," I muttered, wiping the sweat from my brow. I had seen jagged rocks waiting to claim a victim.

She shrugged and took a seat on a flat rock to the left of the bridge. It seemed that, now that we were over here, there was nowhere really to go except back across the bridge. Thus, we huddled on the far bank beside those who had crossed before us, until finally the line paused on the other side to give us a chance to cross back—much to the joy of the bankside spectators, who were by this time placing bets on my expected progress. To their visible disappointment, I crossed safely again.

That experience behind us, we continued our hike on solid ground. Past the bridge, the valley doglegged and became, if possible, even more beautiful than before. We had entered the famous valley Hollywood film producers love so much. Steep, treeless slopes swept gracefully down to the river only to curve up, in a nod to symmetry, on the other side. As we walked, it was not difficult to picture a glacier pushing through 12,000 years ago to carve out this natural wonder; you could have convinced me it had happened last week. Here the hiking consisted of an easy stroll along the valley floor, with the biggest challenge being keeping our feet dry as we passed a series of boggy spots. (All that glacial runoff, I figured.) We eventually crossed a small stream feeding into the Water of Nevis, and shortly thereafter had reached the much anticipated cottage ruins.

There was not much left to see. Just a few crumbled stone walls, really;

though they were still arranged in their original pattern allowing us to discern the different rooms. We poked around for a bit, refreshed ourselves with a snack, and tried to imagine what it must have been like to live out here, herding sheep in the vast emptiness of this singular valley.

"One thing's for sure," Katrina noted, "you could cross 'short talk' off the list of worries."

Had we been so inclined, Katrina and I could have followed the trail on past the ruins and onto neighboring Rannoch Moor, one of the most isolated tracts of land in Britain—a true wilderness, according to our guidebook, covering 150 square miles of "uninhabitable peat bogs, lochs, heather hillocks, strewn lumps of granite and a few gnarled Caledonian pine." The only way in or out, other than on foot was via a lonely outpost of the West Highland Railway known as Corrour Station, which wasn't even serviced by a road. Though we both felt fresh enough to keep walking, we took the decision instead to turn around. We still didn't know where we were sleeping that night, and as good as it felt to be outside, neither of us much fancied the prospect of sleeping in a trackless moor exposed to the elements and stalked by free-range sheep.

• • • • •

Feeling rather pleased with ourselves after our first real highland adventure, we set out next to secure accommodation in an establishment called the Clachaig Inn, described by our guidebook as a gathering place for serious hikers and climbers exploring the area. Nestled in the heart of the Glencoe valley, surrounded by steep peaks and heather-clad slopes, the Clachaig seemed the perfect place for a couple of rugged adventurers like us to swap stories with likeminded souls. I could describe my wire bridge experience, where I defied death from the height of ten feet, and they could tell me about the 3,500 feet of sheer rock they pulled themselves up earlier that day using only their fingernails and teeth.

Finding the inn was no small task, as the Clachaig is located on a back road some three miles from the village of Glencoe. Once there, however, we knew we had made a good choice. The interior served as a shrine to outdoor adventure, with old skis and ice picks decorating the walls. A sign at the front desk warned "No hawkers or Campbells", offering a stoic reminder of the tragic events that had taken place within the valley. We secured a comfortable room (it had a shower I could extend my arms in), scattered our luggage lavishly over the floor, and went down to the pub in the highest of spirits.

After a congratulatory pint, we drove to the nearby Glencoe Visitor Centre where I spent a happy hour reading about the valley's history, geology, wildlife, and climbing traditions. The displays, to the delight of a teacher like me, were extremely well done and included a mixture of video, photography, and even interactive games—these latter being meant undoubtedly for children, but enjoyed equally, I can attest, by a 31-year old man from Ohio. My favorite feature, however, consisted of a wall display full of photographs and quotes from individuals representing all the various constituencies that frequent the valley: hill walkers, ice climbers, shepherds, rangers, environmentalists, musicians, local villagers, all offering their perspective on what Glencoe means to them. I liked this very much.

Feeling enlightened, we returned to the Clachaig to enjoy a hearty meal of steak and ale pie on the outdoor patio while choosing from a vast selection of beverages on tap: Red MacGregor, Three Sisters Pale Ale, Blackthorn Cider, Fraoch Heather Ale, and so on. Having not heard of any of them, I decided to sample several. Thus it was that, by the time we meandered from the dining patio to the pub an hour or so later, any inhibition of short talk was gone and I readied myself for an evening of adventurous tales. To this end, the Clachaig delivered, though the experience would prove more humbling than I had hoped.

There was to be live music tonight, and already a crowd filled the pub when we entered. In Scottish tradition, we approached a booth occupied by just two men and asked if we could join. They nodded consent, and before long we had struck up an amiable conversation with Elan, an East Coast American backpacking around Scotland, and Steve, an oil man from Aberdeen on weekend holiday. (At least, I think Steve was an oil man. He may have been a whale man, or the mayor, for all I know. The Aberdonian accent is notoriously difficult to understand, even by native Scots.) They were both staying at a youth hostel closer to town and had walked over for a pint and music.

"Did you get into the valley yet?" Elan asked.

"Tomorrow," I said, "but we did a great hike in Glen Nevis today." I told him about our earlier adventure, including the hundred-foot high wire bridge I had fearlessly crossed.

This failed to elicit the hoped-for reaction. Instead, Elan bent his head quizzically and asked, "Was the trail crowded?"

"A bit, but not bad," I replied.

"I've found that most serious hikers and climbers in Scotland don't use trails. They just pick a spot on the map and go."

I looked at Aberdonian Steve who nodded in agreement. "Jus' pick a wee spo' n' gae," he affirmed, at which point he and Elan each told us the story of their separate adventures that day. Elan had scrambled to a ridge top and summited a Munro. Steve had flown to France and firebombed parliament. (I may have misunderstood Steve here.)

I looked at Katrina pathetically. We were no strangers to the outdoors. We'd hiked all over America in recent years, including backcountry trips in the Grand Canyon, the Smoky Mountains, the Narrows of Zion, and the wilderness around Tahoe—all of which had entailed fully-loaded packs, multiple-day provisions, and the very real possibility of getting mauled by something larger than a sheep. But on all of these excursions, we'd stuck to a predetermined trail. Suddenly, we felt like a couple of lightweights.

Fortunately, our new companions took pity on us. In a flash, Aberdonian Steve had produced a map from his back pocket, spreading it out on the table between us. And here I should note that the pub of the Clachaig Inn is *exactly* the kind of place one can spread out a topographic map on a table, lean over it with a pint of ale pointing excitedly at its various features and not seem a bit out of place. We did this now, with Steve and Elan making recommendations for us while deciding on their own route for tomorrow. Finally, with a plan in place and the band starting up, I bought a round of pints and relaxed into the ending of what had been as near a perfect day in Scotland as one could possibly conceive—which is saying quite a lot for a day that had started in Fort William.

. . . . .

The next morning found us up early, ready for our day's adventure and anxious to shed any trappings of wimpiness lingering from the night before. Buoyed by a hearty breakfast and provisioned with daypacks bursting with snacks, water bottles, and layers of clothing in case of inclement weather, we bustled into the car. The starting point of our journey lay just a short drive away and took us past the majestic triple peaks of the Three Sisters, which I noted were bereft of tour buses and bagpipers at this early hour. Patches of blue peeked out from behind high clouds, allowing us uninterrupted views of the passing scenery. It promised to be a great day.

Parking the car at the appointed spot, we were presented with a magnificent scene. A stretch of flat grassland rolled out before a long valley—another classic U-shaped, treeless expanse—which dead-ended after several miles into the steep rise of a mighty peak. I checked the scene against our topographic map, considering our route with giddy anticipation. The plan was to walk along the floor of the valley, scramble up to a saddle,* walk along the ridgeline to take in a Munro, and then descend on the far side of the mountain, returning through the adjacent valley. With its grass covered terrain and smooth slopes, the route looked quite literally like a walk in the park. Excitedly, we stepped off the pavement and strode confidently into the wide-open expanse of Glencoe.

Almost immediately, Katrina sunk to her knee in a bog. It was amazing to watch. One moment she walked along jauntily, and the next she resembled a cartoon character, standing at a tilted angle, one leg still firmly on solid ground, the other stuck fast in a slimy underworld of mire. I immediately began hatching a plan for rescue, which consisted of tossing her a granola bar and running to fetch a bagpiper for help. Before I could

---

* Saddles are low-lying ridges between mountain peaks.

255

put such chivalry into action, Katrina rocked back onto the dry ground and slowly, with a wonderful sucking sound, wrenched herself free. Sporting an expression that revealed a fair dose of wonderment ("Now, that was unexpected..."), she stood up to brandish a leg which, from the knee down, showed no differentiation between skin, sock or boot—like the mud-covered stump of a peg-legged pirate.

"Uhh, do you want to go back to the hotel and change?" I ventured helpfully. We were still within fifty feet of the car.

Without a word, Katrina plumped down in the grass, removed her shoe—pouring out copious amounts of black sludge, like a punctured oil pan, as she did so—took off and shook out her sock, and proceeded to wipe off her leg with blades of dry grass until little streaks of skin began showing through. Within minutes, she had reassembled herself, stood up, and with an authoritative "Let's go"—as if we had merely paused to consider the scenery—shouldered her pack and gamely strode on toward the valley. I hastened to follow, thinking what a great story this would make back at the pub, especially once I had moved the location of incident three miles into the interior and added the presence of threatening sheep.

From that point on, the hike proved rather slow going, even though we were theoretically on flat ground. We hopped from dry spot to dry spot along the floor of the valley, until we actually developed some skill at recognizing firm soil, though occasionally we would end up stranded on a closed peninsula surrounded by bog, leaving us no choice but to retrace our steps or slog through wherever it seemed like the ground might best support our weight—a gamble that usually brought on a bout of flailing arms and a string of expletives, as our boots sank to various depths in the mud. Snowshoes would have helped. Webbed feet would have been ideal.

After a couple of miles, we found ourselves beneath a saddle, high on the hill to our right. It was not the saddle we had planned to climb. That one still loomed a considerable way off, but the opportunity to head to higher, and presumably drier, ground proved too irresistible to ignore. Besides, my topographic map showed that once on this saddle we had a nice choice of walking either way along the ridgeline to lofty peaks—not

Munros, but quite respectable nonetheless—or descending down the other side of the mountain to the neighboring valley, all of which was in keeping with our original plan, though it lopped off a considerable distance and the opportunity of summitting a Munro.

"I'm really okay with that," said Katrina, who by this point had fallen several more times and resembled nothing more than a mud wrestler who had lost a recent bout with the swamp creature.

Thus, we abandoned the valley floor and made directly for the saddle, which looked benevolently close, though we would find out just how deceptive distances can be in a treeless expanse where visibility extends for miles in each direction. Scrambling up the slope did prove drier than walking on the valley floor, but the route was considerably steeper than it had looked—like hiking straight up the leaning tower of Pisa—and the further up we went the steeper it got. By the time we were halfway up what had seemed like an innocuous, grassy hillside, we were using our hands as well as our feet, and pausing to rest every few steps to catch our breath, though such breaks also afforded the opportunity to admire the scenery, which, from this new height, was absolutely stunning. The graceful sweep of the valley was even more pronounced from above, and we could look back and see the road, now far off, with more slopes and peaks rising behind it.

With great effort, we finally reached the saddle. It hadn't required any technical climbing per se, just a heavy mix of endurance and perseverance. And it was worth every step. If the views halfway up the hillside had been spectacular, the view from the top was—yes, the word is justified again—breathtaking. We could now look down into two valleys: the one we had come from and the one we would soon descend into. Jagged peaks resembling much higher mountains—the Tetons or Sierra Nevadas—jutted into the sky, though they no longer seemed that far above us. We marveled at our luck with the weather. According to my guidebook, this part of Scotland receives nearly eighty inches of precipitation per year, and on most days would offer views of nothing but white mist. But don't believe it for a second. Beautiful weather, that country.

Taking a better look at my map, I realized we'd gained nearly nine hundred vertical feet in less than a half-mile on our little hillside scramble. I really need to pay more attention to these things before setting off. As a reward for our efforts—and because we were temporarily unable to move—we lingered for a while on the ridgetop, picnicking on a boulder that seemed placed there for just that purpose and enjoying a well-deserved rest in a glorious place. Having reached the ridge, it was tempting to walk along for a while toward the summit, but at this point any trail leading up seemed infinitely inferior to those leading down. Thus, we soon found ourselves involved in a precipitous descent down the other side. Once again, distances proved farther than they first appeared, and several more hours had passed by the time we'd reached the valley floor, rounded the mountain's base and finally found ourselves back at the car, dripping with sweat, caked with mud, and extremely pleased with ourselves.

On the drive back home, we re-passed the Three Sisters overlook, which was now filled with shiny tour buses and people of all ages milling around racks of postcards, and posing with the obligatory bagpiper.

"What a bunch of lightweights," I sneered, as Katrina rolled her eyes and flicked a chunk of dried mud from her boot in my direction.

Back at the hotel, we made a beeline for our room and luxuriated in long showers (arms fully outstretched) and then plopped ourselves on the outdoor patio for a dinner of venison burgers and the first of what would be many pints. Later at the pub, we met up with Aberdonian Steve and Elan and excitedly related our adventures for the day, which I'm sure must have impressed them mightily. On their outing, they had only managed to summit two Munros and descend a precipitous cliff face using nothing but hand and toe holds. What a bunch of lightweights.

# Chapter 21: Men in Skirts

### (A day at the Callander Highland Games)

Here's something fun to try at home. Go out to the yard and cut down a tree, the bigger the better. If you live in a city, a telephone pole will do. Now, stand it on end and hoist it into the air so that the top points straight at the sky and the bottom is cradled at your waist. Feeling a bit wobbly? Well, steady up, because here comes the fun part. Keeping the tree perpendicularly balanced, run across the yard and flip it, end over end, as far as you can. Splendid.

If you liked that, let's try another. Go get a sledgehammer out of the tool shed. I don't mean one of those wimpy five-pound sledges. Grab one of the big boys, a twenty-pounder, something with some persuasion to it. Now, grasping it firmly with two hands, spin it around your head and let it fly. Feels good, doesn't it? For more fun, I might also recommend picking up a rock—one about the size of Gary Coleman—and heaving it like a shot put. If on any of these attempts you hit your neighbor's house across the street, you just may be ready for the highland games. If, as is more probable, you fell somewhat short of your neighbor's house—dropping the object on your toe, for example—might I suggest joining me on the sideline to watch? There is plenty to see.

Besides the aforementioned events, known as the caber toss, the hammer throw and putting the stone, respectively, you will witness other amazing feats of strength at a highland games, like the tossing of a 56-pound weight—the equivalent of a third grader—for height, or a brutal bout of tug of war, with a rope pulled so taut it seems likely to snap before either team gives way. Elsewhere, tests of speed and endurance take place, as athletes attempt the "long leap" or partake in a "hill run". Meanwhile, visitors can enjoy dancing contests, piping contests, and any number of other side shows, usually entailing craft stalls, greasy food stands, and a generous scattering of beer tents, all of which transform a highland games from a mere sporting event into a full-blown community party. Indeed, the atmosphere is reminiscent of a county fair or harvest festival in the American Midwest, where people come in droves to play games, guzzle beer, and ogle a prize-winning squash the size of a refrigerator. ("Damn, Eddie, take a look at that punkin'. It's bigger'n the tires on Vernon's truck.") Perhaps this festive air is why highland games are often referred to as "gatherings".

The origins of these gatherings remain somewhat obscure. They are generally agreed to have begun as a clever way for highland chiefs to identify the best fighting men in their clans. Clearly, it would be an advantage to have the option of picking up and throwing trees at foes. Just how long ago such a tradition took root, however, is unknown. Our guidebook estimated the first games to have occurred in the 14th century, though the Braemar Gathering—the most famous of all highland games*— claims to go back further still, all the way to the 11th century, with the first supposed gathering having been hosted at Braemar by our old friend Malcolm Bighead, Macbeth's murderer.

What *is* certain is that highland games are immensely popular today. Between the months of May and September, spectators in Scotland can attend any of 135 separate highland festivals. In the height of the season a particularly avid fan could travel from event to event, seeing different gatherings every day of the week. These competitions do not take place solely in the north, but are scattered throughout the country, lowland and highland alike. Such is their popularity that the games have even expanded beyond Scotland, taking place around the world wherever Scots have settled: North America, Australia, South Africa. Indeed, Scottish historian Fitzroy McLean, a man who knows his highland games, claims the best gathering he ever attended took place on Grandfather Mountain in North Carolina. These are clearly phenomena with mass appeal.

And just why shouldn't crowds queue up to watch these events, especially when they feature such splendid contenders? Take Donald Dinnie, for example. Dinnie competed in the 19th century, when highland

---

* The Braemar Gathering, held the first Saturday of every September, is annually presided over by the monarchy, often with the Queen herself in attendance—though, sadly, not competing.

gatherings were undergoing a revival in the wake of Queen Victoria's infatuation with all things Scottish. An all-around athlete with a sense of flair, Dinnie excelled at both strength and track events, and was even reputed to do a little dancing in between. Traveling around the world to compete, he became a living legend, drawing bigger crowds in America than championship baseball teams, and so thoroughly dominated each gathering he attended as to be called "the 19th century's greatest athlete" by at least one writer. Such was his strength—and, apparently, his showmanship—that well into his seventies Dinnie would appear at events, hoisting a table over his head while, on top, two dancers performed the Highland fling.

But even Dinnie's individual feats have been surpassed by the giants competing today, who continue to get bigger, stronger and better at throwing heavy stuff around. In 1979, a man named Brian Oldfield heaved a 25-pound stone over 46 feet, a record that still stands at the time of this writing. Had Oldfield been standing in the front of a Greyhound Bus at the time, the stone would have cleared the people seated in the back row. In 1998, a 22-pound hammer was thrown 130 feet. 130 feet! In 2006, a 56-pound weight tossed straight up into the air cleared a 20-foot high bar—the equivalent of throwing a bag of cement onto the roof of a two-storey house. And keep in mind that every last one of these feats was achieved by a man wearing a plaid skirt.

Now, doesn't that sound more interesting than staring at a giant squash?

•   •   •   •   •

I'm sure the reader can imagine our excitement as Katrina and I left Glencoe and started driving toward the town of Callander where a highland festival would be taking place that very afternoon. We had been looking forward to this our whole trip; indeed, we had planned our itinerary around it, booking a reservation at a local B&B for the next three nights. Callander, located smack dab in the center of the country, would serve as headquarters for our last days in Scotland. We could not have chosen better.

For starters, the town's central location made it the perfect place to venture out on daytrips to nearby areas: the historic town of Stirling or the lochs and hills of beautiful Trossachs National Park, for example. Even more exciting for those who go in for this sort of thing, our guest room was located in an establishment known as Arden House, a stately mansion made famous as the TV home of Drs. Finlay and Cameron—Britain's answer to the odd couple—and their trusty housekeeper Janet on a long-running TV series called "Dr. Finlay's Casebook".[*] Having never heard of the show, Katrina and I weren't quite as excited as we were supposed to be by this bit of trivia (had we been staying in the mansion of "The Beverly Hillbillies" now *that* would have been something), but we were pleased to note Arden House's impeccable condition, tidy rooms, well-kept garden and friendly proprietors to look after our every need. Further, the home's location on the edge of town gave us the daily option of going for strolls in the adjacent forest where a waterfall, an ancient Pictish fort, and other woodland pleasures awaited, or, conversely, walking the few blocks into the town center, with its attractive stone buildings lining the main street, a pleasant park with a duck pond, and the smooth waters of the River Teith rolling by. All in all, it seemed a wonderful place to end our stay.

Of course, this would all be discovered in days to come. For now, we were on a mission.

After a brief exploratory walk to get our bearings, we found ourselves following a stream of people across the river and down a road to a large, open field on the outskirts of town. A central area had been roped off to establish a playing field for the athletic competitions. This "Main Arena", as it was generously titled in the program, measured roughly the size of a soccer pitch—indeed, it may have been a soccer pitch—and was ringed on all sides by colorful tents advertising everything from sausage to t-shirts. One tent, placed a little too near the beer tent, it seemed to me, sold various medieval weapons—battle axes, two-handed claymores, broadswords and the like—which I supposed would prove handy should I be suddenly seized

---

[*] The show, which captivated millions of viewers across Britain, ran for ten years (1962-1971), the exact time span during which Americans were likewise mesmerized by *The Beverly Hillbillies*.

with the desire to cut a man in half. I noted with some trepidation the sizable crowd gathered in front of the tent, examining the sharpness of the blades and taking exploratory swipes in the air, and made a mental note to be extra courteous to everyone today.

As we completed our circuit of the tents, people were already getting settled in for the afternoon, setting up lawn chairs or spreading out blankets beside the ring. We ordered two pints from the beer tent and claimed a spot on the grass, thinking how wonderful it was that on a beautiful summer day in Scotland we could sit directly in the sun and not be the least bit uncomfortable. Shortly thereafter, we were treated to one of the most evocative sounds one can experience when sitting in an open field surrounded by rolling hills and a tent full of deadly war implements: the far off sound of droning bagpipes. An excited murmur rose amongst the spectators. The opening parade had begun.

The procession consisted of all the participants in the day's games making their way en masse from town to field. A band of kilted pipers led the way, followed by a marching band which, in lieu of kilts, sported snazzy tartan pants. As the musicians made their way down the road and into the arena, more and more of the parade's participants came into view. It was, to put it mildly, a motley crew. A wild looking group wrapped in traditional highland plaids played a raucous rhythm on drums while various members hopped around brandishing claymores and Scottish flags. A motorcycle stunt team balanced on racing bikes, revving their engines and popping wheelies in dangerously confined quarters. Members of a dueling society attired in 18th century garb engaged in mock sword fighting as they marched. There was even a mysterious fellow accoutered as a one-man band, strumming a ukulele, blowing into a mouth harp, and clashing little cymbals attached to his shoes.

And, of course, there were the athletes. Imagine the offensive line of any NFL team dressed in kilts and you will have a fair idea of the image the competitors presented as they filed into the arena. Except add to that image a handful of equally large and powerful women. The Callander gathering comprised part of the World Championship of Highland Games, meaning the athletes were of the very highest caliber. Indeed, one of the women competing today held four world records.[*] I shivered as she passed.

Showing just how popular highland games have become worldwide, the competitors hailed from all over: Holland, England, even the United States. I was pleased to see two Scots competing as well, with one being a native of the Callander region. The crowd cheered for him wildly as he and the other athletes made a slow circuit of the ring. The scene could have been straight from the Roman Coliseum, except no lion would have been crazy enough to enter the arena.

Shortly thereafter, the honorary Chieftain of the Games, a balding and portly man who looked as likely to compete in a highland games as the Queen must at Braemar, walked onto the field, banged a ceremonial targe and sword in the four cardinal directions, and the competition was underway.

Let me say now that even if someone isn't remotely interested in seeing a highland gathering it is still worth attending the games at Callander just to observe and listen to the Master of Ceremonies, a middle-aged man clad in the most splendidly outrageous outfit I have ever seen. His maroon shirt, kilt of tan tartan, and knee high socks of a similar but badly clashing pattern were topped off with a jaunty Scottish bonnet and pair of square sunglasses, apparently lifted off the set of *The Terminator*. His appearance, however, paled in comparison to the running commentary he kept up throughout the afternoon.

From the moment the games started, he delivered a play-by-play analysis, beautiful for its bluntness and wit, of the athletes and the events. Such commentary resembled what any well-trained, highly paid TV sportscaster would offer, with this very important distinction: whereas TV commentators remain shut away in a booth talking to anonymous people, a great many of whom are comatose on their couches miles away and therefore quite incapable of taking revenge for any comment that may

---

[*] This was Shannon Hartnet, an American competitor who, at the time of this writing, holds the world record for putting the 14 lb. stone (44' 2"), throwing the 28 lb. weight for distance (47' 11.5"), throwing the 12 lb. hammer (120' 1"), and throwing the 28 lb. weight for height (18' 8"), according to www.highlandgames.net/records.html.

offend, the Callander emcee spoke into a microphone in the open air, allowing his every comment to be overheard not just by the crowd, but also—and here is the critical point—by the athletes themselves. Keep in mind these were very large people capable of reducing him to nothing more than a smudge mark in a bonnet without breaking a sweat. Yet, this inhibited him not at all.

Throughout the afternoon, as men looking like they should be named "Ox" or "Killer" would heave a stone or throw a hammer what seemed to be an impressively long distance, the emcee would offer comments like: "Oh, that was disappointing. Ox will have to work on his form to do better than that," or "Oh, my, but that was a bad throw! Not good at all, I'm afraid. Killer can't be happy." Meanwhile, Ox and Killer would be standing a mere fifteen feet away, listening to this commentary echo throughout the valley. I suspected disaster at any moment, and found myself wondering just how far that bonnet would pull down over the emcee's body before his spinal cord gave way and splintered into fine pieces.

Amazingly, disaster never came. To their infinite credit, the athletes took every comment in good humor, even laughing along when their performance earned a particularly cutting remark like: "Well short of anything respectable there," or "Perhaps his sister could take a wee shot at it." And so on.

Thus, far from casting a pall over the event, the emcee's comments—along with the reaction, or lack thereof, from the athletes—helped add to the festive atmosphere of the afternoon. What became very obvious to me was that even though these competitors were deadly serious about what they were doing, and even though there was quite a lot of pride and money at stake, they were still having a good time. I found that wonderfully refreshing, especially given the ridiculous, ego-inspired antics that dominate professional sports in the United States today. Imagine an NBA player sitting passively, or even laughing as a commentator criticized his performance over a loud speaker. It simply wouldn't happen. He'd have his entourage waiting outside the booth by the next time out, and his shoe sponsor would sue for damages. But I digress.

There is something organic about the events of highland games. Watching people run up a hillside rather than on a track seems infinitely more exciting to me, and probably a tad more useful when recruiting warriors for battle, not that this comes into play much these days. This organic nature rings particularly true in the strength events, collectively known as the "heavies". The Callander games focused on the heavies at the expense of speed and endurance events, meaning that, sadly, I didn't get to witness a hill run, though I did watch each of the strength events with increasing fascination.

For "putting the stone", athletes were given a rounded river stone weighing 22-pounds to hurl as far as they could. The stone was smooth all over, but by no means a perfect sphere. We watched the athletes turn the stone around in their palm, searching for the sweetest fit, before heaving it on its way to land with an audible thud in the turf. Throwing the weight for distance involved a 28-pound ball attached to a chain looking very much like something discarded by an escaped prisoner. For this event, the athletes, who proved as quick and graceful as they were strong, would grasp the end of the chain and execute a quick spin maneuver—kilts whirling— before releasing the weight smoothly into the air to sail some ninety feet down field. The hammer throw was equally fun to watch, with the athletes spinning the hammer in a wide arcing pattern around their bodies before releasing it backwards over their shoulders. The hammer itself—a rounded rock affixed to the end of a long wooden stick, like something borrowed from Fred Flintstone's tool shed—made a wonderful projectile, cutting through the air rock-end first, its wooden tail streaming behind like a comet.

As the athletes finished with the hammer throw, I glanced at my program and felt a surge of excitement. The caber toss was next. I'm not sure why this event held such fascination for me, though I suspect its novelty played a role. After all, I could go to any high school track meet to watch events like shot put and discus, which, though somewhat different from putting a stone or throwing a weight on a chain, are certainly in the same spirit. But how often does one get to see a man toss a tree trunk? And then, not just toss it, but flip it end over end, trying to land it as straight as possible. For that is the true object, you see. It doesn't matter how far the caber goes—throw it to the parking lot, if you will—but if it doesn't land straight, it is not a good throw. The best of all possible throws, according to the event's official program, is called a "twelve o' clock", which is one that flips neatly over once and lands pointing straight down the field. Imagine summoning the strength to actually throw a tree trunk end over end only to learn that your efforts were in vain because it landed slightly to the left. Really, I've thought long and hard about this and can't think of a single sport anything like it.

Of course, I have to rely on the program's description of what a good caber toss actually looks like as I have yet to see one. In Callander, not only could the athletes not land the caber straight, they couldn't get it to flip end over end at all. Honestly, they couldn't. I watched with great anticipation as, one by one, each contestant stood the caber upright and lifted it, holding it there for a moment to steady it. This always comprised a somewhat comical moment, as the caber, sticking up some twenty feet in the air, literally dwarfed the athlete and often required him to go into a little drunken sailor routine, weaving around to correct for little shifts in weight that would otherwise cause the caber to topple over. Each weave was accompanied by simultaneous gasps of "Whoooaaa! Whooooooooaaaa!" by the crowd, adding to the drama. Once steadied, the competitor would begin running, slowly at first, but picking up speed until, finally, he reached the climactic moment where he leaned back and heaved with everything he had—only to watch the end of the caber thud into the ground and fall back futilely at his feet. After three attempts each, not one contestant had registered a valid throw.

Naturally, the emcee had a heyday with this, reeling off one lament after another with each passing failure. ("Not even close on that one, I'm afraid. Not at all.") I was disappointed, of course, and was even beginning to feel like the athletes, who had performed so admirably in the other events, were somehow letting the crowd down. Then I heard something come out of the emcee's mouth that changed my perspective entirely. After the last failed attempt, the emcee offered explanatory commentary that included the lines: "Oh, those were valiant efforts, but that is an exceptionally stubborn caber. No one's ever turned it, I'm afraid."

I turned to the man beside me in disbelief. "Excuse me, did he just say no one has *ever* been able to turn that caber?"

"Aye, tha's true," replied the man, a chubby, stubble-faced specimen sprawled in a lawn chair and sipping beer out of a plastic cup. He looked like someone who knew a thing or two about caber tossing, though years of beer intake had given his muscles a bit of a soft jiggle.

"But they can turn other cabers?" I asked.

"Aye, they can," Chubby replied, finishing off the beer and adding it to a collection of discarded plastic cups near his feet.

"So there isn't a standard size for a caber?" I pressed.

"Nae, but they're all close," he informed me, picking up and sipping from a full plastic cup which had been waiting in reserve beside his chair. "Within a certain range more or less. Tho' tha's definitely the biggest."

I don't think I have to tell you what I was thinking here.

"Um, if *no* athlete has *ever* turned that caber," I proffered in a state of genuine wonder, "why don't the officials *GET A SMALLER CABER?*" It seemed so obvious to me. As a teacher, if I gave an exam that students continually failed—and not just the bad students, but the smart ones too, every last one of them, year after year—at some point I'd have to ask myself: "Hmmm, I wonder if there's something wrong with that test? Perhaps I should try making a different one."

Chubby, however, seemed quite taken aback by this notion. "Well, tha's nae really the spirit o' the thing now is it?" he retorted, looking quite offended. "Right now it's gae' a wee bit o' challenge tae it."

And I had to be satisfied with that answer. Not just because it sounded like a wonderfully, adventurous approach to life or because it perfectly captured the "never give up" spirit I had come to admire in Scottish culture, but because I thought I saw Chubby sneak a glance at the weapons tent before turning somewhat irritably back to watch the games. But I still couldn't help feeling I'd missed out on the caber toss.

Fortunately, there were plenty of other novel events to see. In conjunction with the highland games, a strongman competition was being held at the other end of the arena. If the highland games athletes looked large, the strongman competitors were absolutely gargantuan. These are the guys you see on ESPN dragging buses across parking lots or playing Frisbee with manhole covers. Indeed, of the competitors today, one was a five-time winner of the Mr. Universe competition and another held the title of Britain's Strongest Man.*

The competition pitted a team from Great Britain against a team from the Ukraine, with the goal of determining which country was better at lifting and carrying heavy objects. During one event called MacGlashan Stones, competitors had to pick up a 200-pound boulder, carry it for a few wobbly steps, and then lift it onto the top of a whisky barrel, roughly shoulder height. If successful, he got to pick up a heavier boulder and repeat the process. There were five boulders in all, with the last one weighing well over 300-pounds and referred to simply as "the meteorite". Another event, called the Farmers Walk, required competitors to pick up two 300-pound oxygen tanks—one in each hand—and carry them as far as they could before the tanks dropped or their arms fell off. It was all quite insane.

At one point during a break in the action, the motorcycle stunt team took the field revving their engines. For the next twenty minutes, they wowed the crowd with unbelievable stunts: formations requiring precision timing to narrowly avoid collisions with other riders, daredevil jumps through rings of fire—all that kind of stuff. This, combined with the strongman competition, was certainly entertaining, but gave the afternoon a sort of redneck, monster truck rally kind of feel.

"Let's go walk around the tents," Katrina shouted over the roar of the engines. "I want to remind myself that I'm still in Scotland and not Texas."

"Good idea," I shouted back, eyeing a cloud of exhaust heading our direction.

We didn't have to go far. In a large tent behind us, a crowd had

---

* This was Eddie Ellwood (Mr. Universe) and Richard Gosling (Britain's Strongest Man).

gathered to watch a dancing competition just getting underway. That is the great thing about a highland festival: you get all the meaty, muscle-bound, over-the-edge-testosterony stuff going on in one section, and in another, young girls in colorful clothing whirl gracefully to fiddle music. Try that at a monster truck rally and the women had better be dressed in bikinis and dancing on poles. But in Scotland, this was just as much a part of the afternoon as the "heavies". The crowd was enthralled, and so were we.

The dancers, who ranged in age from elementary to high school, were all clad in kilts, vests and knee high socks, though each girl had her own color scheme. We watched as they gave spirited performances of the "sword dance" and the "Highland fling", which have become as much a part of highland tradition as tartan or whisky.

The sword dance, as the name suggests, is danced above two crossed swords laid upon the ground. The dancer leaps and twirls over them, gracefully stepping between the blades, but never touching them. According to tradition, highland warriors would perform this dance prior to combat. Making it through the song without disturbing the swords was a good omen for success on the field.

Very different is the Highland fling, which legend holds was danced by clansmen on their targes, the small leather shields used in battle. To simulate this tradition, dancers performing the Highland fling remain in one spot—a remarkable feat, considering the pace and complexity of the steps. We watched the girls hop around with one leg straight and one bent at the knee, variously crossing their feet, kicking, and spinning, all without wandering more than a few inches from their original starting point. They could have performed the dance in a phone booth. Throughout, the dancers kept one arm curved gracefully in the air above their heads, the other bent at the elbow, the hand on their waist. It was beautiful to watch, and a bit contagious. I may have done a little hopping myself.

The dancing rejuvenated our excitement for the highland games, and we returned to our ringside seats to watch the ending of the competition. Alas, the local contender did not win. That honor went to a giant of a man from Holland, named "Claus the Haus" or some such suitable moniker.

Claus received the ceremonial sword and targe for safekeeping until the next competition. In response, he lifted the weapons above his head and emitted a barbaric scream. Everyone in the crowd wet their pants.

•　•　•　•　•

After the competition, we fell in with a stream of hundreds of people on a march back to town. Excitement filled the air as people relived highlights from the day, with ample hyperbole already creeping into the conversations. It had been an afternoon to remember.

Katrina and I broke off from the crowd in search of dinner and a rest back at our room, but later that night as we strolled through the streets of town, a palpable buzz still hung in the air. This proved especially true at the Claymore Bar, from whose doors the sounds of live traditional music wafted into the night, drawing us in like a tractor beam.

Standing with our pints listening to a pub full of Scots singing their anthems—*Massacre of Glencoe, Skye Boat Song, Loch Lomond,* all of which were familiar to me now—my gaze wandered to a sword and targe hanging on the wall above the band. It suddenly dawned on me just how central to highland culture war and conflict had been. The lyrics we now listened to, as well as nearly everything about the highland gathering we had witnessed earlier, had arisen out of the necessities of battle: the piping and dancing as much as the athletic events. I found myself again in awe of the ability Scots have to pull such beauty and joy out of life's hardest moments. If battle was an inevitable hardship of life, music—whether taking the form of bagpipes, fiddles, singing or dancing—provided the release.

It pleased me greatly to think that these traditions were kept alive today at highland festivals throughout the country, and even more that one can now experience them without the actual danger of being cleaved in two by a claymore, so long as he keeps a wary eye on the weapons tent and doesn't question the caber toss.

# Chapter 22: Biking the High Road

## (A journey to Lochs Katrine and Lomond)

Let's talk enigmas for a moment. I've stumbled upon a good one: Rob Roy MacGregor. The name should be familiar. Rob Roy* comes down to us through folk legend as a Scottish Robin Hood of sorts, someone who operated perhaps a little outside the law, but always for noble reasons and for the overall good of his countrymen.

Well, maybe.

I for one won't pretend to know. So far as I can tell, no one today can say with any certainty just who the man was. Depending on which source one consults, MacGregor was either a thief, a daring hero, a scheming opportunist, a man of unimpeachable integrity, a loyal Jacobite, or a government spy. I suppose it's possible he was a little of each, though some of these concepts seem a little hard to marry. I have yet to meet a scheming opportunist of unimpeachable integrity, for example. What *is* certain is that Rob Roy was born into a clan already notorious for its struggles with authority. Well before his birth in 1671, the MacGregors had managed to run so afoul of the government as to have not only their land confiscated but the very name MacGregor outlawed. Imagine how much you have to peeve the government to have the very usage of your name made illegal.

Rob Roy lived in a complicated Scotland to say the least. On top of his own family's troubles, these were Jacobite times, when the dispute over who was the rightful king of Scotland threatened to destroy the very highland way of life. In this climate, Rob Roy did what many highlanders did: rely on a mixture of cattle reiving and shifting alliances to make it through the days and keep food on the table. Naturally, he made enemies doing so, and when a £1,000 loan he had received mysteriously disappeared, MacGregor could not repay his debt and so took to the hills. Whether he absconded with the money or was himself swindled constitutes a subject of

---

* Roy is a corruption of the Gaelic *ruadh*, meaning red. In this case Rob was called Roy because he sported a fine crop of red hair.

some debate, but the event led to a series of exploits—house burnings, manhunts, captures, escapes, the usual stuff—that gave the name Rob Roy MacGregor considerable notoriety throughout the land. Or at least it would have had anyone been allowed to say the name without getting arrested.

In the face of this high adventure, perhaps nothing reveals Rob Roy's resiliency of character better than how he ended his life. Contrary to all expectation, he was not treacherously shot dead by government snipers or double-crossed by his best friend while hiding out in the hills. Rather, he secured a government pardon and lived out his final days quietly at home in Balquhidder, eventually dying in his bed of natural causes. After a life of infamy, how he accomplished such a quiet end only serves to heighten interest in this most enigmatic of men.

Whatever Rob Roy may have been hardly matters now. Flesh and bone have given way to legend, firmly rooted in Scottish folklore and romanticized over and over again by poets, novelists, and, of course, Hollywood. Remarkably, this transformation from man to myth began in MacGregor's own lifetime. In 1723, eleven years before Rob Roy's death, none other than Daniel Defoe wrote of his exploits in a dubious account called *Highland Rogue*. Eighty years later, William Wordsworth added to the legend, penning a poem called "Rob Roy's Grave", and was shortly followed in these efforts by the ubiquitous Sir Walter Scott, whose book, simply titled *Rob Roy*, became one of the most famous of all the *Waverley* novels. More tributes would follow, culminating in the 1995 Hollywood blockbuster, *Rob Roy*, starring Liam Neeson. The film portrays MacGregor as a hunky but reluctant hero, rooted in a strict code of honor and justice, who would prefer to live a quiet life but is instead forced to avenge the wrongs of evil doers around him. Depending on which review one reads, the movie comprised either a faithful retelling of the life of a great man or a fanciful distortion of the misdeeds of a crafty villain. Again it hardly matters. Movie-goers spent over $31 million on the film, and not just because they wanted to see a sultry Jessica Lange run her hands beneath Liam Neeson's kilt.

Perhaps it is because the story has been covered so often by pop culture, and so successfully, at that, that actual historians tend to shy away from the subject. In his history of the Highland clans—a book one would expect to dedicate an entire chapter to Rob Roy's adventures—MacLean makes only three passing references to the man, though one of these does manage to describe MacGregor as "a swashbuckling character whose arms were reputed to reach a full two inches below his knees." This would be a good time to point out that, besides the fact that no one can agree on exactly who Rob Roy was, certainly no one knows for sure what he looked like—though, based on all of the above, it would appear to have been a cross between Liam Neeson and the Grape Ape.

I bring this up because Callander, where we were staying, had a visitor center dedicated to this simian hero, though a visit after the highland games left me still unable to separate man from myth. This isn't to say the center wasn't well done. In fact it was. I just think the facts are so far gone at this point that the story really is best left to the novelists and Hollywood producers. It seems the directors of the visitor center agreed with me based on the numerous copies of Sir Walter Scott's *Rob Roy* they had opportunistically displayed in the gift shop to ensnare soft-headed romantics. I purchased one immediately.

Rob Roy aside, the visitor center proved well worth the trip on two counts. First, I finally learned all about cattle reiving and the complicated relationship between highlanders and lowlanders. It seems highlanders like Rob Roy made a pretty good living by accepting money from lowland lairds to protect their cattle from theft. Of course, the ones offering protection were most often the cattle thieves themselves, so in a sense the laird paid them to not steal his cattle. Brilliant. The highlanders actually developed a name for this new and very useful system. They called it blackmail.

More importantly, our trip to the visitor center taught us that Rob Roy's stomping grounds, which made up most of the land west of Callander, were beautiful enough to comprise the first, and still most popular, national park in Scotland. The Trossachs, as the region is called, abounds with dramatic peaks, wooded glens, and spectacular lochs, which were already becoming a haven for tourists in the early 19th century thanks to the writings of—need I even say—Sir Walter Scott. Eight years before Scott penned *Rob Roy*, he composed a lengthy poem called *Lady of the Lake*, set on beautiful Loch Katrine in the heart of the Trossachs. The year after its publication in 1810, visitation to the loch shot up from 50 to 270 carriages per year—a larger one-year growth rate than even the *DaVinci Code* could manage for Rosslyn Chapel.

With such landscape located just twenty-odd miles from Glasgow, it's not surprising that this surge of tourism continues today. The bumper-to-bumper traffic creeping along the shores of Loch Lomond, the most famous destination in the park, has become nearly as legendary as Rob Roy himself. And much to the delight of MacGregors everywhere, whose ancestors owned much of the Trossachs before their name became a felony, the land that all those tourists crawl through is now commonly referred to as "Rob Roy country". In a story fraught with ironic developments, I think that's the greatest irony of all.

Taken altogether, this seemed like country worth exploring.

· · · · ·

So it was that I found myself the following day warily eyeing the pair of bicycles we had just rented from a shop on the eastern shore of Loch Katrine and wondering what we had gotten ourselves into. The plan, decided on impulse after perusing a brochure of smiling cyclists at the visitor center the previous afternoon, was to put the bikes on a boat, sail to the far end of the loch, and then cycle back at a leisurely pace along a road lining the northern shore. It had seemed a good idea at the time.

The old saying claims one never forgets how to ride a bike, but this cliché—as is the case with most clichés—misses the point entirely. Though it had been a decade since my last ride, I was indeed still clear on the basics of bicycle operation: spinning the pedals to go, turning the handlebars to steer, pulling the handle-thingy to stop, keeping my mouth shut to avoid snacking on bugs. Naturally, one doesn't forget these things. But it is having the confidence to do them at any speed over "granny-pace" that matters. I was wary to say the least.

We took a test-ride around the parking lot, tentatively weaving through young children, grandmothers, and cars that, though parked, still presented threatening obstacles. Predictably, Katrina took right to it. I, however, felt a long way from my bike-riding youth when I used to terrorize the neighborhood hopping over curbs, weaving effortlessly through traffic, and executing precision maneuvers at speeds that left my mother fretting on the front porch. Mom would have been just fine today though, watching me gingerly test my brakes while executing turns much wider than necessary. So long as the road along the loch shore took the form of a relatively straight, four-lane highway with no traffic, I was going to be just fine.

I had much greater confidence in the boat segment of our journey. Our vessel was an antique steamship called…can you guess?…the *Sir Walter Scott*. Built in 1899, it had been plying the pristine waters of Loch Katrine for over a century, chugging along to this day on its original engine. A sleek looking ship, its long white hull stretched 110 feet from pointed bow to rounded stern. On deck, striped canopies stretched fore and aft of the ship's large smokestack and pilot house, offering shade—or, as the weather may require, shelter—to passengers.

We had unknowingly stumbled upon one of the more popular activities in the area. A long queue of people, the majority of whom toted bikes, lined the dock. It looked like way too many people for the boat, but when the crew lowered the gangplank, we somehow all crammed aboard. Katrina and I stashed our bikes in a holding compartment with the rest and then scrambled to a seat along the port rail near the bow. The deck was so crowded I had to hold my daypack on my lap.

There was good reason for the crowd. Blue skies scattered with white, puffy clouds enabled a clear view of the loch's scenery. The water sparkled in the morning sunshine. Tiny islands dotted the surface, the most notable of which, Ellen's Isle, had provided inspiration for Scott's *Lady of the Lake*. As we quietly steamed past the legendary isle, the loch widened, offering expansive vistas of wooded hills on either side. To the south, these rose up to the 2,370 ft. high eminence of Ben Venue. Other smaller peaks surrounded the rest of the loch, enclosing the whole with their heather clad slopes in a world that seemed completely cut off from the rest of the universe. Suddenly, it made perfect sense why the boat was so crowded: we had stumbled upon one of the most beautiful places on earth.

Besides being a natural wonder luring thousands of tourists to the region each summer, Loch Katrine serves another more practical purpose for Scotland: it is Glasgow's water supply. I was shocked to learn this. The majestic scenery made it hard to comprehend that the country's biggest city lay just over the southern hills, less than an hour's drive away. It also seemed a shame that all this beautiful pristine water was connected via underground pipes to some Glaswegian's grimy toilet. Of course, this constituted a naïve and overly critical reaction. I've thought about it a great deal since and realized that Scotland is lucky to have such a plentiful natural water supply so near its major city. With the frequent rains continually replenishing the loch, Katrine makes a perfect, seemingly bottomless natural reservoir. In order to service the much grimier toilets of Los Angeles and Las Vegas, the United States had to dam the great rivers of the West, flooding canyons of jaw-dropping beauty never to be seen again and draining the mighty Colorado to the last drop. Nary a trickle flows into the Gulf of California today. Against such tragedy, Scotland appears fortunate indeed. But still, I couldn't help gazing at the loch, half expecting to see the water level drop with each flush.

The upshot of the loch serving as Glasgow's water supply is that the surrounding land enjoys protected status. Glaswegians, despite their grimy toilets, don't fancy water full of cattle urine, farm fertilizer, or road runoff, and so the hills sweeping down to Katrine's shores remain virtually untouched. As we cruised the length of the loch, we passed only a handful of buildings, all predating the days of protection and all stunning in their architecture: a stone manor house perched on a hillside on the northern shore, its towers poking through the treetops, Queen Victoria's royal cottage nestled on the southern shore at the loch's midpoint, and, about two-thirds of the way down, a grand-looking Tudor building with the rather daunting name of Stronaclachar. This last marked our docking point, where those of us with bikes would disembark, and the more sensible remainder would stay aboard for the return journey, presumably luxuriating in their newfound space.

I was quite happy to see the dock draw near, not because I felt excited to begin the bike ride, but because I was freezing. From the moment the boat left the shelter of the loch's eastern end, the wind whipping across the water had chilled me to the bone. This, of course, must be taken as a relative notion. Those not from the tropics, which included everyone else on board, didn't seem bothered. Rather, they stood around in their shirtsleeves, pointing at the landscape and jabbering on about the scenery. Meanwhile, Katrina and I huddled on the bench, clutching our bags to our bodies for warmth, and peered at the scenery from beneath the hoods of our rain jackets. My eyes registered the beauty, but my thoughts scanned for warning signs of hypothermia.

Thus it was with some relief that we stepped onto the dock at Stronaclachar. It was nearly noon, and now that we had stopped moving the sunshine overhead had regained some of its warmth. I even peeled off my rain jacket, optimistically stowing it in my daypack. As the boat chugged away, however, the moment was tempered by the now inescapable realization that the only way back to our car was to pedal two rented bicycles fourteen miles through uninhabited Scottish hills.

"Oh, joy," deadpanned Katrina, as the other riders mounted their bikes and pedaled off.

We waited on the dock for a few minutes to let others get well ahead—no need for an audience as we rediscovered our cycling form. Unfortunately, it wasn't just form we lacked. Conditioning apparently also plays a role. Seemingly gentle hills become much more menacing when one attempts to ascend them via a foot-operated crankshaft. Keep in mind, we were in fairly good shape when it came to hiking. Cycling, however, uses totally different muscle groups—and these were groups I had allowed to lay dormant since the Reagan Administration.

We were not the only ones struggling. Within the first half-mile we came across a family of four from England on holiday. The father had thrown his chain, and I lent him my Swiss Army knife to make the necessary adjustments to fix it. As he did this, I surveyed the family. They looked fit enough and still relatively fresh, but I couldn't help thinking it wouldn't be long before the whining started and mom and dad both started accusing the other of coming up with this terrible idea. For now, though, they were all smiles.

"Cheers," the father said, handing me back my knife and turning to lead the family down the next hill. The whoops and hollers of daredevil children shooting down the slope proved somewhat inspiring, and Katrina and I continued on with renewed determination. We would need it.

The next eight miles entailed a slog up and down hills, some relatively easy, some achingly hard, though I prided myself on never having to get off and walk. Instead I pushed on, thigh muscles burning, to each crest, where I would briefly register a spectacular view that would have taken my breath away had I any to give, only to begin a hair raising descent down the other side, hand never far from the brake as I searched for the sweet spot between "granny-pace" and "careening out of control".

Katrina, for her part, employed a different strategy, best described as the "path of least resistance" approach to cycling. Whenever we started up a hill that seemed overly steep, she would dismount about half way up and push her bike the remaining distance, dropping well behind me and out of sight. Once at the top, however, she would remount, give a good push, and start coasting downhill, letting gravity do the work as she picked up a full head of steam, and refusing to touch the brake except in the most dire of circumstances. During these downhill stretches, she would quickly close the gap between us, and at times even shoot by me, laughing hysterically as she barrelled down the hill at brakeneck speed. "Wheeeeeeeeeeeeee!" I would hear her shout, coming up behind me, and then a blur would go by and she was gone until I inevitably passed her going up the next hill. Thus we leap frogged our way around the loch.

We passed some fascinating landmarks along the way: the house where Rob Roy was born at the far western end of the loch, and then, a little later on the northern shore, the Clan MacGregor graveyard. Rob Roy was not buried there, but was rather just over the hills to the north in Balquhidder. Still, the walled graveyard seemed moody enough without him, built on a little spit of land jutting out into the loch. We dismounted at the crest of a hill to read an information sign about the MacGregor graves and treat ourselves to a well-earned snack.

I took this opportunity to study the map obtained from the bike rental shop to see what the coming terrain might offer. This proved a difficult task, as the map was a rather cartoony-looking affair, more like an amusement park guide than a topographic map. Still, it quite clearly showed the road going up and down absurd little hills from Stronaclachar to precisely the point we now stood. From this point on, however, the ribbon of road stretched out rather flatly, seeming to hug the shore all the way back to the dock. We were ecstatic.

Just at that moment, the father who had slipped his chain reappeared with a tired looking brood following him up the hill to the graveyard overlook. We must have passed them at some point without realizing it. The kids, both around ten years old, walked beside their bikes, pushing them uphill. Mom looked like she'd had better vacations.

"Tough hills," dad exclaimed breathlessly, leaning on his handlebars and dripping sweat onto the pavement.

I shared the news that the toughest part was behind him and he brightened considerably. The news had a similar effect on mom and the kids, all of whom had seemed near weeping, but looked upon me now as if I was their greatest hero. With words of gratitude—it seems I had now done them two favors on this trip—they took off triumphantly down the hill and disappeared around the bend.

Minutes later, Katrina and I followed only to round the bend and begin climbing the toughest hill of the day. It seemed twice as steep and much longer than any we had climbed yet, though the let down may have had something to do with it. When Katrina dismounted, I realized she had the right idea, and soon we were both pushing our bikes uphill, thighs screaming in protest. So much for trusting cartoon maps.

We caught up with the English family near the top of the hill. Mom was off and pushing her bike. Dad was pushing his own plus his son's. Son and daughter teamed up on the bike remaining. As we all dropped to the ground at the top, I offered a humble apology, fumbling for my map to show them how it had led me astray. They didn't seem interested in discovering the root of my dangerous incompetence, however, and instead fixed me with four steely glares—the kind reserved for someone who has just run over your dog—before taking off downhill without asking further advice on the terrain. We gave them a good head start.

"Remind me why we're doing this," Katrina asked, as we slowly stood up and remounted our bikes.

"Something about exercise, beauty and solitude," I answered wearily.

"Right. Well, it hurts so it must be good exercise. And when it hurts so much I have to stop, I see that it's beautiful. And now that you drove that family away the solitude seems to be working out. I'd call it a great success." And with that, she remounted, gave a good push, and started coasting down the hill, quickly building up to breakneck speed—a receding "Wheeeeeee!" reaching my ears as she disappeared around the bend.

Happily, the going did get smoother after that, and Katrina would soon be calling the day a great success without a hint of sarcasm. The last five miles or so flattened out considerably, offering a pleasant ride over truly gentle hills. Pedaling along the shore, we were able to concentrate on the stunning views across the loch, and the trip once again seemed like a grand idea. Out on the sparkling water, we saw the *Sir Walter Scott* chugging back up toward Stronaclachar, transporting a new crowd of people awestruck by the scenery. On the private road, however, there were no such crowds. Or if there were, they were spread out over fourteen miles, allowing us to feel like we had the whole loch to ourselves. Adding to the joy of the experience, my confidence in cycling was quickly returning. I felt at home on the bike and was nearly back to curb-hopping, mom-fretting levels. Far from regretting the experience, we suddenly didn't want it to end. But the miles go by rather quickly on a bike, and we soon found ourselves back at the dock, reluctantly returning our mounts to the shop and swearing it would not be another ten years before our next ride.

The last few miles must have rejuvenated the English family as well. We saw them near the dock, eating ice cream and looking very pleased. I gave them a cheerful wave as we passed to see if I was back in their good graces. A derisory grunt from dad and an ice-cream laden tongue from junior informed me that rejuvenation only goes so far.

· · · · ·

Leaving Loch Katrine, we were seized with an idea that on any given summer day occurs likewise to thousands of other tourists and native Scots. We decided to visit Loch Lomond.

Loch Lomond, twenty-three miles long and five miles across at its widest point, ranks as the largest body of fresh water in all of Britain. More impressive than its size, however, is the loch's legendary beauty. Marking the southeast border of the Trossachs, the sparkling water is hemmed in by thick forest and beautiful peaks, most notably Ben Lomond, the southernmost Munro in Scotland. Thirty-seven islands of varying size break the water's expanse, their rounded tops poking through the surface and offering a connect-the-dot marker of the Highland Line, which follows their path directly beneath the loch.

This striking natural wonder provided inspiration for what is arguably Scotland's most famous song:

> *Ye tak' the high road, an' I'll tak' the low road,*
> *an' I'll be in Scotland afore ye;*
> *But me and my true love will never meet again*
> *on the bonnie, bonnie banks o' Loch Lomond.*

The song, actually titled *Loch Lomond*, commemorates a Jacobite soldier, captured and imprisoned in England in the 18th century. After learning he had been condemned to death, the soldier said farewell to his mates, claiming that he would be taking the "low road" of death back to Scotland. His fellow soldiers, meanwhile, who had not been condemned, would be taking the "high road" of life—which apparently was slower, though it did come with the added perk of being alive upon arrival. Having heard the song's evocative lyrics and moody tune performed in pub after pub, Katrina and I were both anxious to see this legendary loch, though we resolved to take the high road to get there, no matter how much longer it took.

Following our guidebook's advice, we stuck to the less-developed eastern shore to avoid the holiday crowds. Upon arrival, we understood "less developed" to be a relative notion. The traffic congestion associated with the loch's western shore may have been missing, but there was no mistaking the hand of man at work.

As we maneuvered the Fiat Crumb up a shore road, the loch's "bonnie banks" presented a splendid view, though this visual splendor was accompanied by a high-pitched auditory whine: the product of jet skis, power boats, and other polluting vessels almost beyond counting playing happily on the water's surface. Apparently, Loch Lomond served as nobody's water supply. Juxtaposed against the tranquility of Loch Katrine, where boat traffic was limited to just a few pre-approved boats like the *Sir Walter Scott*, the waters of Loch Lomond seemed fair game for anyone with an outboard motor and a penchant for hootin' and hollerin'. I'm pretty sure there were aqua sausage rides going on out there somewhere.

We drove to the road's end, halfway up the loch where someone had been kind enough to open a pub, proving that there are some positive byproducts of development. The pub, predictably called the Rob Roy Tavern, was pleasantly situated on the water's edge and seemed the perfect place to sip a pint while absorbing the beauty of the loch and the smell of burning petrol. In this endeavor, we were joined by some unexpected guests. As Katrina and I enjoyed our pints in the beer garden outside the pub, a group of backpackers stumbled out of the woods directly across the road. Gratefully laying down their enormous packs by the pub door, they shortly appeared in the beer garden clutching pints of their own and settled, with a chorus of sighs, into chairs at the table next to us.

These were hikers attempting the West Highland Way, a 95-mile footpath stretching from Glasgow to Fort William. This particular stretch of trail followed the eastern shore of Loch Lomond, conveniently passing within a few yards of an operational beer tap along the way. This last bit was nothing unusual, according to the hikers. Thanks to a plethora of thoughtfully placed hostels and pubs, it seemed one could walk the entire length of the trail in a week, experiencing some of the most wild scenery Scotland has to offer, without ever having to abstain from pub food and alcohol for more than a few hours at a time. This seemed a novel concept. For me, the strapping on of a pack was inevitably accompanied by a period of extreme deprivation when it came to basic needs like cheeseburgers and beer. In my hiking prime, I would have scoffed at these cushy "backpackers", but now they earned my hearty admiration. The fact that I was only two hours removed from a rather humbling bicycle experience may have had something to do with my new perspective.

We enjoyed a quick chat with the group, discovering they were university students on summer holiday. They would be camping tonight a mile or so up the shore from the pub, diverting from the trail just long enough to climb Ben Lomond in the morning before continuing on.

"Best to get a pint first," one of them reckoned.

"Quite right," added another.

Quite right, indeed.


Later that evening, we returned to Callander for some spicy Chinese food and our nightly stroll. The cool Scottish air felt great as we meandered through the public park watching old couples feed the swans and children kick a soccer ball in the nearby field. We had been traveling for nearly two weeks now, but still felt none of the weariness or pining to get back home associated with most lengthy trips. Nevertheless, tomorrow would be our last full day in Scotland, and we had one very important stop left to make.

"Best to get a pint first," Katrina suggested.

"Quite right," I agreed.

# Chapter 23: The Greatest Snub of All

## (A day in Stirling)

On September 11, 1297, 50,000 English soldiers set out to cross the River Forth, their heavy footsteps on the wooden bridge echoing across the Stirling plain. The army, boasting at least 1,000 heavy cavalry, had marched north under orders from Edward I to restore order to an increasingly unruly Scotland. William Wallace, an upstart rebel refusing to submit to Longshanks's rule, had caused quite a stir with his guerilla tactics throughout the summer, and the English had now arrived to teach him a lesson. They could not have chosen worse ground to do so.

Stirling, situated just west of the Firth of Forth, served as the de facto gateway to the highlands. Its castle, perched high on a rocky crag, loomed over the plain below. The River Forth, meandering in a lazy, looping pattern, divided the plain, essentially forming a moat between highlands and lowlands. A single wooden bridge spanned this moat.

Thus, 50,000 men attempted to file over a narrow bridge two by two, which must have made the boarding of the Ark seem a rather speedy process by comparison. The endeavor would have taken hours had the English been allowed to finish it, though this would never come to pass, for after the first few thousand had crossed and were fanning out across the marshy ground north of the river, the Scottish army, which had been waiting in the nearby hills, charged down en masse, screaming and brandishing their weapons.

As the advancing English stopped dead in their tracks, they created a ripple effect of chaos on the bridge behind them, rather like a car testing its brakes in the middle of a congested construction zone. Men and horses bumped into one another on the bridge, causing some to be trampled while others plunged into the deep water below, drowning under the weight of their armor. In the confusion, the charging Scots gained control of the northern end of the bridge, cutting off the retreat of those English already across: a mixture of foot soldiers, archers and heavy cavalry, the latter rendered useless in the marshy ground. The resulting slaughter was horrendous, with the Scots literally hacking to death every last Englishman on the northern bank. This unfortunate lot included one Hugh Cressingham, King Edward's wondrously obese treasurer and personal envoy, who, falling from his horse in the confusion, was too fat to get back on and flee, not that there was anywhere he could have gone.

The rest of the English army, all of whom must never have been so glad to be at the back of a line, watched in horror from the other side of the river before beating a hasty retreat south to the border. Wallace's underdog army, made up of peasants and minor nobility, had routed the English, an unprecedented achievement in the skirmishes between the neighboring kingdoms, and one that up to that very moment had been deemed impossible by the nobility of both sides.

Of course, Wallace had a distinct advantage over his loftier counterparts. Rather than fighting with an army of soldiers who fought only because they were forced to by their noble lord as was standard in the feudal system of the day, Wallace's followers were volunteers who fought because they believed in his promise of freedom—a motivation that would prove effective time and again throughout history, the American Revolution being not the least example. As if to prove its conviction, this peasant army next began the task of liberating Scottish castles and towns from English control and within a month had expelled the southerners from all Scottish lands, at which point Wallace undertook the previously unthinkable task of invading England. He and his men ravaged the English countryside all the way to Newcastle before the onset of winter turned them back to the safety of home.

Prior to this chain of events, the squabbling nobility of Scotland had paid little regard to Wallace, the landless second son of a minor knight. Afterwards, he couldn't be ignored. Swallowing their pride, the Scottish nobles knighted young Wallace, and bestowed upon him the title of Guardian of Scotland—granting him administrative and military authority over Scotland's affairs and leaving him one step short of king. He was not yet 25 years old.

Sadly, the campaign of 1297 would be the highlight of Wallace's brief career. The divided loyalties and continued infighting of the Scottish nobility proved to pose a much greater threat to an independent Scotland than the English army ever had, and Wallace was soon longing for his earlier guerilla days, when his biggest worry was how many English limbs he could detach with the next swing of his claymore. Following a disastrous defeat at Falkirk the following year, a disgusted Wallace resigned the Guardianship and went off to find happier pastures killing Englishmen in France, though his love of Scotland would bring him back a few years later in time to be betrayed, captured by the English and executed in a most hideous fashion.

Though his bid for independence ultimately failed, the movement he inspired did not. Nine years after Wallace's death, Robert the Bruce, the newly crowned king of Scotland, would finish the revolution Wallace had begun by winning a stunning victory at Bannockburn, just a few miles from Stirling. Bruce's victory and subsequent expulsion of English from Scottish soil would ensure Scotland another four centuries of independence.

But this would not be the end of Wallace's influence.

On September 11, 1997, exactly seven hundred years after Wallace's victory at Stirling Bridge (and nearly three hundred since Scotland's annexation by the United Kingdom), Scots voted for the creation of an independent parliament—a referendum that passed overwhelmingly and went into effect two years later. The date of the vote was no accident. It had been carefully selected to capitalize on a swelling of national pride, unmatched since Sir Walter Scott had dressed George IV in flesh colored tights. But this swelling hadn't come about because Scottish voters had suddenly boned up on history. Rather, they had gone to the theaters.

Two years earlier, Paramount Pictures had released *Braveheart*, a film glorifying the life of William Wallace from childhood to his grisly end, with special attention given to the battle of Stirling Bridge and, memorably, three hours of Mel Gibson in a kilt. The movie was rife with historical errors: the battle no longer taking place on or even near a bridge being one glaring example, though my personal favorite was a line noting a group of mourners "playing outlawed tunes on outlawed pipes". Never mind that bagpipes wouldn't be introduced to Scotland for another century at least, and then not outlawed until after the battle of Culloden, a mere 450 years in the future. But who cares? The necessary point was made: the English are an oppressive lot and always have been, and if more people had the cojones of William Wallace, Scotland just might wiggle out from under the Anglo thumb.

Viewers and critics certainly didn't mind the inaccuracies. The movie earned over $200 million and won five academy awards, including best picture, best director, and best portrayal of an English arse-kicking. (That last one may have been unofficial.) Such material success is dwarfed by the effect the film had on the consciousness of a nation. All over Scotland, seemingly content people entered theaters only to emerge three hours later a runnin' for their claymores. Fortunately, they ended up at the polls instead.

The polls and the National Wallace Monument, that is. The latter, built in 1869 overlooking the Stirling plain, was certainly nothing new to Scotland in the 1990's, yet saw a 156 percent rise in visitation the year after *Braveheart's* release. I'm sure the irony of the superhuman Wallace being saved from relative obscurity by an industry as superficial as "show biz" is not lost on the reader, but I suppose it does go to show that Hollywood, despite subjecting the world to *Young Guns II*, can still serve a noble purpose. At any rate, more than a decade after the film's release, over 120,000 pilgrims continue to tour the Wallace Monument each year; and though a great many of them may arrive harboring visions of Mel Gibson in a kilt, they inevitably go away in awe of a national hero.

On our last day in Scotland, Katrina and I intended to be two such pilgrims, though we wouldn't be paying homage to Mel Gibson or a national hero. We would be paying our respects to a revered ancestor.

•　•　•　•　•

Of course, in Scotland, there is always something to see between here and there. To visit the Wallace Monument from Callander, we approached from the west, which meant we were treated to one of the most dramatic views in all of Scotland: the sight of Stirling Castle perched atop 250 feet of sheer cliffs. We could hardly pass by without stopping, and so made a fruitful detour through Stirling's Old Town to take in this fortress which had played such a key role in Scottish history.

Because of the castle's impregnability, Stirling had served as a safe haven for Scottish royalty, especially in the 15th and 16th centuries when the castle housed a succession of juvenile monarchs, including an infant Mary, Queen of Scots, to keep them safe from power hungry nobles. Endearing memories of these fickle Stuart monarchs abounded throughout the tour: here was the courtyard where James V kept his pet lion; here the wall where James II threw a man to his death, and so on. For my money, however, nothing is as impressive as a good old fashioned Great Hall, and Stirling had a fine one. Recently restored, the hall boasted five fireplaces, a high vaulted ceiling supported by beautiful wooden beams, and even a musician's balcony where trumpeters would trumpet while serving wenches brought out the food below. The room had hosted many a banquet for Scotland's 16th century monarchs and seemed like a festive place indeed. We resisted the temptation to linger, however, drawn on by occasional glimpses of a vision beckoning from a hilltop across the valley.

The Wallace Monument seemed to be calling our name.

Built at the height of the Victorian Era and topped with fanciful turrets to prove it, the National Wallace Monument towers above the Stirling plain. A stone structure, 220 feet high, it crowns the top of Abbey Craig, a hill for many years considered the site from which Wallace's troops charged at the Battle of Stirling Bridge, though that theory has been questioned by some given that the descent would have been over a rather sheer cliff, bringing the Scots down upon the English in a hurry, though perhaps not leaving them in the best fighting condition.[*] Regardless, the tower was impressive,

* According to James MacKay (see bibliography), Wallace's army charged from the Ochil Hills, a little to

the Scottish equivalent of the Washington Monument in both grandeur and importance, and containing everything a curious pilgrim could want to know about Scotland's greatest hero.

Well, almost everything.

Parking our car in the lot below, we walked up the path to the top of Abbey Craig. My excitement was palpable. More than a week had passed since we had indulged in any family history, distracted as we'd been by the plentiful diversions of the highlands. After the previous snubs of the Crawford name, however, I felt I needed one last confirmation of ancestral glory before leaving this captivating country. To this end, there seemed to be no more appropriate climax for our trip than a visit to the Wallace Monument. Surely here the Crawford blood coursing through the veins of Scotland's greatest hero would be revealed to the public eye, the proud deeds of his Crawford kin acknowledged for their role in shaping Wallace's legend and preserving the country's independence. We hurried inside.

The tower is divided into five different levels. On the ground floor, we paused at the reception desk long enough to receive a free audio tour device despite my better judgment, given my previous experience at Holyrood. Then a seventy-one step climb up a narrow turnpike stair brought us to Floor 1: the life story of William Wallace. At last.

We entered a fascinating room filled with displays detailing Wallace's transformation from youth to outlaw to guardian of a nation. I traversed the entire floor taking in one story after another, slowly restoring flesh and bone to the man who had become such a legend. The resulting image was impressive. William Wallace, a giant of a man in every sense, grew to be 6' 7" in an age when Mickey Rooney would have been average height. To underscore this point, his claymore, with a blade over five feet long, stood reverently on display in a glass case in the corner. Mickey Rooney couldn't have lifted it off the ground.

"This guy was quite the stud," Katrina expressed in awe.

"Runs in the family," I responded with a grin.

---

the north, as referenced at the beginning of this chapter, though Wallace likely watched the English approach from the Abbey Craig.

"Right, that's what I was thinking."

On top of his tremendous stature, Wallace possessed great skill as an archer and horseman, was a charismatic leader of men, and spoke as many as four languages. In a day when physical prowess, dexterity and wit actually mattered, he really was the Michael Jordan of his time—though even Michael Jordans are mortal, it seems. A multimedia display, complete with a life-sized, slightly spooky, talking Wallace automaton, reminded us of this. It detailed his farcical trial in London and subsequent execution, in which Wallace was drawn behind a cart through the streets, hung and stretched until practically unconscious, cut open while still alive so that he could witness the removal of his own organs, and finally beheaded, with his body being quartered and sent as warnings to the far corners of the realm. The English really, really did not like this man.

By the end of my circuit around the room, however, I too felt like drawing and quartering a few people: the curators of the monument, in this case. To my utter disbelief, I had read every plaque, lingered at every display, listened to every button on the audio tour, but found not a single mention of the Crawford name.

It's worth pointing out that, given the subject material, this omission represented quite an impressive feat. Seeing as how Wallace had a Crawford mother, a Crawford uncle of national prominence who continually sheltered him during his fugitive years, Crawford cousins who fought by his side, and any number of other relatives from his mother's family intricately involved in his adventures, the curators had to go quite out of their way to omit the name. Yet, they did this with commendable aplomb.

Time and again, I read the names of Wallace's fighting companions, like Sir John Graham, or of his minor adversaries, like Sheriff Heselrig. But whenever the opportunity to mention a Crawford came up (which was often, I might add), it was simply "his mother", or "his grandfather", or even "an uncle on his mother's side" in one case. It was uncanny.

No matter, I thought to myself, plenty more still lay ahead. Perhaps one of the upper floors contained a whole room dedicated to Wallace's Crawford kin, and the monument planners simply hadn't wanted to ruin the surprise by mentioning the name down here. I looked at my brochure; it listed the "Hall of Heroes" as the next room.

Yes, that must be it.

We dashed up the next sixty-four steps only to enter a chamber full of marble busts sporting names like Adam Smith, John Knox, and Robbie Burns. Not a Crawford in the bunch. This was getting desperate.

Another sixty-two steps brought us to the "Building of the Monument" exhibit, which was impressive but naturally did nothing to raise Crawford-awareness, while a final climb deposited us onto the viewing platform, overlooking the mighty plain where the battle had taken place. In any other circumstances, the prospect would have been staggering. The River Forth snaked across the fields below; the Ochil Hills swept away to the north, but I was having trouble focusing on such trivial matters. I was scanning the terrain looking for the letters of a familiar surname carved into the surrounding fields of crops, or trimmed out of a garden of box hedges below. As the reader may guess, I searched in vain.

Simply unbelievable. Two-hundred and forty-six steps detailing Wallace's life from beginning to end without once mentioning the Crawford name. It was the ultimate snub.

Even Katrina seemed a little put out by the circumstances, though she showed no hint of surprise. "After all," she pointed out, "wasn't *Braveheart* similarly unkind to Wallace's Crawford roots?"

Indeed it was, writing them out of the script altogether. No Crawford seems to be in the room full of hanging nobles in the early scene meant to recreate the Barns of Ayr incident. In a later scene, Wallace's movie uncle takes on the mysteriously non-Crawford moniker of "Argyll". And as for Wallace's mother, Margaret Crawford, well, she doesn't even appear to exist. When his father and brother go off to war in the movie, young William remains home alone, having apparently been delivered into the world by a stork.

Remembering all this didn't make me feel any better, though I could now view the film in a more sympathetic light. After all, if the screenwriter had conducted his research at the National Wallace Monument, how could he know that Wallace had a mother?

Dejectedly descending the steps, which now seemed much longer than they had going up, we returned to the Fiat Crumb to embark on a half-hearted search for Bannockburn. Signs marked the way for a while, though these mysteriously disappeared as we neared, as if to say "Well, we got you this far. Good luck." Still, the famous battlefield seemed like something worth seeing, so we pressed on. In the end, however, all we found was a suburban sprawl of hideously ugly apartment buildings and traffic circles which left us bewildered.

"What an awful place for a battle," Katrina astutely observed.

Indeed. It was easy to see why the Scots had won. The English couldn't find the battlefield, and if they had they would have fled in horror.

In hindsight, perhaps my mood was tainting my outlook.

•　•　•　•　•

Naturally, this mood couldn't last. A rather stern-faced Katrina informed me of this, declaring in no uncertain terms that she didn't intend to spend her last few hours in Scotland with a mopey husband nursing a bruised ego. Thus, in an effort to shake off this current funk, I spent the drive back to Callander pondering just why the sight of my family name in print suddenly mattered anyway. After all, until just a few weeks ago I had been blissfully unaware of any connection to this place.

But, of course, that was the key phrase: a "connection to this place". With a jolt, I realized that it was precisely this newly discovered family history which provided me a much-desired link to a land I had found more captivating with each passing day. I don't think I realized until that moment the profound effect the past two weeks were having on me. The trip had opened my eyes to a new and wonderful place of which I had been wholly ignorant, much like the first time I had ever snorkeled, sticking my face in the water and seeing a whole world of beautiful reef—the kind I had previously seen only in books or movies—stretching away beneath the surface. My experience in Scotland had proven every bit as exhilarating, but with this very important addition: I had discovered I was related to the fish.

I know this sense of attachment sounds hokey and cheesy and all that, but it was true then and continues to hold true now. The Scotland we had discovered was a beautiful place, a romantic place, a place that honored its past and drew on both its tragedies and glories to inspire an optimistic future. But above all, it was a friendly place, a place where people talked to each other in pubs and sang along with the band, where librarians doted on visitors instead of telling them to shush and old men happily jumped into strange cars to help wayward strangers find their way instead of yelling at them from porches to stay off the lawn. Yes, the more I experienced Scotland, the more I wanted to belong.

Once I understood this, the next revelation was undeniable: my attachment to Scotland, though special, hardly qualified as unique. I thought of the enthusiasm which causes otherwise normal people around the globe to don kilts at clan society meetings and revel in their ancestral attachment, however frivolous, to this proud and wonderful country. I considered the racks upon racks of family crest refrigerator magnets and tartan ties driving Scotland's tourist industry. There is a reason these products sell, and it's not because they're being recommended by interior decorators or wardrobe consultants. No, it has to do with the spirit of Scotland itself, a spirit that gives people a sense that they're in a special place, and makes them want to be part of it.

I wanted to be part of it.

Immediately I felt better. Like an alcoholic confessing his addiction, a burden seemed to lift and I was again free to enjoy the world, perhaps even receive help dealing with my affliction. As always Katrina was there.

"You know what's great to think about?" she asked, as she saw my mood lightening.

I could think of several things, most prominently the fact that someone in my family had a 220-foot tower built in his honor and had inspired a nation for over seven centuries. Katrina was on a slightly different page.

"If Wallace was over six and a half feet tall," she mused, "I guess that means you could actually have tall children, 'cause you know, sometimes height skips a few generations."

"That *is* great, Katrina. Thanks for that."

It's amazing how one can be both humbled and cheered at the same time. But this too was characteristic of the Scotland we had discovered, and seemed an appropriate way to end the trip—though I did find myself sitting up as straight as one can in the driver's seat of a Fiat Crumb all the way back to Callander.

# Epilogue: A Fond Farewell
## (And return)

And so the trip ended.

On the plane ride back, which always seems longer than the plane ride there, I had ample time to reflect on what I had learned. The two biggest revelations—that the trip had unwittingly turned me into a Scot-o-phile and that there was nothing at all unusual about this—we covered in the last chapter. Others, jotted down in a notebook, seem worthy of mention now, as they may be of some value to a first-time traveler to the land north of the Tweed.

Thus, according to my notes, I had learned that Scotland makes a perfect hiking destination so long as one minds the peat bogs, and that its castles offer endless diversions, though sometimes these require a quick trespass through a trailer park. I'd learned that tartan represents much more than a mysterious pattern preferred by American farmers and dads, and, on a more personal note, that Crawfords did indeed play a vital role in the course of Scottish history, though nobody seems to know it. Most importantly, I felt certain that Scotland, with its beautiful landscape, friendly people, and never ending supply of new beers to try, was a place I would see again soon.

This last would prove true two summers later when Katrina and I returned for another two-week tour. On this trip, we revisited many of our favorite haunts, and were delighted to find them much as we'd remembered. At Dunkeld, Balding Guy and Depardieu still presided over the Taybank folk sessions, and even remembered us. Apparently they hadn't had many other visitors from the Caribbean in the interval. At Glencoe, the Clachaig Inn hadn't revised its "No Campbells" policy, and we were again foiled in our attempt to bag a Munro, this time by a rainstorm that blew in from nowhere, whiting out the view and dropping the temperature twenty degrees just as we reached a ridge top. (Okay, maybe it's not *always* sunny in Scotland.) In Edinburgh's Old Town, the ancient White

Hart Inn was now even older and worth another stay at the swanky hotel in the Grassmarket, which, if anything, had become even swankier—though it's just as possible that Katrina and I had simply become more un-hip. We even, I daresay, ventured into the Cowgate under the protective custody of Debbie, a local woman we had befriended, and her teenage daughter. Thus, I discovered that my guidebook had indeed been right about the Cowgate's renaissance, so long as by renaissance it meant a street heaving with drunken, festive crowds. The nearest I came to being mugged was getting leaned on by staggering revelers who desired a little vertical support more than they desired my wallet or car keys.

Oh, and I finally tried haggis, prepared specially for me by an insistent Debbie, which was very kind of her, but was also a lovely reminder to trust my instincts when it comes to local cuisine.

More memorable than the haggis was our return to Craufurdland Castle. I had kept my promise to myself and written ahead to the owners, the Houison Craufurds, to finagle an invitation. Peter, the then laird, and his wife Caroline proved to be a lovely couple, who received my confession of sneaking down their driveway with good humor—though I noted they were waiting outside when we pulled up this time.

They gave us a tour of the grounds, which remarkably had been in the family since 1245, making Craufurdland the oldest estate in Scotland to be inhabited by a single family. To put this in perspective, when Wallace won his victory at Stirling Bridge, he could have come to Craufurdland to celebrate with his Craufurd cousins who had already been enjoying their estate for more than half a century. Inside, we explored the ancient halls in awe, marveling at the entry to the tower house, the turnpike stair, and various secret passageways, and even had the pleasure of meeting their son, Simon, who shared fascinating stories of what it was like to grow up in such a place.

And then it happened.

Like in my fantasy, the tour ended in a snug chamber where I was offered a comfortable chair next to the fireplace. No fire was roaring (it was July, after all), though this hardly mattered given that I was surrounded by books and ancient parchments documenting over 750 years of family history. These Peter shared as he chatted amicably, showing me letters signed by Mary, Queen of Scots, photos of him washing Queen Elizabeth's hands (a ceremonial duty entrusted to the laird of Craufurdland through the Houison side of the family), certified Coats of Arms and tattered family trees that could have kept me occupied for months. If ever there was an antidote to ease the sting of the Crawford snubs suffered on our previous trip, it was an afternoon in this room.

Thinking there was no way the experience could get any better, my attention was suddenly drawn to the open door, where a shadow carrying a tray approached down the hall. Visions of a sassy maid serving up creamy ale flickered through my consciousness, making my heart race and sending me into a slight daydream. Could it be?

When I came to, the vision had been replaced with a smiling Caroline proffering a plate of tea and biscuits. A slight variation to what I had envisioned, but a perfect ending, better than any fantasy.

Once again, Scotland had exceeded my expectations.

It's like that, you know.

# Appendix A: Bibliography

## Guidebook

Humphreys, Rob and Reid, Donald, <u>The Rough Guide to Scotland, Sixth Edition</u>, 2004: Rough Guides, New York, London, Delhi.

>   *This was Katrina's and my bible on the trip. It helped us plan our journey prior to leaving and bumble our way through Scotland while there. Perhaps most importantly of all, it has been a tremendous resource for my research throughout the writing of this book.*

## Books and Articles

Baigent, Michael, Leigh, Richard and Lincoln, Henry, <u>Holy Blood, Holy Grail</u>, 1982: Dell Publishing, New York.

>   *This is the controversial classic delving into freemasonry and a potential bloodline of Christ. It provides interesting insight on the history and symbolism of Rosslyn Chapel.*

Ballingal, James, <u>The Rhynd and Elcho: A Parish History</u>, 1905: David Douglas, Edinburgh.

>   *This was one of our discoveries at the Perth public library. It corroborated the story of Wallace and William Crawford at Elcho.*

Burns, Robert, <u>Selected Poems</u>, 1996: Penguin Popular Classics, London.

>   *The excerpts of Robbie Burns' poetry and songs appearing in <u>Where's Me Plaid</u> were taken from this collection of his work. The preface also provides biographical information, which proved helpful in my discussion of Burns' life.*

Crawford, Kevan, <u>Sons of Freedom: Clan Crawford History, 2<sup>nd</sup> Edition</u>, 2003: Salt Lake City, Utah.

>   *This self-published book by the president of Clan Crawford Association provides an excellent overview of Crawford history, along with an entire section dedicated to William Wallace's exploits. I was able to corroborate many of the stories with my research in the public libraries of Scotland.*

Cunningham, Alastair, <u>A Guide to Dunnottar Castle: Reflecting the History of Scotland</u>, 1998: Gilcomston Press, Aberdeen.

>   *This guidebook, purchased at the entry to Dunnottar Castle, was full of excellent information and anecdotes regarding the castle's history and environs.*

Fraser, William Crawford, <u>Crawford: From the Burning of the Castle by Sir William Wallace to the Visit of King Edward VII</u>, 1909: A. Colthart, Mrs. Muir and R. & J. Murray.

>   *Discovered in the library at Lanark, this book provided valuable information on Wallace's burning of his ancestral castle at Crawford, including the text of Blind Harry's account of the*

*event, reprinted in Appendix C of <u>Where's Me Plaid</u>. Fraser also discusses the rich mining history of the Crawford lands.*

Hayes, Carlton J.H., Clark, Frederick F., <u>Medieval and Early Modern Times: The Age of Justinian to the Eighteenth Century</u>, New York: Macmillan Publishing Co.
*Incredibly, this was one of my old high school textbooks I found sitting on a shelf at home. It helped to refresh my memory on the Elizabethan Era and, later, on Cromwell's battle with the absolute monarchy.*

Lauchland, John, <u>Kilbirnie Auld Kirk: A History</u>, 2000: The Friends of the Auld Kirk Heritage Group, Ayrshire.
*This book chronicles the history of the Auld Kirk, but also contains valuable information on the Crawfords of Kilbirnie. Specifically, it contains a whole chapter on Sir Thomas Crawford of Jordanhill, complete with a first-hand account of his capture of Dumbarton castle, described in a letter Sir Thomas wrote to none other than John Knox.*

Loudoun, Craufuird C., <u>A History of the House of Loudoun</u>, Post-1993: Self-published.
*I stumbled upon this resource in the Kilmarnock public library. It was helpful in establishing a genealogy of the Crawfords of Loudoun.*

MacKay, James, <u>William Wallace: Brave Heart</u>, 1995: Mainstream Publishing, Edinburgh and London.
*This is the comprehensive biography of William Wallace considered by many to be the definitive work. I drew from it heavily for my discussion of Wallace's victory at Stirling Bridge.*

MacLean, Fitzroy, <u>Highlanders: A History of the Scottish Clans</u>, 1995: Viking Studio, New York.
*This excellent book covers the history of highland Scotland from prehistoric times through the diaspora of Scottish émigrés throughout the English-speaking world. It proved invaluable for my discussions on the Battle of Largs, the tradition of crowning kings at Scone, the massacre of Glencoe, the Jacobite movement and tragic events at Culloden, and on the history of clans and tartans in general.*

Marshall, William, <u>Historic Scenes in Perthshire</u>, 1881.
*This is another resource found lurking in the Perth public library which corroborated the story of Wallace at Elcho.*

<u>Our Village: The Story of West Kilbride</u>, 1990: West Kilbride Amenity Society, Ayrshire.
*This book, found in the local library in West Kilbride, discussed the Crawford connection to Crosbie Tower, as well as the Barns of Ayr.*

<u>Particular Description of Cunninghame [Parish of Kilbirnie]</u>
*Loose photocopied pages from this work were found by Katrina in the Kilbirnie Library, Scotland in July, 2004. Based on information found on p. 257, which cites that the Barony*

*of Kilbirnie "has been possessed by, and continues still in the same family, by marriage or by succession, since the year 1397 down to the present times, a period of 443 years," the publication date is assumed to be 1840 or shortly thereafter. The work provided more information about the Crawfords of Kilbirnie.*

Reid, Thomas, <u>History of the Parish of Crawfordjohn, Upper Ward of Lanarkshire, 1153-1928</u>. 1928: Turnbull & Spears, Edinburgh.
*Another book found in the library at Lanark. It contained the excellent description of the peacefulness of Crawfordjohn, excerpted in Chapter 7 of <u>Where's Me Plaid</u>.*

Webster, David P., "Reconsidering Donald Dinnie: A response to Frank Zarnowski's 'The Amazing Donald Dinnie' published in IGH Vol. 5, No. 1", <u>Iron Game History, Vol. 5, No. 2</u>, October, 1998, p. 19.
*One of two accounts of the exploits of Donald Dinnie, the great 19th century highland games athlete. (See Zarnowski, below.)*

Weir, Alison, <u>Mary Queen of Scots and the Murder of Lord Darnley</u>, 2004: Random House, New York.
*Much of the information regarding the life and times of Mary, Queen of Scots, was taken from this excellent read. It proved particularly useful in my discussions of the Darnley and Rizzio murders and Mary's relationship with Queen Elizabeth I.*

Zarnowski, Frank, "The Amazing Donald Dinnie: The 19th Century's Greatest Athlete", <u>Iron Game History, Vol. 5, No. 1</u>, May 1998, pp. 3-11.
*The first article on Dinnie, responded to by Webster, above.*

## Websites

*The following websites all provide background information on a wide variety of topics concerning Scottish history and culture. I referred to them often for background reading, or to cross check information from other sources.*

http://heritage.scotsman.com
http://scotlandvacations.com/robroy.htm
http://en.wikipedia.org
www.electricscotland.com
www.historic-scotland.gov.uk
www.rampantscotland.com
www.tartans.com
www.theheritagetrail.co.uk
www.undiscoveredscotland.co.uk
www.visitscotland.com

*The following websites provide information on specific locations or sites within Scotland discussed in this book.*

www.auldedinburgh.co.uk
www.balmoralcastle.com
www.blair-castle.co.uk

www.castles.org/Chatelaine/CALDER.HTM (Cawdor)
www.cawdorcastle.com
www.glamis-castle.co.uk
www.loudouncastle.co.uk
www.myclan.com/clans/Calder_173 (Cawdor)
www.perthshire.co.uk
www.perthshirebigtreecountry.co.uk
www.rosslynchapel.org.uk
www.scone-palace.co.uk
www.st-johns-kirk.co.uk
www.visitdunkeld.com
www.stbrigids-kilbirnie.com

*Of the thousands of websites discussing Loch Ness and its mysteries, the following supplemented my research for Chapter 19.*
www.lochness.co.uk
www.lochness-centre.com
www.lochnessguide.com
www.loch-ness-scotland.com
www.museumofhoaxes.com/nessie.html
www.nessie.co.uk
http://ourworld.compuserve.com/homepages/lesj/deepscan.htm

*The following websites provide information on the Edinburgh Festival.*
www.edfringe.com
www.edinburghfestivals.co.uk
www.eif.co.uk

*The following websites provide information on the connection between Scottish and American music.*
www.ibma.org/about.bluegrass/history/index.asp
www.mtsu.edu/~tah/currunits/scotsirish/essay.pdf
www.scotlandintune.com/enjoy/bow_to_the_west.html

*The following websites provide various versions of the ghost stories surrounding Glamis Castle.*
www.castleofspirits.com/glamis2.html
www.clanlindsayusa.org/castles_glamis.html
www.dundeemessenger.co.uk/myths/ghosts.htm
www.mysteriousbritain.co.uk/hauntings/glamis.html

*Other websites proving helpful for various statistics or facts found in Where's Me Plaid include:*
http://experts.about.com/e/s/ss/ss_sir_walter_scott.htm
http://scotland.ask.dyndns.dk/
www.boxofficemojo.com/movies/
www.edinburghliterarypubtour.co.uk/pubtours/pubs.html
www.electrum.co.uk/pubs/tour/pubs/whitehart
www.ellisislandimmigrants.org

www.enchantedlearning.com/usa/states/area.shtml
www.geologyshop.co.uk/ukvolc.htm
www.golftravelengland.com/destguide/geographic.asp
www.great-britain.co.uk/history/history.htm
www.highlandgames.net/records.html
www.jimwillsher.co.uk/Site/Hills
www.magicdragon.com/Wallace/Wallace7.html
www.nostalgiacentral.com/tv/drama/drfinlay.htm
www.rosebankhouse.co.uk/scotland.html
www.royalty.nu/Europe/England/Windsor/QueenMother.html
www.samueljohnson.com
www.scotexchange.net/txtonly/aillst_2003-2.pdf
www.siliconglen.com/Scotland/11_24.html
www.spartacus.schoolnet.co.uk/USAscotland.htm
www.timeanddate.com/worldclock/astronomy.html
www.worldwaterfalls.com/waterfall.php?num=687

## Other Helpful Sources, Some Quite Random

Information on the history of the White Hart Inn came from a menu insert left on the table of that venerable establishment and shamelessly lifted by the author during the summer of 2004.

Information on Neil Gow was taken from a framed print of the artist on the wall of the Taybank Hotel during our trip.

Information on Rosslyn Chapel visitation was provided by Stuart Beattie, Director of Rosslyn Chapel in private email correspondence with the author dated March 20, 2006.

Information on the cultural and natural history of Glencoe was provided by the many excellent exhibits on display in the National Trust of Scotland Visitor Center in Glencoe.

Information on William Wallace and his exploits was gleaned from <u>The True Story of Braveheart</u>, a History Channel documentary produced in 2000 as part of the "History's Mysteries" series.

*The following brochures and pamphlets proved particularly helpful in providing information about specific places and regions we visited:*

Official brochure from the Palace of Holyroodhouse, Edinburgh. The Royal Collection © 2004, Her Majesty Queen Elizabeth II.

"Perthshire: Big Tree Country" put out by the Perthshire Tourist Board with the cooperation of the Forestry Commission based in Edinburgh.

"Perthshire: Outdoor Activities" also put out by the Perthshire Tourist Board.

"Blair Castle: Ancient Seat of the Dukes and Earls of Atholl", published in 2004 by the Blair Charitable Trust, which manages the castle.

"Scone Palace: Information for Visitors", given to us upon entering the Palace grounds.

"Urquhart Castle: The Guardian of the Glen", published by Historic Scotland, 2004

"Walks in Glen Nevis", published by The Highland Council Ranger Service

Official brochure for the 2006 Braemar Gathering, published by the Braemar Royal Highland Gathering Ltd. Society Office, Braemar AB35 5YH

"World Highland Games & Ladies' International Highland Games & World's Strongest Man Team Challenge Souvenir Programme" published in 2004 by Callander & District Round Table.

# Appendix B

# Auld Lang Syne

By Robert Burns[*]

Should auld acquaintance be forgot,
    And never brought to min'?
Should auld acquaintance be forgot,
    And auld lang syne?

        For auld lang syne, my dear.
            For auld lang syne.
        We'll tak a cup o' kindness yet,
            For auld lang syne.

We twa hae run about the braes,
    And pu'd the gowans fine;
But we've wander'd mony a weary foot,
    Sin' auld lang syne.

We twa hae paidled i' the burn,
    From morning sun till dine;
But seas between us braid hae roar'd,
    Sin' auld lang syne.

And there's a hand, my trusty fiere,
    And gie's a hand o' thine;
And we'll tak a right guid-willie waught,
    For auld lang syne.

And surely ye'll be your pint-stowp,
    And surely I'll be mine;
And we'll tak a cup o' kindness yet,
    For auld lang syne.

---

[*] (From Burns, Robert, <u>Selected Poems</u>, 1996: Penguin Popular Classics, p. 263.)

# Appendix C

# Excerpts from "Wallace"

By Blind Harry[*]

Schyr Jhone the Grayme, and gud Wallace in feir,
With thaim fourtye off men in armes cleir,
Through Craufurd mur as that thai tuk the way,
On Ingliss (men) thar mynd ramaynit ay.
Fra Crawford Jhon the wattir doune thai ryd;
Ner hand the nycht thai lychtyt apon Clyd;
Thar purposes tuk in till a quiet waill.[1]      [1] valley
Than Wallace said: 'I wald we mycht assail
Craufurd Castell, with sum gud jeperte[2]      [2] warlike enterprise
Schir Jhon the Grayme, how say yhe best may be?'
This gud knycht said: 'And the men war without.
To tak the hous thar is bot litill doubt.'
A squire than rewllyt that lordschip haill,
Off Cummyrland borne, his name was Martyndaill.
Than Wallace said: 'My self will pass in feyr,
And ane with me, off herbre for to speyr.
Folow on dreich[3], giff that we mystir ocht.'      [3] slow
Edward Litill with his mastir furth socht,
Till ane oystry[4], and with a woman met.      [4] inn
Scho tald to thaim, that Sothroune thar was set:
'And ye be Scottis, I consaill yow pass by;
For, and thai may, yhe will get ewill herbry.
At drynk thai ar, so haiff thai bene rycht lang;
Gret worde thar is of Wallace thaim amang.
Thai trew that he has found hys men againe:
At Lowchmaben feyll[5] Inglis men ar slayne.      [5] many
That houses is tynt[6]; that geris[7] thaim be full wa:      [6] lost; [7]makes
I trow to God that thai sall swne tyne ma.'
Wallace sperd[8], of Scotland giff scho be.      [8] asked
Scho said him: 'ya, and thinkis yet to se
Sorow on thaim, throw help off Goddis grace.'
He askit hyr, quha was in to the place.
'Na man of fens is left that houses within,
Twenty is her, makand gret noyis and dyn.
Allace,' scho said, 'giff I mycht anys se,
The worthy Scottis maist maister in it to be.'
With this woman he wald no langer stand;

---

[*] (From Fraser, William Crawford, <u>Crawford: From the Burning of the Castle by Sir William Wallace to the Visit of King Edward VII</u>, 1909: A. Colthart, Mrs. Muir and R. & J. Murray, pp. 6-9.)

A bekyn he maid, Schyr Jhon come at his hand.
Wallace went in, and bad *Benedicite*.
The capteyne speryt: 'Quhat bellamy[9] may thow be,
That cummys so grym? Sum tithandis[10] till vs tell.
Thou art a Scot; the dewyll thi natioune quell.'
Wallace braid[11] out his suerd with outyn mar;
In to the breyst the bryme[12] captayne he bar,
Throuch out the cost[13], and stekit him to ded.
Ane other he hit awkward vpon the hed.
Quham euir he strak he byrstyt bayne and lyr[14];
Feill off thaim dede fell thwortour[15] in the fyr.
Haisty payment he maid thaim on the flur;
And Eduuard Litill kepyt weill the dur.
Schir Jhon the Grayme full fayne wald haiff bayne in;
Eduuard him bad at the castell begyne;
'For off thir folk we haiff bot litill dreid.'
Schir Jhon the Grayme fast to the castell yeid.
Wallace rudly sic routis[16] to thaim gaif,
That twenty men derffly[17] to dede thai draiff.
Fyfteyne he straik, and fyfteyne has he slayne;
Edward slew five quhilk was off mekill mayne.[18]
To the castell Wallace had gret desyr.
Be that Schir Jhone had set the yet in fyr;
None was tharin at gret defens couth ma,
Bot wemen fast sar wepand in to wa.
With out the place ane ald bulwark was maid;
Wallace yeid our with out langer abaid.
The wemen sone he sauffyt fra the dede;
Waik folk he pu, and barnys, off that stede.
Off pursiaunce thai fand litill or nane;
Befor that tyme thar wictaill was all gayne.
Yeit in that place thai lugyt still that nycht;
Fra oystre' broucht sic gudis as thai mycht.
Wpon the morn the houses thai spoilye fast,
All thing that doucht out off that place thai cast.
Tre wark thai brynt, that was in to tha wanys;
Wallis brak doun that stalwart war off stanys;
Spylt at thai mycht, syne wald no langer bid;
On till Dundaff that sammyn nycht thai ryde;
And lugit thar with myrthis and pleasance,
Thankand gret God that lent thaim sic a chance.

[9] friend
[10] tidings
[11] drew quickly
[12] fierce
[13] side of the body
[14] flesh
[15] cross
[16] severe blows
[17] vigorously
[18] moan

*Note to reader: In the above poem, original spellings have been preserved. As will be noted in several cases, the same word is often spelled in different ways within the body of the poem. This was common in the 15th century when the poem was composed. The printing press was still a new invention and spelling had not yet been standardized. Because of this, the poem is much better comprehended through an oral recitation of the poem, which would have been the normal method of delivery, rather than through the reading of a written version. Try phonetically reading the poem above, and I think you'll find this is true.*

**500 A.D.**

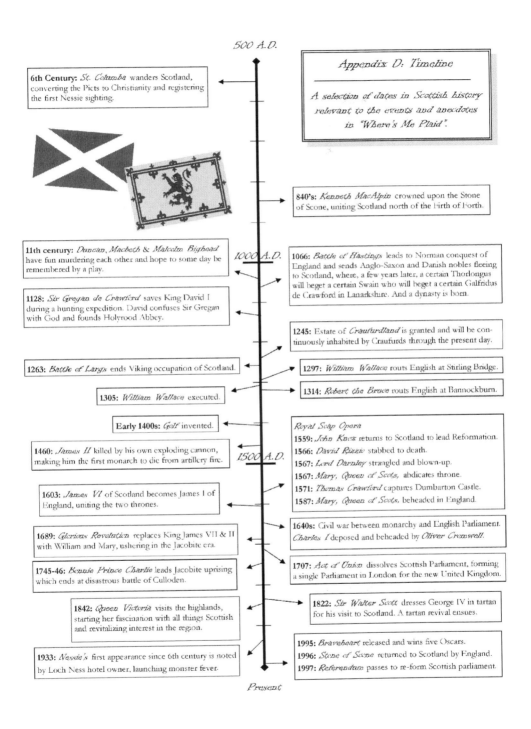

**6th Century:** *St. Columba* wanders Scotland, converting the Picts to Christianity and registering the first Nessie sighting.

**840's:** *Kenneth MacAlpin* crowned upon the Stone of Scone, uniting Scotland north of the Firth of Forth.

**11th century:** *Duncan, Macbeth & Malcolm Bighead* have fun murdering each other and hope to some day be remembered by a play.

**1000 A.D.**

**1066:** *Battle of Hastings* leads to Norman conquest of England and sends Anglo-Saxon and Danish nobles fleeing to Scotland, where, a few years later, a certain Thorlongus will beget a certain Swain who will beget a certain Galfridus de Crawford in Lanarkshire. And a dynasty is born.

**1128:** *Sir Gregan de Crawford* saves King David I during a hunting expedition. David confuses Sir Gregan with God and founds Holyrood Abbey.

**1245:** Estate of *Craufurdland* is granted and will be continuously inhabited by Craufurds through the present day.

**1263:** *Battle of Largs* ends Viking occupation of Scotland.

**1297:** *William Wallace* routs English at Stirling Bridge.

**1314:** *Robert the Bruce* routs English at Bannockburn.

**1305:** *William Wallace* executed.

**Early 1400s:** *Golf* invented.

*Royal Soap Opera*
**1559:** *John Knox* returns to Scotland to lead Reformation.
**1566:** *David Rizzio* stabbed to death.
**1567:** *Lord Darnley* strangled and blown-up.
**1567:** *Mary, Queen of Scots,* abdicates throne.
**1571:** *Thomas Crawford* captures Dumbarton Castle.
**1587:** *Mary, Queen of Scots,* beheaded in England.

**1460:** *James II* killed by his own exploding cannon, making him the first monarch to die from artillery fire.

**1500 A.D.**

**1603:** *James VI* of Scotland becomes James I of England, uniting the two thrones.

**1640s:** Civil war between monarchy and English Parliament. *Charles I* deposed and beheaded by *Oliver Cromwell*.

**1689:** *Glorious Revolution* replaces King James VII & II with William and Mary, ushering in the Jacobite era.

**1707:** *Act of Union* dissolves Scottish Parliament, forming a single Parliament in London for the new United Kingdom.

**1745-46:** *Bonnie Prince Charlie* leads Jacobite uprising which ends at disastrous battle of Culloden.

**1822:** *Sir Walter Scott* dresses George IV in tartan for his visit to Scotland. A tartan revival ensues.

**1842:** *Queen Victoria* visits the highlands, starting her fascination with all things Scottish and revitalizing interest in the region.

**1995:** *Braveheart* released and wins five Oscars.
**1996:** *Stone of Scone* returned to Scotland by England.
**1997:** *Referendum* passes to re-form Scottish parliament.

**1933:** *Nessie's* first appearance since 6th century is noted by Loch Ness hotel owner, launching monster fever.

*Present*

309

Made in the USA
Middletown, DE
22 October 2020

22602248R00172